BURPEE
GARDENING
CYCLOPEDIA

A CONCISE, UP-TO-DATE REFERENCE
FOR GARDENERS AT ALL LEVELS

Allan Armitage
Maureen Heffernan
Chela Kleiber
Holly H. Shimizu

Edited by Barbara W. Ellis

RUNNING PRESS
PHILADELPHIA • LONDON

9   8   7   6   5   4   3   2   1
Digit on the right indicates the number of this printing

Library of Congress Cataloging-in-Publication Number 2001094429

ISBN 0-7624-1211-9

Cover design by Bill Jones
Interior design by Jan Greenberg
Edited by Sara Phillips
Typography: Garamond and Optima

This book may be ordered by mail from the publisher.
Please include $2.50 for postage and handling.
But try your bookstore first!

Running Press Book Publishers
125 South Twenty-second Street
Philadelphia, Pennsylvania 19103-4399

Visit us on the web!
www.runningpress.com

Photography Credits

Pamela Harper: cover (bottom right), spine (top), spine (bottom), 578 (bottom left), 579 (top left), 579 (bottom right), 580 (top left), 580 (top right), 581 (top right), 581 (bottom left), 582, 583 (top left), 583 (bottom right), 586 (top right), 586 (bottom left), 586 (bottom right), 587 (top right), 587 (bottom left), 587 (bottom right), 588 (top right), 588 (bottom left), 588 (bottom right), 589 (top left), 589 (bottom left), 589 (bottom right), 590 (top left), 590 (top right), 592, 593, 595 (top left), 596 (top left), 596 (top right), 597, 598, 599 (top right), 600

W. Atlee Burpee Co.: cover (top left), cover (top right), cover (bottom left), 577 (top left), 577 (top right), 577 (bottom left), 578 (top left), 578 (bottom right), 579 (bottom left), 580 (bottom left), 581 (top left), 581 (bottom right), 583 (top right), 583 (bottom left), 586 (top left), 587 (top left), 589 (top right), 590 (bottom left), 590 (bottom right), 591, 594, 595 (top right), 595 (bottom right), 599 (top left), 599 (bottom right)

Stan Green: cover (top center), 577 (bottom right), 578 (top right), 579 (top right), 588 (top left), 596 (bottom left), 596 (bottom right)

Barbara W. Ellis: 580 (bottom right), 599 (bottom left)

Special Thanks

This book is the product of many hands and many talents —writers, photographers, designers, and editors have all played a part in its production. But we owe special thanks to the gardeners who grew the plants and created the scenes shown in the photographs in this book. We express our gratitude to them all, and especially to the following: Trevor and Janet Ashbee, Elsa and Mike Bakalar, Arlene Bartlett, Shirley Beach, Elda and Ray Behm, Dan Borroff, Sydney and Martin Eddison, Jerry Flintoff, Barbara Flynn, Lee Goosens, Mary Henderson, Mrs. Julian (Polly) Hill, Mrs. Calvin Hosmer, Gladys and Alain Huyghe, Daniel John, Louise Kappus, Liz Knowles, Mrs. Gavin Letts, Mary Ley, Shiela Magullion, Kathryn McHolm, Phoebe Noble, Lee Nydegger, John and the late Jane Platt, Loleta Powell, Rob Proctor, Joanna Reed, Mr. And Mrs. J. P. Smith, Bill and Bunny Soltis, Sir John Thouron, Mr. and Mrs. A. Van Vlack, Louise Weekes, Norma and Gerald Wilson, Wayne Winterrowd, and Joe Eck.

TABLE OF CONTENTS

PART III
THE PRACTICAL GARDENER 446

INTRODUCTION

Next to language, the richest expression of diversity in America is found in our home gardens. Gardeners across this vast country have developed a fascinating array of unique regional gardening styles. These styles—developed in response to the local climate, ethnic traditions and a myriad of other factors—range from urban aesthetic statements to deceptively simple gestures that communicate the values of country living. But make no mistake: In this land of "do it yourself," each and every garden, regardless of its style, reflects its owner's personality and individuality.

Nowadays, we approach gardening with the same vigor and determination we bring to fixing up our houses. No other nation can claim to have as many hardware stores, and our passion for weekend home-improvement projects has inspired both serious and comic television programs. *The Burpee Gardening Cyclopedia* was written with that same do-it-yourself spirit in mind. It is designed to help and inspire gardeners at every level— to make your newfound passion a long-term commitment, stimulate a neglected "green thumb," or help you express your own individuality through your garden.

Happy gardening!

GEORGE BALL, JR.
President, W. Atlee Burpee & Co.

PART I

GARDENING FROM THE GROUND UP

GARDENING IS BOTH AN ART AND A SCIENCE. Designing a pleasing garden layout, and creating gorgeous plant groupings within that layout, allow nearly endless scope for exploring your creativity. As with art, making a beautiful garden can be a transcendent experience—one that restores and renews your heart, mind, and soul. Creating a great garden is a real challenge, but it can bring you, and everyone who visits your garden, a great deal of pleasure and joy.

Before mastering the *art* of gardening, however, you need to understand the *science* that makes it work. In the following chapters, you'll find out how knowing about your soil and climate can help you create a beautiful, thriving garden. You'll also find all kinds of tips and techniques that will help you design your garden— from mapping your site to planning its layout and working with color and texture. When you combine this knowledge with your own outdoor experience and common sense, you'll be well on your way to creating your own garden masterpiece.

CHAPTER ONE

GETTING STARTED

The first rule of successful gardening is to work with, not against, the natural setting. While it's possible to grow plants that aren't well adapted to your climate and conditions, it takes a lot more fussing, and the results may not be worth the trouble. For instance, shade-loving plants, such as impatiens and hostas, will suffer in a hot, sunny garden no matter how much you pamper them. But when you match the right plant with the right place, you've set the stage for healthy, vigorous growth, prolific flowering, and generous harvests.

So how do you know which plants are right for your yard? The key is knowing what growing conditions—what kind of climate, how much light, and what kind of soil—your yard has to offer. Once you know these factors, you can read the plant portraits in later chapters to learn about the needs of the plants you'd like to grow. When you find a match between the plants' needs and what you can provide, you're in business!

UNDERSTANDING YOUR CLIMATE

"Climate" is a catch-all term that combines many different factors, including high and low temperatures, frost dates, rainfall, and wind. All of these factors will affect the way your plants grow.

TEMPERATURE

Although you can change some growing conditions, such as the quality of your soil, there's not much you can do to change the yearly high and low temperatures your garden experiences. That makes it especially important to choose plants that can tolerate those temperatures.

The United States Department of Agriculture (USDA) has determined that there are distinct temperature zones (called hardiness zones) for the United States, including Alaska and Hawaii. They have produced a zone map that is absolutely indispensable for all gardeners who want to know which perennials, trees, and shrubs are likely to thrive in their area. (These zones don't apply to annuals, such as marigolds, since these plants naturally die before winter anyway.)

The USDA Plant Hardiness Zone Map divides the country into 11 different temperature regions, based on the average annual low temperatures. It assigns a zone number to each region, which corresponds to a range of low temperatures. (For example, if you live in Philadelphia, you live in Zone 6. That means that your average annual minimum temperatures range between 0° and -10°F.)

To find out which hardiness zone you live in, turn to the official USDA Plant Hardiness Zone Map on page 584 and locate where you live on the map. Jot down your area's specific zone number with your garden notes, and keep it in mind anytime you buy perennials, trees, shrubs, and other permanent plants from catalogs or garden centers.

FROST DATES

If you're raising annual flowers and vegetables, hardiness zones won't tell you if the plants you want to grow will thrive in your temperatures. For these plants, you need to know the average dates of the first and last frost in your area. These fixed dates determine the beginning and end of your regular growing season.

The average last spring frost date is particularly important if you grow your own transplants from seed. It will give you a guideline for knowing when it's time to start seed indoors, as well as when it's safe to sow seed outdoors or set out transplants. The average date of the first fall frost will tell you when to dig up or protect tender plants that could get damaged or killed by freezing. The number of days between these two dates is the average length of your growing season. This is important to know for vegetables, since it will tell you if a particular crop can produce a harvest in the growing season your garden offers.

The last and first frost dates are fixed averages for a given area, based on many years of tracking weather patterns. To find the average dates for your particular area, call your local Cooperative Extension Service office, which is listed in the county or city government listings of your telephone directory. Or ask at your local garden center or nursery. Keep in mind that these are averages, so the actual date of the last spring or first fall frost will change a bit from year to year.

RAINFALL

The amount of water a garden receives is not necessarily restricted to natural rainfall patterns. For instance, if you live in a dry climate, you can still grow moisture-loving plants if you are willing to spend the time and money needed to provide extra water. However, this is working against your natural environment and not *with* it.

As water becomes more of a precious resource, it is increasingly important to plan your garden with water-saving techniques in mind. To do that, you need to be familiar with the average rainfall patterns in your area. If you've lived in one area for years, you probably already know roughly how often it rains, and whether dry spells are common. If you're new to an area, ask neighboring gardeners or the local Cooperative Extension Service office about the amount of rainfall you can expect through the year.

To find plants that are adapted to your area's natural moisture, check the plant portraits later in this book.

You can also find out about plants that do well in your area by visiting parks and cemeteries, where plantings are usually left to grow without a lot of fuss. If plants are thriving there with no watering, chances are good that the same kinds will do well in your yard, too.

WIND

The amount of wind a site gets is another important climatic factor to consider before planning your garden. Strong summer winds can topple tall flowers and vegetables, while dry winter winds may damage soft-leaved evergreen trees and shrubs.

Knowing where strong winds may be a problem will prevent you from placing plants that are susceptible to wind damage in exposed locations. If your entire garden area is exposed to strong winds, you may need to install fencing or plant a natural windbreak of cold-hardy evergreen trees and shrubs.

LEARNING ABOUT LIGHT

Before you can plan a garden or choose plants for it, it's critical to know how many hours of sunlight the site receives each day. While you can get very specific about light conditions, most references break light levels down into three simple groups: full sun, partial shade, and full shade. (Some books and catalogs use the term "partial sun," which is really only another way of saying "partial shade.")

As the earth moves around the sun, the amount of light either increases or decreases during each season. The three basic light classifications are usually meant to describe the amount of sun during the prime growing months, which for most parts of the country are April through August.

FULL SUN

"Full sun" generally means that a site receives, or a plant needs, at least 6 hours of sun each day between 10 A.M. and 6 P.M. In cooler northern gardens, plants needing full sun do best with 8 or more hours of sun, since the light is not as intense there as in the warmer southern zones. Full sun is best for most vegetables, herbs, fruit trees, and roses, as well as many kinds of flowers.

PARTIAL SHADE

Partial-shade plants don't need either full, direct sun or full shade. They prefer dappled shade, where the light is filtered through the leaves of deciduous trees, such as maples or dogwoods, during the summer months. A partially shaded site gets either dappled light all day or some direct sunlight for less than 6 hours each day.

FULL SHADE

A fully shaded site receives no direct light. Full shade is common on the north side of a house, and in spots sheltered by evergreen trees and shrubs. While full shade limits your plant choices fairly dramatically, you may still be able to create beautiful plantings with shade-lovers such as hostas, rhododendrons, ferns, and mosses.

UNDERSTANDING YOUR SOIL

IS IT CLAY, SAND, OR LOAM?

Soil mineral particles are divided into three basic groups—sand, silt, and clay—depending on their size. Soils from different areas, even from different parts of your yard, can vary noticeably in the proportions of sand, silt, and clay they contain. A soil with balanced amounts of sand, silt, and clay is called a loam. Each kind of soil has different traits.

Clay Soil: The bane of many gardeners, clay soil is mostly composed of tiny particles less than 1/12,500 of an inch across. Their tiny size means that the particles are easily compacted. Compaction of clay particles leads to two common clay soil problems: waterlogging (after heavy rain or irrigation) or crusting (after a dry spell). When clay soil is wet, it clings to your shovel and looks like a dense, heavy, cloddy paste. When clay soil is dry, the surface looks like cracked, hard pottery pieces.

If your soil is on the clayey side, don't despair—it is still possible to create a gorgeous garden. In fact, there are some advantages to clay. For one thing, clay soil holds more moisture and nutrients than sandy or loamy soil, so it is better suited to plants that appreciate extra moisture. And clay soil doesn't require frequent fertilizing.

You can moderate many of the problems of clay by digging generous amounts of organic amendments, such as compost, peat moss, or leaf mold, into the soil. Garden gypsum (hydrated calcium sulfate) can also be added to clay soil to loosen up the compacted particles, although it may increase the acidity of the soil.

Sandy Soil: Sandy soil contains tiny mineral pieces that are significantly bulkier than clay particles. Unlike clay soil, sandy soil has a light, loose feel, and water drains through it quickly. In fact, sandy soil may drain so quickly that the water is gone before the roots can reach it. As the water drains through, it also picks up nutrients and carries them downward, out of the reach of plant roots.

Sand is terrific for plants that like very dry and well-drained soil. But for most plants, sandy soil needs frequent watering and fertilizing to supply what they require to grow.

Digging in a layer of compost, chopped leaves, or other organic matter before planting, and adding more each year, will turn a dry, sandy soil into a great growing site for a wide variety of garden plants.

Loamy Soil: Loamy soil contains a good balance of large sand particles, tiny clay particles, and medium-sized silt particles. If your garden site has naturally loamy soil, consider yourself very lucky; it provides excellent growing conditions for most garden plants. The sand particles contribute a loose feel and good drainage, while the silt and clay particles hold the nutrients and water that roots need.

WHAT KIND OF SOIL DO YOU HAVE?

To determine if your soil is sandy, clayey, or loamy, pick up a handful of lightly moist earth from your garden and rub it between the palms of your hands. Look at the result, then match it with what you've already observed about your soil:

• Does the soil in your hand form a sticky ball that doesn't fall apart when you tap it? After a rain, does water seem to take a long time to drain away? If so, you have clay soil.

• Does the soil run through your hand without forming any kind of clump or ball? When you water your garden, does the water quickly soak right in, with little runoff? If so, your soil type is sandy.

• Does the soil in your hand form a ball that crumbles easily when you tap it? Does your soil naturally seem to be evenly moist but never waterlogged? If so, you probably have loamy soil.

WHAT IS THE PH?

Along with their mineral content, soils are also classified by their pH—their level of acidity or alkalinity. The pH scale ranges from 1.0 to 14.0, with 7.0 being neutral. If a soil's pH is higher than 7.0, it is alkaline; if the pH is below 7.0, it is acidic. Most garden soils in the United States fall somewhere between 4.5 and 8.0.

It's important to know what pH you're dealing with, because it can have a great effect on which nutrients are available to your plants. When the pH is too high or too low, your plants may get too much of some nutrients and too little of others. At a high (alkaline) pH, for instance, calcium and iron get chemically "locked" into the soil, so they are not available to plant roots.

Soil pH also affects the balance and health of soil microorganisms. Earthworms, for example, do not tolerate very acidic soil. A pH between 6.0 and 7.0 is best for most beneficial soil microorganisms. This same range is ideal for most plants; a slightly acidic 6.5 is optimal. (Acid-loving plants, such as rhododendrons, azaleas, camellias, dogwoods, and blueberries, prefer a lower pH, from 4.5 to 6.0.)

Testing Soil pH: Checking soil pH is fairly easy. Do-it-yourself soil-testing kits are available from garden supply catalogs and most garden centers. A very quick and easy way to measure pH is to use one of the metal probe-type pH meters: You insert the probe into the soil, wait 60 seconds, and then check the gauge to find out the pH level. There are also soil-testing kits that use a chemical solution to test soil pH and nutrient content. When testing your garden soil, be sure to take readings or soil samples from different sites, since pH and nutrient values can vary even within a small area.

Adjusting Soil pH: If your pH tests show that your soil is between 6.0 and 7.0, you really don't need to bother adjusting the pH (unless, of course, you're growing acid-loving plants such as rhododendrons or camellias).

If your pH is too low, you'll need to add lime to your soil. Garden lime (calcium carbonate) is readily available at garden centers, hardware stores, and discount home-and-garden centers. Applying about 5 to 10 pounds of garden lime for every 100 square feet of garden area will raise the soil pH by one full number (from 5.0 to 6.0, for instance). Add the right amount for your needs, based on the results of your soil analysis, and work it into the top few inches of soil. You can apply lime any time of the year, but it's best to add it several months before planting time. (Just leave several weeks between applying fertilizers and adding lime; the two don't mix well.) Once the pH is in the right range, continue to check it every few years, and add more lime as needed.

If alkaline soil is your problem, you need ground sulfur, calcium sulfate, iron sulfate, aluminum sulfate, or garden gypsum. Like lime, these materials are readily available from garden centers. Apply them according to the package directions, depending on how much you need to lower the pH. Pine needles, pine bark, peat moss, and manure can also lower soil pH, although they work much more gradually. Once you get the pH to the right level, mulching plants with pine needles or pine bark can help keep the soil balanced.

HOW'S THE FERTILITY?

A fertile soil is rich in the major nutrients that plants need to develop and grow. Plants absorb all of these nutrients through their root systems.

The primary nutrients are nitrogen, phosphorus, and potassium. Nitrogen is the essential element that plants break down to make their own food through photosynthesis. When nitrogen is lacking, plants will grow slowly, producing weak stems and yellowish leaves. An infusion of nitrogen into the soil has an immediate effect, stimulating plant growth and greening up the foliage. Too much nitrogen, however, promotes soft, succulent growth that is prone to damage and disease. It also encourages leafy growth at the expense of blooms, so flowering plants may produce few, if any, flowers in high nitrogen soil.

Phosphorus is critical for good root, seed, flower, and fruit development, since it promotes cell division. If your soil is deficient in phosphorus, you will see a reddish to purple color develop on the leaves and stems of plants. It is a good practice to sprinkle some phosphorus—in the form of colloidal phosphate or rock phosphate—into freshly dug garden beds so the roots will have easy access to this important nutrient.

Potassium, or potash, promotes photosynthesis and root development, and builds strong cell walls. It also helps plants retain moisture and keeps them from drying out in the summer and winter. A lack of potassium in the soil will show up in poor root development, susceptibility to wilting and wilt diseases, and a bronzy color on the foliage. Potassium is highly soluble, so it leaches out of the soil fairly quickly. If your soil is naturally low in potassium, it's a good idea to add a boost of high-potassium fertilizer (such as potassium sulfate or potassium nitrate) at the beginning of each growing season.

WHAT'S THE DRAINAGE LIKE?

Poor drainage is the cause of many untimely plant deaths. When the soil is filled with water, roots can't get the air they need to function, and they suffocate. The symptoms of waterlogged soil are similar to those of too-dry soil: wilting and eventual death.

Garden sites that have poor drainage are often at the bottom of a slope. Flat or low-lying areas can also be prone to waterlogging. Clay soils, as well as shallow soils over hard, rocky subsoil, are often wet, too.

Testing Drainage: Fortunately, it is relatively easy to diagnose poor drainage problems in soil. If you can still see standing water in areas of your yard several hours after a heavy rain, your soil is probably not well drained, and chances are, it is not good for most garden plants. To get a more accurate picture, try this simple test:

1. Take a 46-ounce aluminum can (like the kind Hawaiian Punch comes in) and remove its top and bottom.
2. Dig a 4-inch-deep hole in an area of your yard where you want to measure soil drainage.
3. Set the can securely in the hole, and back-fill the soil firmly around the outside of the can.

4. Fill the can with water up to the top, and check how far the water level drops in hour.

If you have well-drained soil, the water level should drop about 2 inches in an hour. This drainage rate is ideal for most garden plants.

If the water level drops more than 4 to 5 inches in an hour, your soil drains too quickly; add more organic matter.

If the water level drops less than 1 inch in an hour, your soil is poorly drained and needs serious help to make it suitable for most plants.

Improving Drainage: There are several ways to speed up soil drainage. If the soil is compacted or high in clay, organic matter is probably the answer. Dig or till in generous amounts of compost, chopped leaves, or other organic matter regularly. Do so before planting every year, if you're growing vegetables or annual flowers. For more permanent plantings, such as perennials and shrubs, till in organic matter at least a year ahead and again before planting.

Loosening the soil with digging and organic matter can also help to improve drainage in low-lying areas.

If your site is flat, and tilling and adding organic matter doesn't help, you will probably need to install a drainage system. Unless the drainage problem is very extensive and unusually severe, you may be able to install a system yourself without having to hire a professional contractor.

Yet another way to cope with poor soil—no matter what the cause—is to create raised beds. Raised beds are garden areas where you build up the soil so that the surface is above the normal soil level. If drainage problems aren't too severe, you can rake the soil into broad mounds a few inches high. To make beds higher than about 6 inches, build frames from landscape timbers, cinder blocks, or rocks to hold up the soil. (Avoid pressure-treated timbers or creosoted railroad ties, which can release harmful substances into the soil.) Loosen the top layer of existing soil within the frame by digging in a 2- or 3-inch layer of organic matter. Fill the frame the rest of the way with a mixture of good topsoil and organic matter. When the mixture settles in a few weeks, it should be 1 to 2 inches below the top of the frame.

CHAPTER TWO

DESIGNING YOUR GARDEN

If you're new to gardening, the idea of designing your own landscape can seem rather intimidating. Even more advanced gardeners may shy away from writing down their ideas, preferring to dig rather than draw. And there's no doubt about it—you *can* create a nice garden without ever putting pencil to paper.

But before you skip to the next chapter, consider the following advantages of creating a customized plan for your plantings:

• Garden planning can be lots of fun. It doesn't necessarily mean sitting at a desk, drowning in papers and protractors: It's looking at books, magazines, and catalogs for ideas; visiting other gardens for inspiration; and daydreaming about what you always wanted to have in your garden.

• Planning can save you money. Deciding now what you want for your garden can prevent you from making costly mistakes and help you keep an eye out for bargains, so you can phase in your design.

• Garden planning can save you time, too. Advance planning lets you look at your property as a whole, rather than in bits and pieces, so you can design your yard for easy maintenance from the start.

In this chapter, you'll learn all the basics of creating a great garden plan, from making a site map to deciding what kind of and how many plants to buy. Along the way, you'll find lots of exciting and inspiring ideas to help you plan a landscape that's perfectly suited to your own wants and needs.

START WITH A SITE MAP

The best way to begin your dream garden is with a site map—a plan of what already exists on your property. You don't need to be an experienced architect or draftsman to create a usable map; as long as you can read it, it doesn't matter how rough it is. What's important is the actual process of making the map. By spending a little time really looking at your yard, measuring and observing the existing features, you can create a layout that takes full advantage of what your site has to offer.

Follow these steps to create your site map:

1. Carefully measure the boundaries of your garden site with a 50– or 100–foot carpenter's measuring tape.

2. As best you can, draw the site to scale on a piece of graph paper. A scale of 1 inch on paper to 1 foot on the ground should give you enough room on the map to write in some details. If you can't fit your whole yard on one sheet, either tape several sheets together or use a smaller scale (such as 1 inch on paper to 2 feet on the ground).

3. For future reference, draw an arrow on the sketch to indicate which way is North.

4. Sketch in any existing features—for example, the house and other structures, trees, shrubs, flower beds, vegetable gardens, driveways, sidewalks, and patios or decks.

5. Indicate on the sketch the location of overhead power and telephone lines, as well as underground electric cables, water pipes, sewer lines, and septic

tanks. If you don't know exactly where these lines are located, call your local utility services.

6. Go back to the notes you made as you learned about your site in Chapter 1. On your map, mark where particular spots have special features, such as summer shade, poor drainage, or exposure to strong winds.

IDENTIFY YOUR NEEDS

Once you know what you have, it's time to think about what you need. Sit down with a pencil and your garden notebook, and start writing down the practical things that you know you need to consider in your plan—for instance, a path between the house and the mailbox, an area for kids and pets to play, or a place for a clothesline. This list should include features that you feel you absolutely must have in your yard, such as a vegetable garden for fresh produce, a flower bed to brighten a dull corner, or a tree to shade a porch or patio.

MAKE A WISH LIST

Now comes the fun part: thinking about what you'd really like to put in your garden. You probably already have some ideas, inspired by things you've seen in books, magazines, catalogs, and other gardens. A wish list gives you a place to put down those ideas so you can remember them when it's time to actually lay out the plan.

MAKING A ROUGH PLAN

Start by taking a copy of your site map and sketching in the features from your needs list. Also, mark any changes you definitely plan to make, such as removing overgrown shrubs or redirecting awkward paths. Now, look at your wish list and see which of those ideas would work. If you have lots of room, you may be able to fit in everything you want.

You'll also need to consider how much time and garden. Despite wishful thinking, there is no such thing as a no-maintenance garden. Be realistic about how much time you can spend on mowing, pruning, staking, weeding, and watering. When you don't have the time to care for it, even the best design will soon look neglected and shabby. If you are a beginning gardener, or a busy person without a lot of extra time, you're better off keeping the design simple, at least for a few years. As your skills, wants, and needs change, you can always go back and add features later on.

FINE-TUNING YOUR MASTER PLAN

It's time to put the finishing touches on your landscape plan. The key to a professional-looking layout is to use the same principles the pros use:

Repetition: Repeating different design elements is an important part of creating a sense of unity. These elements include both the "hardscape" features and the plants themselves. "Hardscape" refers to the constructed features of a landscape, such as paths and walkways, decks and patios, and walls and fences.

Balance: Achieving balance is critical in good garden design. When you look at the garden, it should not appear greatly weighted to one side or one area. While one area may have a captivating specimen tree or an eye-catching island flower border, it shouldn't overwhelm the entire garden.

LAY OUT BEDS AND BORDERS

Now that you know where you want everything to go in your garden, you can start thinking about the details, such as the size and shape of the planting areas. There is no right or wrong shape or size—it depends on the amount of room you have and on the look you're striving for.

A great way to try out different shapes before digging is to outline the bed with a hose or rope. Move the hose or rope around until you find a shape you like. If necessary, adjust the shape of the bed to create the most pleasing view.

PICK PLANTS FOR YOUR PLANS

Once you've determined the exact shape and size of the bed or border, you're ready to design the planting scheme for that space. The best way to do this is to make an enlarged drawing of the garden bed.

Take the exact measurements of the bed and draw it to scale on graph paper, as you did for the master plan. Next to the outline, jot down everything you know about the site, including the amount of sun and shade it gets, the soil type, the drainage characteristics, and the soil fertility.

Armed with all this information, you can start selecting the plants. Make a list of plants that appeal to you, then go through the list to make sure they will grow well in the conditions available on your site. Then check to make sure you've included some plants for all seasons to ensure that the landscape will be interesting year-round. Finally, decide how to group the plants to create the most pleasing combinations.

TURN YOUR DREAM INTO REALITY

You have your maps and your plant lists. Now it's time to move to the next step: installing the garden. Don't think you have to do it all at one time. Now that you have a plan, it's easy to phase in the garden over several years, as time and finances permit.

Ideally, you should begin with the big projects. Start by removing any unwanted trees and shrubs. This is also the time to do any major regrading of the soil and to put in drainage pipes or trenches. Next, plant larger trees, privacy hedges, and wind screens so they'll get established as soon as possible. Then construct any raised beds, garden walls, or other masonry structures. It's also helpful to lay out your paths before you plant.

Of course, it's not much fun to wait several years before starting on your actual garden plantings. To spruce up your yard in the meantime, experiment with container plantings and annual flower beds. If you have time, you may even want to start a small, temporary perennial garden. When you're ready to start the permanent plantings, you can dig up the perennials, divide them, and use them to fill your new gardens.

PART II

PLANT PORTRAITS

Deciding what to grow is one of the most enjoyable aspects of gardening. What gardener hasn't spent an enjoyable few hours pouring over the pages of a catalog, or wandering the aisles of the local garden center? There are always new plants to try, whether they are old favorites your grandmother once grew or plants you've never heard of before. But deciding what to grow can be intimidating, too. It can also be frustrating if your new purchases don't perform well in your garden.

In the chapters that follow, you will find all the information you need to grow a host of annuals, perennials, bulbs, roses, vegetables, herbs, groundcovers, and vines. You will find photographs and descriptions of hundreds of terrific plants, along with tips for growing them from seed, ideas for using them in the garden, problems to watch out for, and much more. For a successful, thriving garden that is easy to care for, use this information to fill your garden with plants that will grow vigorously in the sun, soil, and climate conditions your yard has to offer.

CHAPTER THREE

ANNUALS
AND
BIENNIALS

Dependable and easy to grow, annuals and biennials are the backbone of many American flower gardens. Marigolds, petunias, geraniums, and other favorites offer colorful flowers and season-long bloom that can brighten up any yard and add a welcoming touch to entryways. In this chapter, you'll learn about the many exciting advantages of growing these beautiful and versatile plants. Plus, you'll find a gallery of plant portraits to help you choose the best annuals and biennials for your yard.

WHAT ARE ANNUALS AND BIENNIALS?

Technically, an annual is any plant that completes its life cycle in one year: It germinates, grows leaves, blooms, produces seed, and dies all in one growing season. Marigolds, cosmos, and sweet peas are all examples of true annuals. Biennials, such as foxgloves, complete the same cycle, but over two years. They produce only leaves the first year, waiting until the second year to flower, set seed, and die.

While these definitions can be helpful, plants don't always fit neatly into categories. As some gardeners say, plants don't read books, so they may not behave the way books say they should! Petunias, impatiens, and geraniums, for example, are staples of the annual garden, but botanically speaking, they are actually perennials. (In most areas, they are killed by frost at the end of the season.) And some biennials, including forget-me-nots, will grow, bloom, and set seed in just one year if you start them indoors in late winter. Many biennials also produce lots of seedlings, so they may bloom in your garden for many years, as perennials do.

So, while it's helpful to know how an annual or biennial is supposed to act, it's more important to consider how the plant will actually grow in your garden. In the plant portraits in this chapter, in seed catalog descriptions, and on seed packets, you'll see that the plants commonly grown as annuals are classified as "tender," "half-hardy," or "hardy," depending on their tolerance for cold temperatures.

Tender annuals, such as petunias and begonias, have no tolerance for frost. They must be sown indoors in spring and transplanted outside after all danger of frost has passed, or sown directly in the garden when the soil is warm. Snapdragons, dusty miller, and other half-hardy annuals can be sown outdoors a few weeks before the last frost, but after the last heavy frost. If they self-sow (drop seeds that grow into new plants), their seed can often survive the winter and may germinate the following year. Hardy annuals, including sweet peas and larkspur, can tolerate a light frost. Sow them outdoors as soon as you can work the soil in spring. If they self-sow, their seed can survive the winter and germinate the following year.

PLANT PORTRAITS

The following plant portraits are by no means an exhaustive list of the many fine annuals and biennials that North American gardeners can grow and enjoy. The plants covered here were selected for their superior garden performance, reliability, popularity, or special qualities. They are also easy to find, either as seed from mail order catalogs or as bedding plants at local garden centers.

GROWING TIPS AT A GLANCE

Each of the following plant portraits includes simple symbols to highlight special features you need to know about each annual and biennial. If you're not sure what any of the symbols mean, refer back to this key.

○ Full sun (more than 6 hours of sun a day; ideally all day)

◑ Partial sun (some direct sun, but less than 6 hours a day)

● Shade (no direct sun)

✳ Drought-tolerant

❄ Prefers cool temperatures

✿ Good as a cut flower

✾ Good as a dried flower or seedpod

❦ Fragrant

▼ Grows well in containers

Ageratum houstonianum

ad-jer-AY-tum hew-stow-nee-AY-num.
Ageratum, floss flower. Tender annual.

Characteristics. Height: 6 to 30 inches. Colors: Blue, purple, pink, and white.

With their tight clusters of powder-puff blooms, ageratums add a soft, almost fluffy texture to beds and borders. The flower buds are darker in color than the fully opened flowers, and because they don't open all at once, the clusters often have an interesting two-toned look. The plants are mound-shaped, forming undulating ribbons of color when they are in full bloom. Ageratums come in a wide range of blue shades, from light powder blue through deep oceanic blue to lavender as well as white and pink. Many cultivars are named after bodies of water, including 'Blue Danube Hybrid', 'Blue Lagoon', 'Pacific', and 'Adriatic'. Some names, such as 'Blue Mink', suggest the luxuriant texture of the flowers.

Because of their reliable garden performance, ageratums are favorite annuals for use in flower beds or wherever a broad sweep of color is desired all summer long.

How to Grow. Sow seed indoors about 6 weeks before the last frost. The seeds need light to germinate, so just scatter them over the planting medium and press them lightly into the surface. Keep the medium moist by covering the trays or pots with clear glass or plastic until seedlings appear. Transplant hardened-off seedlings to the garden when all danger of frost has passed. Bedding plants are readily available at garden centers.

Ageratums grow best in a warm, rich, well-drained soil in full sun, or plant in light shade where summers are long and hot. They tolerate heat and drought but should be watered during prolonged dry periods for continuous bloom. Deadheading keeps the plants looking tidy and encourages more blooms to form.

Uses. The compact dwarf ageratum cultivars, including 'Blue Danube Hybrid', are at their best in mass plantings. They make excellent edging plants and blend well with other low-growing annuals in window boxes and other containers. The taller cultivars, such as 'Blue Horizon Hybrid', are ideal for annual or mixed borders. The flowers are excellent for cutting for fresh or dried bouquets.

ALYSSUM, SWEET. See *Lobularia maritima*

Antirrhinum majus

an-ter-EYE-num MAY-jus.
Snapdragon. Half-hardy annual.

Characteristics. Height: 6 to 36 inches. Colors: Pink, red, salmon, yellow, orange, white, and bicolors.

Snapdragons are long-time garden favorites for their elegant, lightly fragrant flower spikes in a wide variety of compatible colors. Besides soft pastels, deep reds, and burgundies, Snapdragons come in an exquisite range of bicolors. Bicolor combinations include orange with yellow, salmon with apricot, cherry red with rose, and many lighter and darker shades of the same color. The florets on the flower spikes resemble tiny dragons' heads, which snap open and shut when you squeeze the "jaws." Part of the charm of snapdragons, no doubt, comes from our childhood memories of snapping snapdragon flowers—an irresistible urge some of us have not outgrown.

Snapdragons are tender perennials that are normally grown as tender or half-hardy annuals. They can remain outside all winter in frost-free areas. They also do well in greenhouses.

How to Grow. Because snapdragons bloom best in cool weather, you should start the seed indoors 8 to 12 weeks before the last frost. The seed needs light to germinate, so scatter it over the surface of the planting medium. Cover trays or pots with glass or plastic to keep the medium moist while the seeds are sprouting; remove the cover when seedlings appear. When the seedlings are 3 to 4 inches tall, pinch the tops off to encourage better branching. Snapdragons tolerate light frost, so you can transplant hardened-off seedlings to the garden after the last heavy frost. Bedding plants are readily available at garden centers.

Snapdragons bloom best in well-drained, moist soil, in cool late-spring or early-summer temperatures. They can tolerate light shade but bloom much better in full sun. Snapdragons tend to stop producing flowers when hot weather arrives, but they will usually re-bloom when the weather cools off in late summer if you cut back the spent flower stalks. The flowers that follow the initial bloom tend to be smaller than the first flowers, but there are often more of them. Taller cultivars need staking. Snapdragons are susceptible to rust fungus, which appears as orange or brown spots on the underside of the foliage. If the disease is a problem in your garden, try growing resistant cultivars.

Uses. Snapdragons are available in a broad range of heights, so they can be used in many ways in the garden. The very small cultivars, such as 'Floral Carpet Hybrid', work well as an annual groundcover, as an edging, or in pots or window boxes. The spiky form of taller cultivars adds an attractive accent to annual and mixed borders. (Deadheading is particularly important in these spots, to keep the plants flowering.) Tall snapdragon cultivars also make remarkably long-lived cut flowers.

BABY'S BREATH. See *Gypsophila elegans*

Begonia X semperflorens
Beh-GO-nee-uh sem-per-FLOR-enz.
Wax begonia. Tender annual.

Characteristics. Height: 6 to 12 inches. Colors: Pink, red, white.

Wax begonias are among the most versatile and reliable annuals available They grow well in sun or shade, are rarely bothered by pests or diseases, and require very little maintenance in the garden. Wax begonias tend to have a uniform growth habit and bloom freely from early summer to frost, making them popular subjects for mass plantings or formal designs where color and form must be constant all season.

Wax begonia flowers are generally 1 to 2 inches across, although cultivars are available with flowers up to 3 inches wide. The plants bloom so freely that the flowers create masses of color in the garden. The light or dark green, bronze, or red foliage provides an attractive contrast to the flowers. The common name 'wax begonia' refers to the waxy texture of the leaves.

How to grow. Since wax begonias take several months to bloom from seed, you'll need to sow the seed indoors 12 weeks before the last frost. The seeds are so small, some Burpee customers have complained they didn't get any seeds in the packet—only dust! Because the tiny seeds are difficult to handle, you might want to mix them with a little sand to help you sow them more evenly. Begonias require light to germinate, so just scatter them as evenly as you can over the surface of the planting medium. Cover the posts or trays with glass or clear plastic to keep the seed from drying out; remove the cover when seedlings appear. Adding bottom heat will speed germination.

When the seedlings are large enough to handle, transfer them to 6 inches apart in the flat, or move them to individual posts. Transplant hardened-off seedlings to the garden when all danger of frost has passed. The stems and foliage of wax begonias are brittle and break easily, so handle the plants carefully. Bedding plants of begonias are always available at garden centers.

Wax begonias grow easily in most soils but prefer rich, well-drained soil. They tolerate full sun to fairly dense shade. These dependable plants need little maintenance and are rarely bothered by pests or diseases once they are established in the garden.

Uses. Wax begonias are the perfect bedding plant for sun or shade. They make colorful edgings and fill window boxes and other containers with masses of color. They also make good houseplants, since they stay compact in pots and do not require bright light to bloom well.

BLUE LACE FLOWER. See *Trachymene coerulea*

Brachycome iberidifolia
BRAK-ee-kohm eye-ber-id-ih-FOE-lee-uh.
Swan River daisy. Tender annual.

Characteristics. Height: 10 to 18 inches. Colors: Pink, blue, violet, and white.

Swan River daisy produces masses of small, lightly scented, daisylike flowers on mounded plants with delicate, feathery foliage. When they bloom, the bright little daisies are so prolific that they almost cover the foliage. The bloom period is unfortunately short—from 3 to 6 weeks—but the spectacular display outweighs this drawback. The short bloom season makes Swan River daisy a good subject for containers, particularly hanging baskets, which can be removed easily. (Make successive sowings into several hanging baskets so you'll have a new basket ready when the previous one is starting to look tired.) The common name refers to the region of Australia where the plant grows wild.

How to Grow. Where summers are short, it is best to start seeds indoors 6 weeks before the last spring frost. Set hardened-off seedlings in the garden after the last heavy frost. You can also sow seed directly in the garden after all danger of frost has passed. Make successive sowings every 3 weeks for continuous bloom all summer. Plants in hanging baskets are sometimes available at better garden centers.

The plants prefer full sun, cool temperatures, and well-drained, rich, sandy soil. They benefit from extra fertilization throughout the summer. Deadheading will prolong the flower display.

Uses. Swan River daisy is ideal for hanging baskets and other containers, and is an excellent choice for rock gardens. It is also good for edging and beds, as long as you can replace it with fresh plants for continuous bloom. The mildly fragrant flowers make enchanting small bouquets.

BUSY LIZZIE. See *Impatiens* spp.

Calendula officinalis
kuh-LEN-dew-luh off-ish-in-AL-iss.
Pot marigold. Hardy annual.

Characteristics. Height: 10 to 24 inches. Colors: Yellow, gold, orange, and cream.

In Shakespeare's time, pot marigolds were more likely to be found in kitchen and herb gardens than in ornamental flower borders. Their edible flowers and foliage have long been used to flavor soups and stews, and the flowers used to be grown for medicinal purposes, including the removal of warts.

Nowadays, these charming annuals are popular for adding cool-season color in the flower garden. The bright yellow, gold, orange, and cream flowers resemble chrysanthemums, both in looks and in fragrance. Single and double forms are available. Dwarf cultivars are ideal for flower beds; tall cultivars are good for cutting. Children love growing pot marigolds because the seeds are easy to handle and grow quickly. The bright blooms make pretty and fragrant bouquets.

In public gardens, pot marigolds are often planted with pansies in early spring, replaced in summer with warm-season annuals, then brought back for the cool weather of fall. At home, however, you don't need to take as much trouble with them. Pot marigolds will tolerate some hot summer weather if you keep the roots cool with a light mulch and water the plants regularly. They are not at their best in the heat of summer, but they should revive when cool weather returns.

How to Grow. After the last hard frost in spring, direct-sow the seeds where you want the plants to grow in the garden. Pot marigold seeds resemble comma-shaped worms, and more than one Burpee customer has sent back seed packets with a note indicating that the seeds were devoured by the worms in the packet! When the seedlings are 3 to 4 inches tall, thin them to 17 to 15 inches apart. In areas with mild winter weather, you can sow seed in the garden in fall for early-spring bloom. Plants are sometimes available at garden centers.

Pot marigolds thrive in well-drained soil and full sun. Deadheading encourages continuous blooming. The spent flower heads look somewhat like the flower buds. However, if you look closely, you'll notice that the spent heads have green, wormlike seeds that are beginning to form in the center.

Uses. Easy-to-grow pot marigolds are ideal plants for children and other beginners. Compact cultivars add cool season color to beds, edgings, and containers. The rich gold and yellow shades combine beautifully with blues and purples. The taller cultivars make terrific cut flowers. These old-fashioned favorites also deserve a place in herb gardens, as well as Shakespearean and Colonial American period gardens.

CALIFORNIA POPPY. See *Eschscholzia californica*
CARNATION. See *Dianthus* spp.

Catharanthus roseus
kath-uh-RAN-thus ROH-zee-us.
Vinca, periwinkle. Tender annual.

Characteristics. Height: 4 to 15 inches. Colors:
Pink, purple, and white.

Vinca is a very satisfying annual to grow. It is rarely
bothered by pests and diseases, it tolerates drought without wilting, and it does not need deadheading or staking.
Plus, it continues blooming all summer through heat,
humidity, and drought, right up to the first frost in fall.
Five-petaled flowers bloom profusely on well-branched
plants with glossy, dark green foliage. Newer cultivars
have larger flowers (up to 2 inches across) that come in a
wider range of colors, including deep rose and orchid.
Many flowers have a center "eye" of a contrasting color.

How to Grow. Start seed indoors 10 to 12 weeks
before the last spring frost. The seed needs light to germinate well, so just scatter it over the surface of the

planting medium. Cover the flats or pots with glass or clear plastic until the seedlings emerge. Transplant hardened-off seedlings to the garden when the danger of frost has passed. Bedding plants are always available at garden centers.

Vinca tolerates a wide range of soil conditions, but prefers well-drained, sandy soil. Plants grow best in full sun or partial shade. They need little care once they are established in the garden.

Uses. Vinca is a reliable plant for beds and borders in full sun or partial shade. Because of its uniform growth and compact size, it makes an ideal edging or annual groundcover. Vinca is also great for window boxes and other containers. The pastel pink shades contrast beautifully with deep blues and purples.

Chrysanthemum ptarmiciflorum
kris-ANN-the-mum tar-mih-sih-FLOR um.
Dusty miller. Half-hardy annual.

Characteristics. Height: 6 to 10 inches. Colors: Silver foliage, yellow flowers.

The name "dusty miller" actually refers to several different silver-leaved plants—most commonly *Chrysanthemum ptarmiciflorum* and *Cineraria maritima*. *C. maritima* 'Silverdust' has finely cut, velvety silver foliage. *Chrysanthemum ptarmiciflorum* 'Silver Lace' has a finer, more delicate texture and a stiffer habit. Both have a compact habit, making them ideal companion plants for other low-growing annuals. Dusty miller will bloom, but most gardeners prefer to cut off the small flowers.

How to Grow. Start seed indoors, as dusty miller tends to grow slowly. Sow 'Silver Lace' 12 weeks before the last expected spring frost and 'Silverdust' about 2 weeks later. Transplant hardened-off seedlings to the garden when the danger of frost has passed. Dusty miller is readily available at most garden centers.

Dusty miller prefers well-drained, sandy soil but is easy to grow in any soil. It requires full sun and will become lanky in the shade. The plants need little maintenance once they are established.

Uses. Dusty miller is invaluable for its velvety, silvery foliage, which looks very attractive when contrasted with pinks, blues, purples, and even whites. It makes an excellent edging, border, rock garden, or container plant. Use the cut foliage for contrast in fresh flower arrangements.

Cleome hasslerana

klee-OH-mee has-ler-ANN-uh.
Spider flower. Hardy annual.

Characteristics. Height: 3 to 6 feet. Colors: Pink, purple, rose, and white.

These towering background annuals make a dramatic statement in any garden. From early summer to frost, the bushy, well-branched plants are topped with airy heads of spidery flowers in soft pastel colors. The blooms are followed by long, narrow seedpods, each full of a long row of seeds. The foliage has a distinctive fresh fragrance somewhat like that of tomato foliage. Spider plants have two kinds of foliage: long, narrow lower leaves and deeply cut, handlike upper leaves. Mature plants develop short thorns along the stems, so beware when thinning plants or cutting flowers.

Cleome self-sows furiously—a drawback or a virtue, depending on how you look at it. While the seedlings are prolific enough to be weedy, they are easy to pull out, and they won't return if you don't let them bloom. And this ability to self-sow can be a bonus if you want cleome in your garden the following year, since you won't need to sow it. It also gives you plenty of seedlings to share with family, friends, and neighbors. Start fresh seeds every few years to keep your cleome patch vigorous.

How to Grow. Start seed indoors 6 weeks before the last spring frost, or sow outdoors where you want the plants to grow, after the danger of heavy frost has passed. Seeds need light for germination, so leave them uncovered, but keep them moist until they sprout. When outdoor-sown seedlings are about 4 to 5 inches tall, be sure to thin them, or they'll become crowded and leggy. Bedding plants are sometimes available at garden centers.

Cleomes are easy to grow in most soils but prefer a rich, well-drained site. They tolerate drought conditions. The plants bloom best in full sun but will flower in partial shade. Give them plenty of room, since individual plants can spread 2 to 3 feet wide. They require little maintenance once established, never need staking, and are rarely bothered pests and diseases.

Uses. Cleomes make striking, fast-growing annual hedges. Their thorns and dense foliage create an effective barrier, while the prolific pink, purple, rose, and white blooms create a pleasing mass of color that is easily visible from a distance. The tall plants are welcome additions to the back of annual or mixed borders for their long period of bloom and airy flower heads. Cleomes also make dramatic cut flowers.

Consolida ambigua

kon-SOL-ih-duh am-BIG-yew-uh.
Rocket larkspur. Hardy annual.

○ ❄ ✂❀ ❀

Characteristics. Height: 2 to 4 feet. Colors: Blue, pink, red, purple, lavender, burgundy, and white.

Rocket larkspurs are beloved for their tall, showy flower spikes, which look wonderful in the garden or indoors in fresh or dried arrangements. These versatile plants are as at home at the back of a formal mixed annual and perennial border as they are in an informal setting, such as a wildflower meadow or cottage garden. Best of all, they are so easy to grow that even novice gardeners are seldom disappointed.

Closely related to delphinium, rocket larkspur is known by several botanical names, including *Delphinium ajacis* and *D. consolida*. It is no surprise that one of the common names of this familiar favorite is annual delphinium.

How to Grow. Rocket larkspur is easy to grow from seed sown directly in the garden where the plants are to grow. In early spring, after the last heavy frost, prepare a seedbed and sow the seed. Be sure to keep the seedbed moist until the seedlings appear. For earlier bloom, start seeds indoors 6 to 8 weeks before the last frost. In frost-free areas, sow them in the fall for late-winter and early-spring bloom. Fall sowing for spring flowers sometimes works in areas as cool as southern portions of Zone 6 if the winter is mild. The plants will also self-sow in mild-winter areas. Rocket larkspur is not readily available as bedding plants.

These plants grow best in rich, well-drained, slightly alkaline soil, with full sun and cool night temperatures. They bloom all summer in areas where summer nights are cool and moist. In warmer regions of the country, rocket larkspurs are at their best in late spring and early fall. Most cultivars need staking.

Uses. Tall cultivars of rocket larkspur—such as 'Giant Imperial Mixed'—make excellent background plants at the back of a border. They also work well as accent plants or temporary annual hedges. Grow shorter cultivars in containers or in the middle of annual or mixed borders. All rocket larkspurs make dramatic cut flowers, fresh or dried.

Cosmos spp.
KOZ-mohs.
Cosmos. Half-hardy annual.

Characteristics. Height: 1 to 5 feet. Colors: Crimson, rose, pink, white, yellow, and orange.

Two species of cosmos are commonly grown in the garden, but the one that most gardeners are familiar with is *Cosmos bipinnatus*. This species has feathery foliage and reddish, pink, rose, or white flowers. The popular 'Sensation' series produces plants that grow to 5 feet tall, with flowers up to 5 inches across. 'Sensation Mixed' comes in various shades of pink, burgundy, and white. The flowers of 'Seashells' have unique rolled, tubular petals. Shorter cultivars, such as 20-inch-tall 'Sonata', are attractive in patio containers.

The species *C. sulphureus* may be slightly less common, but it is equally as beautiful. As its name suggests, the flowers come in shades of yellow, orange, and orange-crimson. The foliage is less finely cut than that of *C. bipinnatus*, and the plants do not grow as tall. The All-America Selections winner 'Sunny Red' is a very intense orange-crimson color and looks outstanding in borders; it is breathtaking next to deep purples or blues. 'Bright Lights', a mix of yellows and oranges, is popular for cutting, borders, and containers.

How to Grow. Both species are easy to grow from seed sown directly in the garden after the danger of heavy frost. You can also start them indoors 5 to 6 weeks before the last spring frost. Transplant hardened-off seedlings to the garden when the danger of frost has passed. Cosmos seedlings are readily available at garden centers.

Cosmos tolerates a wide range of soil types, particularly poor soil. In fact, too-rich soil can encourage lush foliage at the expense of flowers. Pinch off spent flowers to encourage continuous bloom. These durable plants withstand heat and drought, and are rarely bothered by pests and diseases. They need full sun to bloom well. Tall cultivars require staking to prevent their thick, hollow stems from breaking due to heavy rain or wind.

Uses. Tall cultivars of *C. bipinnatus* add a soft, airy touch to the back of an annual or mixed border. You can also use them as a fast-growing annual hedge or in a cutting garden. Since the taller cultivars are not always uniform in height, they're perfect for adding an informal look to cottage gardens. Shorter cultivars of both species are ideal near the front of the border, in containers, or as edgings. They also make beautiful cut flowers. Because cosmos is easy to grow and the seeds are large and easy to handle, it is a good choice for a children's garden.

DAISY, SWAN RIVER. See *Brachycome iberidifolia*

Dianthus spp.
dy-ANN-thus.
Pinks, carnation, sweet William. Hardy annual or biennial.

Characteristics. Height: 6 to 18 inches. Colors: Pink, red, purple, yellow, white, and bicolors.

The genus *Dianthus* includes many species of annual, biennial, and perennial garden flowers. All dianthus have fringed edges on the flower petal which look as though they've been cut with pinkie shears—hence the common name "pinks." (Even though many cultivars *are* pink in color, the name has no connection to the color.) Most dianthus species also have smooth, long, narrow leaves in various shades of blue and green.

The species usually called annual dianthus (*D. chinensis*) is a popular bedding plant for borders and containers. In areas with mild winters, annual dianthus may actually grow as a perennial. The compact plants are covered with flat, round, single flowers about 1 inch across. Colors include pink, red, white, and many bicolors with picotee edges All-America Selections winner 'Ideal Violet' is an unusual dark violet color with a rich, velvety look.

The familiar long-stemmed florist carnation (*D. caryophyllus*) is generally not suitable for gardens, but compact types are charming for bedding, containers, and small bouquets. They have the same spicy fragrance as the long-stemmed carnations, and make attractive, long-lasting cut flowers. They come in red, yellow, pink, salmon, purple, and white.

Sweet William *(D. barbatus)* is a biennial that blooms the second year from seed. Sweet Williams are senti-mental favorites that give an old-fashioned look to the garden. They are covered with clusters of exquisite tiny, round, flat, single flowers for several weeks in spring.

The small flowers resemble those of annual dianthus. Tall and dwarf cultivars are available in a wide range of colors, both solid and bicolored.

How to Grow. Start annual dianthus and carnations from seed sown indoors 8 weeks before the last hard frost in spring. Just barely cover the seed with the growing medium. Transplant hardened-off seedlings to the garden after the last heavy frost. Annual dianthus is commonly available at garden centers as bedding plants.

For sweet William, sow seed in midsummer in a protected area of the garden. Sprinkle soil over the seeds until they are barely covered, and keep the area moist. Move the seedlings to their blooming locations in late summer or early fall for spring bloom. You can also start the seed indoors in late spring or summer, then transplant the seedlings in late summer or early fall. Plants are sometimes available at garden centers.

Once you've planted sweet William, you probably won't have to worry about starting or buying plants again. Like many biennials, it readily self sows in the garden. Dig up the seedlings in the fall and move them to wherever you want them to bloom the next year.

All pinks prefer well-drained soil and full sun. They can tolerate drought but appreciate extra watering in dry weather. They are sensitive to excess nitrogen and may develop brown leaf tips if you overfertilize them. Remove spent flowers to prolong the bloom season (but leave a few flower heads on sweet Williams if you want them to self-sow).

Uses. Annual dianthus and compact carnations are excellent in beds, borders, containers, and window boxes from summer to fall. Sweet Williams are showy in beds, borders, and edgings in spring. All pinks are great for cutting, and many cultivars have very fragrant flowers.

Digitalis purpurea
dih-jih-TAL-iss per-per-EE-uh.
Foxglove. Biennial.

Characteristics. Height: 3 to 4 feet. Colors: Pink, purple, creamy yellow, and white.

Biennial foxglove forms a basal rosette of leaves the first season from seed and blooms early the following summer. The huge flower stalks are covered with bell-shaped blooms that resemble the fingertips of gloves. The inside of each flower is irregularly marked with rather sinister-looking spots. The flowers at the bottom of the spike are the first to open. These elegant plants are popular for formal borders because they are easy to grow and provide a dramatic, colorful vertical accent in shady or sunny locations. They are also marvelous for informal woodland gardens, since they self-sow reliably, providing plants for the following year without your having to scatter fresh seed.

'Excelsior' is a popular cultivar that produces florets all around the spike rather than on one side, as most foxgloves do. 'Foxy', an annual cultivar, blooms in just five months from seed.

How to Grow. Sow foxglove seed in midsummer in a protected part of the garden. Scatter the seed over the planting area and press it lightly into the soil surface. Keep the area moist until seedlings appear, then move them to their permanent location in early fall. You can also start the seed inside in spring and move the seedlings outdoors in early fall. Plants are often available at garden centers in spring and fall. You may also be able to buy them through mail-order catalogs.

Foxgloves thrive in rich, moist, well-drained soil. They grow best in partial shade but can tolerate full sun if you water them regularly in dry weather. The plants generally do not require staking in informal settings. In formal borders, however, you may want to stake the stems to keep them upright and to prevent them from being damaged by wind.

If you cut the stalks back right after bloom, you may get a second flush of flowers in late summer or early fall. But if you allow the spent flower stalks to dry on the plant before deadheading, foxgloves will almost always self-sow. You may find seedlings in unexpected places far from the mother plants. Once you learn to recognize the seedlings, you can dig them up in early fall and move them to where you would like them, or share them with friends and neighbors.

Uses. Foxgloves are at home in woodland gardens and make attractive accents at the back of mixed borders. The flowers are terrific for cutting. Keep in mind that foxgloves are highly toxic and therefore unsuitable for gardens visited by small children.

DUSTY MILLER. See *Chrysanthemum ptarmicidorum*

Eschscholzia californica

eh-SHOL-zee-uh kal-ih-FOR-nih-kuh.
California poppy. Hardy annual.

Characteristics. Height: 10 to 12 inches. Colors: Orange, pink, red, yellow, and white.

California poppy is not a true poppy (of the genus *Papaver*), but it has poppylike flowers. The plants are low-growing, with a spreading habit and ferny foliage. As its common name indicates, California poppy is native to California, where it carpets hillsides in spring. This delicate-looking flower is popular all over the United States as a cool season annual. The wild form is orange, but cultivars come in a broad range of colors, including pink, red, yellow, and white. Some double-flowered cultivars are available.

How to Grow. California poppy does not transplant well, so plant the seed directly in the garden in early spring, after the danger of heavy frost has passed. Scatter the seed over the growing area, press it lightly into the soil, and keep the seedbed moist until seedlings appear. Thin the seedlings to about 6 inches apart when they are

3 to 4 inches tall. Bedding plants are not readily available at garden centers.

California poppy prefers sandy, well-drained, alkaline soil in full sun. It blooms best in cool temperatures and can die out in the hot summer heat. This low-maintenance, drought-tolerant plant is generally free of pest and disease problems. Like true poppies, California poppies often self-sow and will naturalize in favorable locations.

Uses. California poppy is pretty in beds, borders, and pots, and is an ideal plant for sunny rock gardens. In masses, it makes a showy annual groundcover. Try it as a cut flower, too.

Eustoma grandiflorum
yew-STOH-muh gran-dih-FLOR-um.
Lisianthus. Half-hardy annual.

Characteristics. Height: 18 to 36 inches. Colors: Blue, pink, and white.

Prized for its exceptionally elegant, satiny, funnel-shaped flowers, lisianthus is gaining popularity as a cut flower and as a garden plant. This native American wildflower is sometimes called prairie gentian, since it is native to the dry prairies of the Southwest. It bears its poppylike blooms in delicate shades of deep gentian blue, silvery pink, and creamy white, all of which blend easily with other colors in the garden and in bouquets. A variety of single and double forms are available. 'The Blue Rose' is a new double-flowered cultivar that bears striking, deep purple-blue blooms with flaring petals that really look like roses! Cultivars with deep rose-pink to nearly red flowers are available as well.

Lisianthus plants can look lost in the garden if they are planted sparingly. Grown in masses, however, they are truly magnificent and sure to evoke praise from the most jaded visitor.

How to Grow. Sow seed at least 12 weeks before the last frost in spring. Press the tiny seeds into the surface of the planting medium, and cover the trays or pots with glass or clear plastic until seedlings appear. To encourage branching, pinch the seedlings several times before transplanting. After all danger of frost, carefully transplant the hardened-off seedlings to the garden. Transplants are available at well-stocked garden centers.

Lisianthus is not an easy annual to grow, since the seed tends to germinate slowly and the plants take a long time to bloom from seed. The seedlings do not transplant happily, either, so be sure to handle them carefully when transplanting. Once established in well-drained soil and full sun, however, lisianthus requires little care. It can tolerate drought and will bloom continuously until the first frost.

Uses. Lisianthus is grown primarily for its stunning, long-lasting cut flowers. The shorter cultivars are attractive in containers. All types can be used in borders or as edgings, as long as they are spaced closely together.

FLOSS FLOWER. See *Ageratum houstonianum*
FORGET-ME-NOT. See *Myosotis sylvatica*
FOUR O'CLOCK. See *Mirabilis jalapa*
FOXGLOVE. See *Digitalis purpurea*
GERANIUM. See *Pelargonium* spp.

Gypsophila elegans
jip-SAW-fill-uh EL-eh-ganz.
Annual baby's breath. Tender annual.

Characteristics. Height: 18 to 24 inches. Colors: White or pink.

Baby's breath is the common name for both annual and perennial species of *Gypsophila*. Annual baby's breath has tiny white or pink blooms that are widely dispersed on delicate, well-branched stems. The leaves are very fine and narrow. In the garden, baby's breath has a lighter-than-air texture, with clouds of tiny flowers blooming continuously for 5 or 6 weeks at a time. 'Covent Garden', a popular cultivar, offers masses of tiny, single white flowers on billowy, 18-inch plants.

How to Grow. For early bloom, start seeds indoors 4 or 5 weeks before the last spring frost. Seeds need light to germinate, so scatter them over the surface of the planting medium. Keep the medium moist by covering the trays or pots with glass or clear plastic until seedlings appear. Transplant hardened-off seedlings to the garden when all danger of frost has passed. Annual baby's breath also grows easily from seed sown directly in the garden after danger of heavy frost. Because the bloom time is relatively short, many gardeners sow annual baby's breath every 3 weeks until summer to ensure a continuous display. Annual baby's breath does not tend to be readily available as bedding plants, possibly because of its short life span.

This annual prefers, but does not require, alkaline soil. It will grow well in most well-drained soil in a sunny location. The plants are rarely bothered by pests or diseases.

Uses. Like the perennial species, annual baby's breath is grown primarily for its tiny flowers, which are ideal for fresh arrangements and for drying. The plants add an airy look to borders and rock gardens.

Helianthus annuus

hee-lee-ANN-thus ANN-yew-us.
Sunflower. Half-hardy annual.

Characteristics. Height: 18 inches to 10 feet. Colors: Yellow, red, and brown.

Sunflowers are often listed in both the flower and vegetable sections of seed catalogs: as flowers, for their ornamental value, and as vegetables, for their edible seeds. The ornamental kinds are available as single or double flowers and come in many colors, including shades of red and mahogany. The new dwarf cultivar 'Sunspot' grows only 18 inches tall and looks delightful in containers or as an edging. All sunflowers are so named because they turn toward the sun during the day. Keep this in mind when you decide where to plant these annuals, since a north-facing site may leave you with a crop of sunflowers that always turn their backs on you.

How to Grow. Sunflowers grow so quickly that they are normally sown directly in the garden after all danger of frost. Plant the seed about ½ inch deep. Thin the plants to about 2 feet apart when they are 3 to 4 inches tall. Plants are rarely available at garden centers.

Sunflowers are easy to grow in any soil, in full sun. They benefit from extra fertilization and watering in dry weather when they begin blooming. They are rarely bothered by pests or diseases.

Uses. Dwarf sunflower cultivars are fascinating in patio tubs, and the small-flowered types are good for cutting. Tall cultivars make dramatic background plantings, annual hedges, or garden accents. They attract birds to the garden, which is a disadvantage for the vegetable garden but an advantage for the flower garden. Because sunflowers are so easy and fast-growing, they are ideal plants for children's gardens.

Heliotropium arborescens
hee-lee-oh-TROH-pee-um ar-bor-ESS-enz.
Heliotrope. Tender annual.

Characteristics. Height: 8 to 18 inches. Colors: Purple, violet, and blue.

Heliotrope is valued for its exquisite fragrance and regal blue-purple color. You'll enjoy the vanilla-like fragrance best when the plants are sited near a resting place, such as a patio or garden bench, or by an open window. The intense deep purple, violet, or blue color combines well with silver, white, pink, yellow, and orange.

How to Grow. For early bloom, start seed indoors about 6 to 8 weeks before the last frost in spring. The seeds need light to germinate, so just scatter them over the surface of the planting medium. Keep the medium moist by covering the trays or pots with glass or clear plastic until seedlings appear. Transplant hardened-off seedlings to the garden when all danger of frost has passed. You can also sow the seed directly in the garden after the danger of frost has passed. Bedding plants are available at well-stocked garden centers.

Heliotrope prefers rich, well-drained soil in a sunny location. It is generally reliable and requires little care, other than an extra drink of water during dry spells.

Uses. Heliotrope makes a wonderful addition to beds, borders, containers, and edgings for its gorgeous color and delicious fragrance.

HONESTY. See *Lunaria annua*
IMMORTELLE. See *Xeranthemum annuum*

Impatiens spp.
im-PAY-shenz.
Busy Lizzie, impatiens. Tender annual.

Characteristics. Height: 8 to 20 inches. Colors: Pink, purple, red, orange, salmon, light blue, and white.

Busy Lizzie (*Impatiens wallerana*) is America's favorite bedding plant for shade, and for good reason. The plants are neat, well branched, and fairly uniform. The many brightly colored flowers often cover the foliage, and they bloom nonstop from early summer to frost. The flowers come in an immense range of colors, many with splashes or "eyes" of contrasting colors. 'Super Elfin Swirl' is coral pink with a deep rose edge. 'Cherry Vanilla' is a clear white with a bright cherry splash in the center. Double-flowered forms, which look like exquisite miniature roses, are also available. Some cultivars have bronze- or chocolate-colored foliage, or variegated foliage with a creamy white edge.

The plants tend to be bushy, spreading wider than they grow tall. Older cultivars required pinching to maintain their bushiness, but newer cultivars remain compact and well branched without pinching. Taller cultivars are still available and tend to have a more old-fashioned look.

But busy Lizzies aren't the only kind of impatiens worth growing. The showy New Guinea hybrids are also gaining in popularity as newer cultivars become available. They used to be sold primarily as houseplants and were relatively expensive to produce, since they were grown from cuttings. New seedgrown cultivars have been developed that perform better in the garden, and they tolerate more sun than busy Lizzies. 'Tango', an All-America Selections winner, offers orange flowers measuring more than 2½ inches across on 2-foot plants. The 'Spectra Hybrid' series has green or variegated foliage and flowers in shades of pink, rose, red, lavender, and white. Some plants have such attractive leaves that they could be grown for their foliage alone.

How to Grow. Both kinds of impatiens are slow to grow to blooming size, so start the seed indoors 10 to 12 weeks before the last frost in spring. The seeds need light to germinate, so scatter them over the surface of the planting medium. Keep the medium moist by covering the trays or pots with glass or clear plastic until seedlings appear. Transplant hardened-off seedlings to the garden when all danger of frost has passed.

Busy Lizzies may self-sow in the garden, but seedlings of hybrid cultivars probably won't resemble the parent plants. To get particular colors, you should start new plants from fresh seed every year. If there's a favorite color that you absolutely must have, or if you want to grow impatiens as house plants for the winter, take cuttings of either kind from garden plants before the first fall frost. To take cuttings, cut 3 to 4 inches of healthy new growth. Remove the lower leaves and set the stems in a glass of water to root, or insert the bottom half of each stem into a pot of moist growing medium. Plants are always available at garden centers. However, mail-order seed catalogs usually offer the best selection of colors and types.

Busy Lizzies thrive in partial to full shade, while New Guinea impatiens can take more sun. Both kinds of impatiens prefer evenly moist soil. Busy Lizzies in particular will wilt dramatically in dry soil. They recover remarkably well once they are watered, but can only take so much neglect before suffering, so check them daily in hot, dry weather. Wilting occurs most often when the plants are growing in sunny locations, in containers, or under mature trees that rob the surrounding soil of precious water. For this reason, busy Lizzies do not perform as well under shallow-rooted trees, such as dogwoods and maples, as they do under deep-rooted trees, such as oaks. If the plants have rich, cool, moist soil, they will thrive, spread, and bloom continuously until frost.

Uses. Both busy Lizzies and New Guinea impatiens stay neat and attractive in patio containers, hanging baskets, and window boxes. Busy Lizzies are essential in shady borders, as edgings, and as an annual groundcover under trees. They also make good houseplants because of their tolerance for low light conditions. Add extra humidity to the dry winter air in your house by placing the pots on a bed of moist pebbles.

LARKSPUR, ROCKET. See *Consolida ambigua*

Lathyrus odoratus

LATH-ih-rus oh-door-AY-tus.

Sweet pea. Hardy annual.

Characteristics. Height: 9 inches to 5 feet. Colors: Blue, pink, purple, red, orange, and white.

At the turn of the century, sweet peas were one of the most popular garden annuals in America, and they were on the cover of many early Burpee catalogs. They were eventually surpassed in popularity by more heat-tolerant bedding plant introductions, such as marigolds and zinnias. However, sweet peas still have a pleasant, old-fashioned association for many people, and no one can grow them without friends and neighbors stopping by and exclaiming, "You're growing sweet peas! My mother (or grandmother) used to grow them!"

Sweet pea flowers are deliciously fragrant and make superb cut flowers. They come in soft, pastel colors and many rich shades of deep rose and cherry red. Early cultivars grew as vines; the vining types are still available, but dwarf forms suitable for containers have also been developed. The newer cultivars have larger flowers than their ancestors, although some have lost their fragrance in the breeding process.

How to Grow. Sweet peas, like garden peas, thrive in cool weather, so plant them early in spring (or in fall for winter bloom in frost-free areas). Direct-sow the seed ½ inch deep as soon as you can work the soil. To encourage faster germination, nick the seed coat with a nail file or soak the seed overnight before planting it. You can also start sweet peas indoors in mid- to late winter. Set the seedlings out in early spring, after hardening them off. They are not readily available as bedding plants.

Sweet peas prefer rich, moist, well-drained soil and full sun. Climbers need some kind of support to wrap their tendrils around. In a greenhouse, they climb nicely on strings or wires strung from floor to ceiling. Outside, they can climb a fence, trellis, or tall tripod. Dwarf cultivars need no support.

Uses. In the cool weather of spring, sweet peas add a wonderful old-fashioned feel to flower beds, trellises, and containers. Grow some in a cutting garden, too, for indoor enjoyment. Sweet peas make excellent cool greenhouse plants for winter cut flowers.

LISIANTHUS. See *Eustoma grandiflorum*

Lobularia maritima

lob-yew-LARE-ee-uh muh-RIT-ih-muh.
Sweet alyssum. Hardy annual.

Characteristics. Height: 3 to 6 inches. Colors: White, pink, lavender, and purple.

Sweet alyssum is a popular annual with very tiny flowers in pastel shades of lavender, pink, and rose, as well as deep purple and white. (The name of the cultivar 'Easter Basket' captures the mood of the pastel colors available.) This low-growing plant combines well with many other bedding annuals, especially as a filler plant in patio container plantings, window boxes, and hanging baskets. It has a spreading habit on the ground and a cascading habit in containers.

Sweet alyssum has a delicious, meadowy sort of fragrance, but the scent is easy to miss, since the plants are so low-growing. To enjoy your sweet alyssum to the fullest, plant it in a window box under an open window, in a planter on a deck or patio, or by a garden bench. Or try planting it along the top of a retaining wall or in a raised bed or rock garden.

How to Grow. Sow seed directly in the garden after danger of heavy frost. As a hardy annual, sweet alyssum can tolerate a light frost. Scatter the seed over the planting area as evenly as you can, and just barely cover it with a sprinkling of soil. The seed is small and easy to oversow. This is not normally a problem, however, as the plants can tolerate overcrowding. Sweet alyssum tends to self-sow if it likes the location. Bedding plants are usually available at garden centers.

Sweet alyssum can tolerate a wide range of soil conditions and is easy to maintain in the garden. It blooms best in full sun but tolerates partial shade well. It prefers cooler temperatures and tends to go to seed in hot weather. Shearing the plants back after they bloom will usually cause them to produce a new flush of growth.

Uses. Sweet alyssum is excellent for hanging baskets, window boxes, strawberry jars, and other containers where it is allowed to billow over the side. Use it as a low-growing spreader for sunny to lightly shaded beds, borders, and rock gardens. In masses, sweet alyssum makes an effective annual groundcover.

Lunaria annua

lew-NARE-ee-uh ANN-yew-uh.

Honesty, money plant. Biennial.

Characteristics. Height: 30 inches. Colors: Purple or white flowers; silvery seedpods.

Honesty is grown primarily for its papery, pearly white seedpods, which add a unique look to dried bouquets. It is a biennial, producing scalloped, wedge-shaped foliage the first year, and flowers and seedpods the second year. Its pretty purple or white spring flowers make it an excellent choice for flower borders or woodland plantings. The flowers are followed by seedpods in late summer or early fall. The seedpods turn from green to brown, and eventually the outer casing starts to peel away. At that point, you can gently peel it off to reveal the shimmery white center of the pod. If you try too early, you can easily tear the center part of the pod; wait until the casing almost comes off by itself.

How to Grow. If you really want flowers and seedpods in 1 year, you can try starting the seed indoors 8 to 10 weeks before the last frost; set the seedlings out after danger of heavy frost, after hardening them off. In most cases, however, honesty grows best from seed planted directly in the garden after all danger of frost; the plants will produce flowers and seedpods the following year.

Like many biennials, honesty self-sows reliably. You can peel the outer casing from the pods right in the garden and allow the seeds to drop on the ground, then transplant the seedlings—carefully—in late summer or fall. Plants are not normally available at garden centers.

Honesty is not fussy about soil conditions and will grow and bloom well in full sun or partial shade.

It does not require staking or deadheading. (If you do remove the flowers, the seedpods will not form.

Uses. While honesty is primarily grown for its ornamental seedpods, the flowers are also decorative in beds and borders. The blooms are attractive in fresh arrangements, too.

MARIGOLD. See *Tagetes* spp.

Mirabilis jalapa

mih-RAB-ih-liss huh-LOP-uh.

Four o'clock. Half-hardy annual.

Characteristics. Height: 2 to 3 feet. Colors: Pink, purple, red, orange, yellow, white, and multicolor combinations.

Four o'clock plants grow 2 to 3 feet tall and are well branched and bushy. The botanical name *Mirabilis* refers to the miraculous diversity of flower colors produced on a single plant. Not only are individual flowers often multicolored, but different flowers on the same plant may be different colors. The funnel-shaped blooms resemble petunia flowers and only open for part of the day, theoretically starting at four o'clock (hence the common name). They often stay open all day in cloudy weather. The fact that the flowers open so late in the day bothers some people, but is not usually a problem for those who return home from work every day just when the flowers are opening to greet them.

Every year some Burpee customers ask why their four o'clocks bloom even later than four o'clock—sometimes as late as eight or nine o'clock in the evening. No one knows for sure, but it may have something to do with the heat. We know the flowers cannot tolerate the hot, mid-afternoon sun. It's possible that they open later if the plants are located in an area that captures heat or is exposed to the late-afternoon sun.

How to Grow. Start seed indoors 4 to 6 weeks before the last frost in spring. Sow the large seeds ½ inch deep. Transplant hardened-off seedlings to the garden when all danger of frost has passed. You can also sow seed directly in the garden after the danger of frost. Bedding plants are not readily available at garden centers.

Four o'clocks are easy to grow in most soils and can withstand heat, humidity, and drought. They require full sun to bloom well but also will tolerate light shade. The plants are rarely bothered by pests or diseases.

Uses. Four o'clocks are colorful annuals for beds, borders, and containers. They make poor cut flowers because they cannot be relied on to remain open. Four o'clocks are good flowers for children to try, since they are colorful, easy to plant, and fast growing.

MONEY PLANT. See *Lunaria annua*
MOSS ROSE. See *Portulaca grandiflora*

Myosotis sylvatica
my-oh-SOH-tiss sil-VAT-ih-kuh.
Forget-me-not. Hardy annual or biennial.

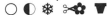

Characteristics. Height: 12 inches. Colors: Blue, pink, lavender, or white.

Forget-me-nots bloom for several weeks in spring with literally unforgettable, tiny, intense blue flowers over low-growing mounds of long, narrow foliage. They are also available in shades of pink, lavender, and white, but the dainty blue flowers are what people are usually talking about when they say that a plant has "forget-me-not flowers."

Because they bloom at the same time as many spring bulbs, forget-me-nots are excellent companions for tulips, daffodils, and other early bulbs. These sturdy little plants often grow as biennials, so you can even plant them in the fall, after you plant your bulbs, for a memorable spring show.

How to Grow. Sow seed in late summer or fall for blooms the following spring. Or sow seed indoors 6 to 8 weeks before the last frost. Cover the seed with a thin layer of planting medium. Transplant hardened-off seedlings to the garden when the danger of heavy frost has passed. Plants are usually available at garden centers.

Forget-me-nots prefer cool, moist soil in partial shade or full sun. They require little care once they are established, and they are rarely troubled by pests and diseases.

Uses. Forget-me-nots are ideal for cool-season color in containers, flower beds, edgings, and even rock gardens. They are also perfect for naturalizing in woodlands. They make delightful, long-lasting cut flowers for small bouquets.

NASTURTIUM. See *Tropaeolum majus*
PANSY. See *Viola X wittrockiana*

Papaver spp.
PAP-uh-ver.
Poppy. Hardy annual.

Characteristics. Height: 15 to 36 inches. Colors: Pink, purple, red, orange, salmon, and white.

Poppies have many associations—some cheerful,

some serious. They have been immortalized in the paintings of the Impressionists, and they are somber memorials of the dead of World War I. And with their gorgeous colors and crinkly petals, poppies are sure to bring joy to any garden planting.

Every year customers ask Burpee if the poppies it sells are the same as those that grew in France, on Flanders fields, at the end of World War I. The poppy they are referring to is *Papaver rhocas*, commonly called Flanders poppy. Flanders poppies have silky, crinkled, clear red petals that form a delicate, cup-shaped bloom about 1 inch across. Although the original red Flanders poppy is still available, it has been used to produce new strains called Shirley poppies. Shirley poppies come in a wider range of colors—including pinks, whites, and bicolors—and a broader range of flower types, including doubles and semidoubles.

While Flanders and Shirley poppies are hardy annuals, Iceland poppy (*P. nudicaule*) is actually a perennial that can be treated as an annual. Its flowers look similar to those of Flanders and Shirley poppies, but the color range includes oranges and yellows.

All poppies have a basal rosette of serrated or ferry-textured leaves, thin stems, and pendulous flower buds that straighten up as they open. Annual poppies add bright summer color to the garden, generally blooming from June to the end of August.

How to Grow. Poppies have easily damaged taproots and seriously resent transplanting. Fortunately, they are easy to grow from direct-sown seed. In early spring, scatter the seed over the soil where you want the plants to grow, and keep the soil moist until seedlings appear. (In mild-winter areas, sow in fall for earlier blooms the next year.) While poppies are offered occasionally at garden centers, sowing seed is best, since they don't transplant well.

Poppies thrive in rich, sandy soil and full sun. For the most continuous bloom, remove the spent flower stems frequently. Toward the end of the season, leave some flowers to form seed; poppies often reseed when they are happy in their location.

Uses. Enjoy the beautiful blooms of these easy annuals in beds and borders. Poppies make wonderful cut flowers. Cut the flower when it is still in bud, and seal the cut end of the stem with a lighted match to prevent rapid water loss. Poppies are also excellent flowers for naturalizing in a wildflower meadow.

Pelargonium spp.

pel-ar-GOH-nee-um.

Geranium. Tender annual.

Characteristics. Height: 10 to 18 inches. Colors: Pink, magenta, red, orange, salmon, and white.

Geraniums are among the most popular flowers in American houses and gardens. These dependable plants add bold, bright colors to beds, borders, and containers from early summer to the first frost in fall. In protected locations, they can even tolerate a light frost and may be among the last annuals in bloom in the garden in autumn. You can bring them indoors to continue their display in a sunny window all winter, until it's time to put them in the garden again in the spring. Geraniums are easy to maintain, requiring only deadheading and some extra watering in dry weather.

Many types of geraniums are available for the garden as well as the house and greenhouse. The familiar zonal geranium (*Pelargonium* X *hortorum*) has big, ball-shaped flower heads in bright shades of red, magenta, orange, pink, and white. The plants have an upright habit and rounded, scallop-edged leaves, which are plain green or have a dark ring near the edge.

Ivy-leaved geranium (*P. peltatum*) has foliage true to its common name and a cascading habit that makes it well suited for hanging baskets. The flowers are less showy than those of zonal geranium, with looser flower clusters. Martha Washington or regal geraniums (*P. X domesticum*) have large, crinkled leaves with a maple-leaf shape. Their gorgeous flowers bloom in astonishing bicolor combinations. They do not tolerate the hot, humid summer weather common in much of the country and are often grown in greenhouses or as houseplants.

Beautiful flowers aren't the only reason to grow geraniums; some have delightful foliage as well. Scented geraniums come in a wide array of foliage fragrances, including chocolate, peppermint, and lemon. They are usually grown in greenhouses or as houseplants, but they add a nice touch to herb and flower gardens, too.

How to Grow. Geraniums take a long time to bloom from seed, so start them indoors 10 to 12 weeks before the last frost in spring. Cover the seed with a thin layer of growing medium. Transplant hardened-off seedlings to the garden when all danger of frost has passed. Most garden centers sell pots of geraniums in spring.

Because geraniums are really tender perennials, you can keep them over the winter as houseplants. Bring the plants indoors in the fall, or take cuttings from healthy stems and root them for houseplants. You can then take more cuttings from the houseplants during the winter and root them for next year's garden.

Geraniums prefer rich, well-drained soil in full sun. They will also tolerate light shade. Deadhead them periodically to promote continuous bloom. The lower leaves have a tendency to turn yellow or dry up, especially on container-grown plants; remove the off-color leaves to keep the plants neat, and fertilize the containers to add needed nutrients.

Uses. Geraniums are popular outdoors in beds, borders, and containers of all sorts—especially window boxes. They also make excellent houseplants for a sunny spot indoors. The flower clusters add bright color to fresh bouquets. Cascading cultivars are ideal for hanging baskets.

PERIWINKLE. See *Catharanthus roseus*

Petunia X hybrida

peh-TOON-yuh HY-brih-duh.

Petunia. Tender annual.

Characteristics. Height: 12 to 15 inches. Colors: Blue, pink, purple, red, yellow, white, and bicolors.

Another of America's top-ten bedding plants, petunias are loved for the bright color they provide all summer until the first frost. They also have a delicious fragrance, which is often overlooked when they are planted in small numbers among plants with a stronger fragrance. If you are fortunate enough to find a bench in front of a large planting of petunias, the unforgettable scent will entice you to linger.

Petunias are sometimes classified as multiflora or grandiflora types. The multifloras produce many small flowers, while the grandifloras produce fewer, larger flowers up to 5 inches across. Double and single forms are available for both types.

How to Grow. Petunias take a long time to bloom from seed, so they need an early start. Sow the seed indoors 10 to 12 weeks before the last frost in spring. The tiny seed needs light to germinate; scatter it as evenly as possible over the surface of the planting medium. Keep the medium moist by covering the trays or pots with glass or clear plastic until seedlings appear. Transplant hardened-off seedlings to the garden when all danger of frost has passed. Most garden centers offer a broad selection of petunias as bedding plants.

Petunias grow best in full sun and rich, well-drained, sandy soil. Pinch off spent flowers for continuous blooming. Many cultivars of petunias, especially grandiflora types, tend to droop in rainy weather and take some time to recover before they continue their floral display. Petunias are also subject to botrytis, a fungal disease that causes spotting on the flowers, particularly after rainy weather. The multiflora types are more rain-tolerant and botrytis-resistant.

Around the end of July, cut your petunias back to about 4 to 6 inches, and give them a feeding of 5-10-5 or 5-10-10 fertilizer. They will come back in a few weeks and bloom all the better for this treatment, right up to the first frost.

Uses. Petunias are perfect for sunny beds and borders, and in mass plantings for a great sweep of color. They are particularly impressive cascading from hanging baskets, window boxes, and other containers. Petunias are actually tender perennials, so you can grow them on a sunny windowsill as houseplants. They are also popular for greenhouse growing in winter.

Phlox drummondii

FLOKS druh-MON-dee-eye.
Annual phlox. Hardy annual.

Characteristics. Height: 6 to 18 inches. Colors: Blue, pink, lavender, red, salmon, white, and many bicolors.

Annual phlox is a bright, summer-blooming annual with clusters of small, round, single or semidouble flowers in a range of colors on sturdy, mound-shaped plants. The flowers have a faint, sweet fragrance, which is most noticeable when the plants are located in raised beds or containers, or in mass plantings. You can also enjoy the fragrance by cutting the flowers for small bouquets.

How to Grow. After the last heavy frost in spring, sow the seed directly in the garden where you want the plants to grow. You can also start them indoors 6 to 8 weeks before the last frost, then transplant the hardened-off seedlings to the garden when all danger of frost has passed. The seeds need darkness to germinate, so cover them with ⅛ inch of soil. Indoors, cover the flats with a sheet of newspaper until the seeds sprout. Bedding plants are not usually available at garden centers.

Annual phlox thrives in rich, well-drained soil in full sun. The plants may need extra water in dry periods but are generally tolerant of high heat. Pinch off spent flowers for continuous bloom. Otherwise, the plants require little care in the garden.

Uses. This colorful annual can be used in beds, borders, rock gardens, edgings, containers, and cutting gardens. It looks marvelous in masses as an annual groundcover.

PINKS. See *Dianthus* spp.
POPPY. See *Papaver* spp.
POPPY, CALIFORNIA. See *Eschscholtia californica*

Portulaca grandiflora
por-tew-LAH-kuh gran-dih-FLOR-uh.
Moss rose. Hardy annual.

Characteristics. Height: 5 to 6 inches. Colors: Pink, magenta, red, orange, yellow, salmon, and white.

Moss rose is a low-growing, succulent annual popular for its remarkable tolerance for heat and drought. It is ideal for rock gardens and desertlike patches in the garden where few other long-blooming, colorful annuals can thrive. The brightly colored flowers may be single, semidouble, or double, like miniature roses. They bloom on spreading plants with short, narrow, succulent foliage resembling that of rosemary. The flowers stay closed all day in cloudy weather, or open during the day and close late in the afternoon in sunny weather. This can be a drawback for those people who work outside the home and return every day to see the flowers closed. (They might want to plant *Mirabilis jalapa*, commonly called four o'clocks, instead!) New cultivars, such as the 'Sundial Hybrid' series, have been developed to bloom for longer periods.

How to Grow. For earliest bloom, start seed indoors 6 to 8 weeks before the last frost in spring. The seeds need light to germinate, so just scatter them over the surface of the planting medium. Keep the medium moist by covering the trays or pots with glass or clear plastic until seedlings appear. Transplant hardened-off seedlings to the garden when the danger of frost has passed. You may also want to try sowing the seed directly in the garden after all danger of frost. The seed is quite small, however, and it is likely to dry out when sown in the dry areas moss rose loves. Keeping the seedbed evenly moist—just until seedlings appear—may encourage better germination. Bedding plants are readily available at garden centers.

Moss rose prefers sandy, hot, dry locations in full sun. It is rarely bothered by pests or diseases and requires almost no maintenance after it has become established in the garden. The plants often reseed in favorable locations.

Uses. Moss rose is perfect for rock gardens and for beds and borders in drought-prone areas. It grows nicely between paving stones. The plants have a spreading habit, so they cascade gracefully from hanging baskets and window boxes. They also make a great annual groundcover.

POT MARIGOLD. See *Calendula officinalis*
ROCKET LARKSPUR. See *Consolida ambigua*
SNAPDRAGON. See *Antirrhinum majus*
SPIDER FLOWER. See *Cleome hasslerana*
SUNFLOWER. See *Helianthus annuus*
SWAN RIVER DAISY. See *Brachycome iberidfolia*
SWEET ALYSSUM. See *Lobylaria maritima*
SWEET PEA. See *Lathyrus odoratus*
SWEET WILLIAM. See *Dianthus* spp.

Tagetes spp.

TAH-jeh-teez.

Marigold.Half-hardy annual.

Characteristics. Height: 8 to 36 inches. Colors: Yellow, orange, red, white, and bicolors.

Marigolds owe their popularity to their cheerful, summery blooms, which blanket sturdy, easy-care plants from midsummer to fall. They are available in a wide range of shapes and sizes, with single or double flowers that may resemble daisies, anemones, or carnations. Marigolds come in sunny shades of yellow, gold, orange, and rust-red, in both solid colors and bicolor combinations. White cultivars are also available, providing a welcome contrast to the hot colors.

Marigold flowers and foliage have a characteristic pungent scent that many people like—and many more dislike. Odorless cultivars are available for the latter group. The odor, however, can serve a purpose, as it is thought to repel insects. For this reason, vegetable gardeners have traditionally planted marigolds around their crops. Research has also indicated that the roots of French marigolds emit a substance that deters root-damaging nematodes in the soil. But perhaps the best reason to plant these annuals around vegetable or herb gardens is that they are edible, and their petals make colorful additions to salads.

In seed catalogs, you'll see marigolds divided into four groups: American or African marigolds (*Tagetes erecta*), French marigolds (*T. patula*), signet marigolds (*T. tenuifolia*), and triploid hybrids. Each group has different traits and uses in the garden.

American marigolds are medium to tall, stocky, hedge-type plants with blooms up to 4 inches across. They are available in shades of yellow, gold, orange, and white. These durable plants are most frequently used in mass plantings or large containers, as floral hedges, or for cutting. Cultivars in Burpee's award-winning 'Lady Hybrid' series are among the best American marigolds available, with sturdy stems and fully double flowers.

French marigolds are shorter than the American types and tend to bloom earlier. They have single or double flowers in shades of yellow, gold, orange, and rust, as well as intense rust-and-yellow bicolors. French marigolds are perfect for beds, borders, edgings, and containers. The 'Disco' series has exquisite single flowers in a wide range of solid colors and bicolors.

Signet marigolds have dainty single flowers on short, mounded plants with ferny foliage. They look so different from their more familiar American cousins that many people do not recognize them as marigolds. These plants are becoming more popular for rock gardens, containers, herb gardens, beds, borders, and edgings.

Triploid marigolds are a combination of American and French types, with the best qualities of both: vigor, compact habit, early and prolific bloom, and large flower size. They are also "mule" types, which means that they do not produce seeds; instead, they direct all their energy to producing flowers. Triploids are among the best performing marigolds available.

How to Grow. Marigolds grow easily from seed sown directly in the garden after all danger of frost. For earlier bloom, start seed indoors 6 to 8 weeks before the last frost. Just barely cover the seed with the soil or planting medium. Transplant hardened-off seedlings to the garden when all danger of frost has passed. Bedding plants are always available in a wide array of colors and types at any garden center.

Marigolds can adapt to most kinds of garden soil, but prefer a well-drained soil that is not overly rich. They must have full sun. The plants resist both heat and drought. The taller cultivars may need staking, and all types require deadheading.

Marigolds are susceptible to aster yellows, a disease that causes the plants to turn a greenish yellow color and makes the foliage texture rougher; remove infected plants immediately if you notice these symptoms. Aster yellows and insect problems tend to be worse for the odorless cultivars and the older white cultivars.

Uses. Marigolds are great for almost all sunny garden spots, including beds, borders, edgings, containers, cutting gardens, rock gardens, cottage gardens, mass plantings—even herb and vegetable gardens! These colorful, easy-to-grow annuals are perfect confidence-builders for beginning gardeners of all ages.

Trachymene coerulea
tray-KIH-men-ee see-RULE-ee-uh.
Blue lace flower. Tender annual.

Characteristics. Height: 24 to 30 inches. Colors: Blue. This unusual tender annual looks like a lovely blue version of Queen-Anne's-lace. The flowers are a unique shade of icy blue and add a delicate, airy texture to the border. They are most effective in the garden when planted in large numbers. The flowers have a delicate, sweet fragrance that can be lost when surrounded by more fragrant flowers. You'll appreciate the scent most when you cut the flowers and bring them inside.

The upright plants spread about 12 inches wide and have lacy, medium green foliage. They bloom best in cooler temperatures. Where summers are hot, blue lace flower may not bloom until temperatures begin to cool off in late summer.

How to Grow. Blue lace flower dislikes being transplanted. After all danger of frost has passed, sow the seed directly in the garden where you want the plants to grow. Just barely cover the seed with soil, and keep the seedbed moist until seedlings appear. When the seedlings are 4 to 5 inches tall, thin them to 9 to 12 inches apart. Bedding plants are generally not available at garden centers.

Blue lace flower prefers rich, sandy, well-drained soil in full sun. The plants may require staking. They are rarely bothered by pests and diseases.

Uses. Blue lace flower is beautiful in the middle of a border or in a cottage garden. It also makes a lovely, long-lasting cut flower. If you have a greenhouse, you can grow it in winter. While blue lace flower is not a native plant, its resemblance to Queen-Anne's-lace makes it look at home in a wildflower meadow.

Tropaeolum majus
troh-pee-OH-lum MAY-jus.
Nasturtium. Hardy annual.

Characteristics. Height: 1 foot (bedding types) to 6 feet (vining types). Colors: Orange, pink, yellow, red, mahogany, and white.

Nasturtiums are popular for their vibrant, sweetly fragrant blooms and interesting foliage, which resembles miniature lily pads. They are available as low-growing, bushy bedding plants up to 1 foot tall; as semidwarf, mound-shaped plants up to 20 inches tall; or as vines that climb 6 feet or more.

The foliage is usually light to medium green, although 'Alaska' has unusual variegated foliage and is attractive even without flowers. The edible foliage and flowers of nasturtium have a peppery flavor and add color to salads or garnishes.

How to Grow. Nasturtiums grow quickly from seed sown directly in the garden after danger of a heavy frost. Plant the large, pealike seeds ½ inch deep. Thin the seedlings to 12 inches apart when they are 3 to 4 inches tall. For earlier bloom, you can sow seed indoors 6 weeks before the last frost. Transplant hardened-off seedlings to the garden when the danger of frost has passed. Bedding plants are not normally available, possibly because nasturtiums are so easy to grow from seed.

Nasturtiums prefer poor, well-drained soil in full sun. Too-rich soil encourages leafy growth at the expense of flowers. The plants grow best in cooler temperatures. They tend to bloom less in the heat of summer but revive beautifully in the first cool weather of late summer. Deadhead regularly to prolong blooming. Tie vining types to a latticelike support if you want them to climb. Nasturtiums almost always have aphids on the succulent new leaves and flowers; control the pests with insecticidal soap.

Uses. Short cultivars are useful for beds, borders, and edgings. Vining types are attractive as a temporary climbing screen or cascading out of window boxes and hanging baskets. All kinds make excellent cut flowers. Nasturtiums are good plants for children to grow because they are fast, easy, and reliable.

Verbena spp.

ver-BEE-nuh.
Verbena. Half-hardy annual.

Characteristics. Height: 6 inches to 4 feet. Colors: Blue, pink, purple, red, apricot, salmon, and white.

Verbena X *hybrida* is a popular, low-growing bedding annual with bright clusters of dainty blooms that resemble primrose flowers. They come in a wide range of colors, including blue and purple shades, Valentine's Day red, all shades of pink, and white. Some cultivars bloom in solid colors; others have a gleaming white "eye" in the center of each flower. 'Peaches & Cream' is a recent All-America Selections winner that offers a subtle blend of blush and apricot shades—unique colors for verbena. The color is breathtaking when placed next to deep purple or blue flowers.

Another new annual verbena All-America Selections winner is *V.* X *speciosa* 'Imagination'. This is a spreading type that can grow 2 feet tall, with intense violet-blue flower clusters on long stems. The foliage is feathery, almost like asparagus fern. This annual looks stunning cascading out of window boxes and hanging baskets.

V. bonariensis is a lesser-known verbena that is really a tender perennial grown as an annual. It grows 2 to 4 feet tall and has very long stems topped with flattish clusters of violet-blue flowers. Even with its long stems, it never needs staking. *V. bonariensis* is not as easy to site in the garden as the other annual verbenas, as it can look gawky and insignificant unless planted in masses. It often reseeds, producing seedlings that can pop up in unexpected locations; leave these alone if they look right, or move them to a more pleasing location in spring. The plants may also overwinter in areas with mild winters.

How to Grow. Verbenas take a long time to bloom from seed. To get an earlier start, sow the seed indoors 10 to 12 weeks before the last spring frost. The seed needs light to germinate, so just scatter it over the surface of the planting medium. Keep the medium moist by covering the trays or pots with glass or clear plastic until seedlings appear. Transplant hardened-off seedlings to the garden when the danger of frost has passed. Bedding plants of *V.* X *hybrida* are readily available at garden centers; plants of the other verbena species are less commonly available.

These annuals prefer rich, well-drained, sandy soil and

full sun. They do not perform well in wet or heavy soil; take care not to overwater them. Deadhead periodically to prolong the bloom season. The plants are susceptible to spider mites in very dry weather, but are rarely bothered by other pests and diseases. In general, verbenas require little maintenance once they are established in the garden.

Uses. *V.* X hybrida is popular for beds, borders, edgings, rock gardens, and window boxes and other containers. The fragrant flowers are delightful for small bouquets. *V.* X *speciosa* is ideal for containers, beds, and borders; it's also great as an annual groundcover. *V. bonariensis* works well as an accent in mixed borders.

VINCA. See *Catharanthus roseus*

Viola X wittrockiana

vy-OH-luh wit-rok-ee-AY-nuh.
Pansy. Hardy annual or biennial.

Characteristics. Height: 6 to 7 inches. Colors: Blue, pink, purple, red, orange, and white.

Pansies are practically synonymous with spring. They

are classic companions for early bulbs, such as tulips and daffodils, in beds or window boxes. But spring isn't the only time you can enjoy them. These cool-loving plants are also valuable for fall bloom.

Pansies are available in a wide array of colors, many with the familiar faces and whiskers we remember so well from childhood. 'Maxim Marina' is a rare sky blue with dark blue blotches surrounded by a border of white. 'Padparadja' is a very striking, brilliant, solid orange, named after a famous orange sapphire of Sri Lanka. It has a longer bloom period than other pansies and is tolerant of summer heat.

How to Grow. For spring bloom, sow the seed indoors—covered with a thin layer of planting medium—in December or January, and transplant the hardened-off seedlings to the garden after the last heavy frost. Or sow seed in midsummer in a sheltered location in the garden, and move the seedlings in fall to their spring-blooming locations. In areas with mild winters, you can sow pansies in the fall for flowers the following spring. Pansies are commonly available as bedding plants at garden centers in early spring.

For fall-blooming pansies, sow seed in early summer in a protected garden area, and move the plants to their blooming locations in early fall. Or transplant spring-blooming plants to a sheltered location in early summer, and move them back to the garden in early fall.

Pansies prefer cool, moist soil and partial shade or full sun. They are seldom bothered by pests and diseases, and require very little maintenance once they are established in the garden. If slugs are a problem, control them with diatomaceous earth or slug bait.

Uses. Pansies are perfect for cool-season color in beds, borders, rock gardens, and edgings. They are also delightful in small bouquets as well as patio containers and window boxes.

WAX BEGONIA. See *Begonia* X *semperflorens*

Xeranthemum annuum

zer-ANN-the-mum ANN-yew-um.

Immortelle. Tender annual.

Characteristics. Height: 2 to 3 feet. Colors: Pink, red, and white.

Like strawflower, immortelle is grown for its silky-textured, daisylike flowers, which are easy to dry for everlasting arrangements. The flowers come in double and semidouble forms. They bloom on 2- to 3-foot plants for a relatively short period of several weeks in summer.

How to Grow. For earliest bloom, start seed indoors 6 to 8 weeks before the last frost in spring. The seed needs light to germinate, so just scatter it on the surface of the planting medium. Keep the medium moist by covering the trays or pots with glass or clear plastic until seedlings appear. Transplant hardened-off seedlings to the garden when all danger of frost has passed. Or sow seed directly in the garden after all danger of frost in spring. Bedding plants are not generally available at garden centers.

Immortelle prefers sandy, fertile soil in full sun. It may need extra watering during extended dry periods in summer. The plants are rarely bothered by pests and diseases, and require little care once they are established in the garden.

Uses. Immortelle is primarily grown for dried flowers; try just-picked blooms in fresh bouquets, too. The flowers are also attractive in beds, borders, and large containers.

Zinnia spp.

ZIN-ee-uh. Zinnia.
Tender annual.

Characteristics. Height: 6 to 36 inches. Colors: Pink, red, orange, yellow, green, and white.

As symbols of summertime, zinnias are rivaled only by marigolds. They bloom nonstop from midsummer to the first frost in fall, creating cheerful masses of color in the garden and providing cut flowers for the house all summer long.

Zinnia elegans is the zinnia grown most often in American gardens. The single, semidouble, or double flowers come in bold shades of pink, magenta, orange, yellow, and white, in both solid colors and bicolors. They range from quilled "cactus" types to ruffled and semiruffled "dahlia-type" flowers. The well-branched plants are fairly stiff and upright, and usually behave well in the garden. However, the tall cultivars can topple dramatically during summer storms, uprooting themselves and sometimes their neighbors. (Staking is the key to preventing this problem!)

Many cultivars of this garden favorite are available. 'Envy' is a fascinating green-flowered cultivar. 'Candy Cane Mixed' has pink, rose, and cherry stripes on gold flowers, which are also flecked with orange. 'Firecracker' has big double blooms with twisted, yellow-tipped petals, which really do look like exploding firecrackers.

Z. angustifolia, also known as *Z. linearis*, is a narrow-leafed zinnia with daisylike flowers in shades of yellow, orange, and white, all with orange centers. The single flowers grow 1 to 2 inches across. The graceful plants are quite different in texture from *Z. elegans*, and have a looser, more informal look. They tend to sprawl gently on the ground, often rooting along the stems. They cascade elegantly from window boxes and patio containers, and can even be used as an annual groundcover.

Z. angustifolia has been gaining in popularity since Burpee's introduction of 'Star White', a welcome new color that has made this species easier to combine with other plants. (The original orange does, however, make a striking display with blues or purples.) One of the best things about *Z. angustifolia* is that it is resistant to the two scourges of zinnias: powdery mildew and alternaria. It also tolerates more shade, heat, and drought than *Z. elegans*, and tends to self-sow. In addition, the plants do not seem to require as much deadheading as *Z. elegans.*

The 'Pinwheel' series, developed by Burpee, is a cross between these two species, combining the larger flower size of *Z. elegans* with the mildew resistance and single flower form of *Z. angustifolia.* These cultivars are available in cherry, orange, rose, salmon, and white.

How to Grow. Sow seed directly in the garden after all danger of frost. Or, for earlier bloom, start seed indoors 6 to 8 weeks before the last frost. Sow seed ¼ inch deep. Transplant hardened-off seedlings to the garden when all danger of frost has passed. Bedding plants are sometimes available at garden centers.

Zinnias are obliging, easy-care plants that tolerate a wide range of soil conditions. They do, however, grow best in fertile, well-drained soil in full sun. Constant deadheading is a must for all cultivars of *Z. elegans.* (Frequently cutting flowers for fresh arrangements serves the same purpose and is much more fun.) Taller cultivars need staking to stay upright. But if you neglect to stake your plants and they sprawl, don't despair! Zinnias have the ability to send out roots along stem that are in contact with the soil, which in turn enables them to fill empty spots in beds and borders without your help. You can even encourage this process by pinning stems to the ground with hairpins or padded wire to keep them in contact with the soil.

Zinnias are susceptible to two fungal diseases: powdery mildew, which causes powdery white patches on the leaves; and alternaria, which causes leaf spots. Space the plants generously to allow for good air circulation around the leaves, and pinch off any infected leaves as you spot them. In areas with humid summers, it is almost impossible to avoid these two diseases, but fortunately, they do not tend to attack plants until fairly late in the summer. If these diseases are a yearly problem in your garden, try growing *Z. angustifolia* or the 'Pinwheel' series. Japanese beetles can be a problem in July in areas where they thrive; unfortunately, there are no easy controls.

Uses. Zinnias are prized for beds, borders, edgings, floral hedges, containers, cutting gardens, and cottage gardens. They are perhaps at their best in mass plantings. Zinnias are excellent flowers for children to grow, since the large seeds are easy to handle and the flowers are reliably colorful. *Z. angustifolia* looks at home in wildflower meadows.

CHAPTER FOUR

PERENNIALS

Gardeners have been growing and enjoying peonies, irises, primroses, pinks, and many other delightful perennials for hundreds of years, and with good reason. With a little care, these beautiful, dependable plants return year after year to show off their stunning flowers and fabulous foliage. Plus, it's easy to find the perfect plant for virtually any site, since perennials come in an incredible array of colors, shapes, sizes, and bloom times. In this chapter, you'll discover dozens of exciting perennials, along with inspiring ideas for including them in every part of your yard.

WHAT IS A PERENNIAL?

Before you start choosing your perennials, it's helpful to understand some of the lingo associated with them. A perennial is any plant that can live for more than two years. Technically, this includes woody-stemmed plants, such as trees, shrubs, and many vines. Sometimes the term "herbaceous perennial" is used to differentiate the soft-stemmed perennials from those that have longlived woody stems. In most cases, though, gardeners simply call daylilies, phlox, asters, and other plants that die back to the ground each year "perennials."

While all perennials have the ability to grow and bloom for several years, they can't all persist in every climate. Some—including petunias, impatiens, and wax begonias—can only survive from year to year where winter temperatures stay above freezing. In most areas of the country, these tender perennials are grown as annuals. (That's why you'll find these and other tender perennials covered in Chapter 3 of this book.) The perennials discussed in this chapter are called hardy perennials, since they can send up new shoots from their roots even after their tops have been killed by frost.

All hardy perennials can survive frost. However, the amount of winter cold they can tolerate varies. That's why descriptions of hardy perennials indicate a range of hardiness zones (such as "Zones 5 to 9"). These ranges correspond to the USDA Plant Hardiness Zone Map, which divides the country into 11 zones based on average winter low temperatures. The hardiness range does not account for hot temperatures in summer, summer night temperatures, rainfall, or other climatic factors that can affect how well a certain perennial will grow in a given area. But this information can at least help you narrow your plant choices to those that should thrive in your climate. If you don't know what hardiness zone you live in, check the USDA Plant Hardiness Zone Map on page 584.

PLANT PORTRAITS

The perennials described in the following plant portraits were selected for their superior garden performance, popularity, versatility, ease of care, and long season of interest. Also included are a few particularly beautiful perennials that are worth the extra special care they need to thrive. You can find all of these perennials—either seed or plants—in mail-order catalogs or at local nurseries and garden centers.

GROWING TIPS AT A GLANCE

Each of the following plant portraits includes simple symbols to highlight special features you need to know about each perennial. If you're not sure what any of the symbols mean, refer back to this key.

○ Full sun (more than 6 hours of sun a day; ideally all day)

◑ Partial sun (some direct sun, but less than 6 hours a day)

● Shade (no direct sun)

❋ Drought-tolerant

❄ Prefers cool temperatures

✂❀ Good as a cut flower

❁ Good as a dried flower or seedpod

❦ Fragrant

▼ Grows well in containers

Achillea spp.

ah-KILL-ee-uh.

Yarrow, sneezewort. Summer. Zones 3 to 9.

Characteristics. Height: 2 to 5 feet. Colors: Yellow, bronze, pink, lilac, red, and white.

Yarrow has showy, flat, disklike flower clusters and finely divided, ferny foliage. Several species are commonly grown in gardens. Common yarrow (Achillea millefolium) features masses of pink, red, bronze, or white flower clusters on low-growing plants with feathery foliage. The plants have a tendency to sprawl, especially in hot summer weather, and they spread quickly. They are attractive in the front of the border and in patio containers. The All-America Selections winner 'Summer Pastels' blooms the first year from seed and comes in a wide range of antique-looking pastel colors, including rose, lavender, bronze, red, yellow, and white.

Fernleaf yarrow (*A. filipendulina*) comes in shades of yellow or gold on tall, strong plants with ferny, gray-green foliage. 'Gold Plate' grows to 5 feet tall and has deep yellow flower heads. 'Moonshine' is a hybrid with remarkably beautiful, creamy primrose-yellow flower heads; the 2-foot-tall plants have attractive, silvery gray foliage. 'Coronation Gold', one of the most popular hybrids, offers deep yellow flower heads and gray-green foliage on sturdy, 3-foot plants, which never need staking.

Sneezewort (*A. ptarmica* 'The Pearl') has a sprawling habit and masses of dainty, double white flowers reminiscent of baby's breath. The green foliage is narrow and airy, but not divided—very different from that of other yarrows.

How to Grow. Yarrow species and some culti vars will grow from seed sown in midsummer and bloom the following summer. Sow seed directly in a protected area of the garden. Move the young plants to their permanent locations in fall or early spring. 'Summer Pastels' blooms the first year from seed sown indoors 8 to 10 weeks before the last frost date. Cultivars are readily available as plants from garden centers and by mail-order.

Yarrows are vigorous growers and benefit from being divided every 2 or 3 years in spring or fall. The stems are often strong enough to be self-supporting, but taller cultivars may need staking. The plants are drought-resistant and rarely troubled by pests or diseases. Once they are established in the garden, they are trouble-free.

Uses. These long-blooming, easy-to-grow perennials are popular for both formal borders and informal cottage gardens. They also make ideal fresh cut or dried flowers. Shorter cultivars are suitable for patio containers. Taller cultivars look at home in wildflower meadows.

Alcea rosea

AL-see-uh ROH-zee-uh.
Hollyhock. Summer. Zones 4 to 8.
○

Characteristics. Height: 6 to 10 feet. Colors: Pink, red, yellow, purple, white, and black.

These stately, old-fashioned favorites have the remarkable ability to evoke memories of visiting country relatives in summer—even if you never had any! Names such as 'Old Farmyard' conjure up images of neglected stands of hollyhocks coming back year after year in front of an old barn wall, or against a farmhouse in need of new paint. While some hollyhock plants can survive for many years, they are usually described as short-lived perennials. Since hollyhocks can bloom quickly from seed, they can even be grown as annuals or biennials.

Hollyhocks are related to hibiscus and have the same flower form, with large, overlapping petals and a long, narrow column of fused reproductive parts in the center. The flowers bloom on tall spikes on big plants with large, rounded leaves. Single-, semidouble-, and double-flowered forms are available. The more old-fashioned-looking single-flowered types were once very difficult to find, but are becoming popular again.

These perennials are susceptible to several serious pest and disease problems, including rust and mites. People who love hollyhocks grow them in spite of these problems, since no other plant can take their place in the garden or in the heart.

How to Grow. Hollyhocks are easy to grow from seed sown indoors 8 weeks before the last frost date. To aid germination, soak the seeds overnight. They need light to germinate, so just press them lightly into the surface of the planting medium. Transplant hardened-off seedlings to the garden when the danger of frost has passed. Hollyhock plants are sometimes sold at garden centers.

The plants prefer a well-drained, moist soil enriched with plenty of organic matter. They do best in full sun, and may need staking in exposed locations.

Uses. Hollyhocks provide dramatic screening when planted along a fence or wall. They are also excellent plants for the back of the border. Hollyhocks always make a statement planted as a garden accent.

Alchemilla mollis
al-kuh-MILL-uh MOL-iss.
Lady's-mantle. Early summer. Zones 4 to 7.

◗ ● ✁

Characteristics. Height: 18 to 24 inches. Colors: Greenish yellow.

This striking perennial features clouds of tiny flowers that are held above lobed, light green leaves. The flowers bloom for several weeks in June and often grow so heavy that they fall back and rest on the foliage. They are a very unusual shade of chartreuse, which blends beautifully with pinks and deep purples in flower borders. The leaves have an undulating, pleated look and are covered with tiny hairs that catch and hold water droplets, giving them a fresh look after a rainfall. (Unfortunately, their tendency to hold moisture can cause plants to rot, especially in areas with hot, humid summers.) The foliage is so attractive that lady's-mantle is often used as a leafy groundcover.

How to Grow. Start with purchased plants, which are available from garden centers and through mail-order catalogs.

This charming perennial prefers cool, moist, rich soil in partial shade or full sun. It tolerates more light in cooler areas; partial shade is important in warmer regions. Divide crowded plants in spring or fall. Lady's-mantle is rarely bothered by pests or diseases.

Uses. Grow lady's-mantle as a spring-to-fall ground-cover or as an edging for beds and borders. It also looks great in woodland gardens. The blooms make interesting and attractive filler flowers in cut flower arrangements.

Amsonia tabernaemontana
am-SOH-nee-uh tay-ber-nee-mon-TAN-uh.
Blue starflower. Early summer. Zones 3 to 9.

Characteristics. Height: 2 feet. Colors: Light blue.

This reliable, easy-to-grow plant isn't grown often enough in American perennial gardens. The well-behaved, 2-foot-tall, bushy mounds have handsome, willowlike leaves. The leaves are attractive in the border all season, but are especially eye-catching when they turn fiery yellow-orange in the fall. The plants bloom in June, with pretty balls of star-shaped, steel blue flowers.

How to Grow. To raise your own plants, sow seed in midsummer directly in a protected area of the garden. Move the young plants to their permanent locations in fall or early spring. If you prefer, you can purchase plants of blue starflower, which are available at some garden centers and through mail-order catalogs.

The plants prefer a moist, well-drained soil enriched with plenty of organic matter. They perform best in full sun but can tolerate light shade; in too much shade, they grow tall and leggy. Cut the plants back by one-third after flowering, to encourage neater, more compact growth. Clumps can live for many years without division, but you can divide them in spring or fall for propagation. Blue starflower is rarely bothered by pests and diseases, and is easy to maintain through the season.

Uses. Blue starflower is a handsome plant for the middle of the border. It is one of the few herbaceous perennials that can be grown for its fall color alone. The flowers are good for cutting.

Anemone X hybrida
ah-NEM-on-ee HY-brih-duh.
Japanese anemone. Fall. Zones 5 to 8.

Characteristics. Height: 2 to 4 feet. Colors: Pink or white.

Graceful Japanese anemones add elegance to perennial gardens, woodland plantings, and shrub borders in fall, when tired summer plantings are just beginning to revive for their end-of-the-season show. The blooms resemble fully open poppy flowers, on long, waving stems that seem to be constantly in motion. They are available in single-, semidouble, and double-flowered forms, in shades ranging from deep rose to shell pink to white. 'Alba' offers pristine white, single flowers on 2-foot plants. 'Margarete' has deep rose, semidouble flowers that contrast beautifully with blue asters. 'Queen Charlotte' bears semidouble flowers in a lovely, gentle pink.

How to Grow. Japanese anemones are usually grown from purchased plants. They are available from mail-order catalogs and at some garden centers.

The plants grow best in rich, well-drained, moist soil

and partial shade or full sun. They may need extra watering in dry conditions. They are relatively slow to mature and may take 2 or 3 years to bloom. Deadheading will prolong their blooming period. In northern areas, Japanese anemones need a protective winter mulch. If you want to propagate clumps, divide them or take root cuttings in spring.

Uses. Japanese anemones are wonderful in the back of the perennial border. They are perfect companions for asters and Kamchatka bugbane (*Cimicifuga simplex*). Japanese anemones also naturalize well in woodlands. The flowers are good for cutting.

Aquilegia spp.
ak-will-EE-jee-uh.
Columbine. Spring. Zones 3 to 8.

Characteristics. Height: 2 to 3 feet. Colors: Blue, purple, pink, yellow, red, white, and bicolors.

Columbines are among the most welcome flowers of spring. The flowers always look perfect, with long, narrow sepals and cup-shaped petals, often in a contrasting color. Many cultivars have long, elegant spurs; others have shorter, inward-curving spurs; and some have no spurs at all. The green or gray-green foliage is deeply lobed and attractive enough to make a lightly textured groundcover even when the plants are not in bloom. When columbines are planted in the open, their long stems sway in the wind, making the delicate flowers look as though they are constantly in motion.

Wild columbine (*Aquilegia canadensis*) is a native American wildflower with small red-and-yellow flowers that bloom for up to 6 weeks in May and June. The plants require little assistance in the garden, taking good care of themselves and self-sowing where they are happy. They are ideal for naturalizing in woodlands or wild-flower meadows, and make charming cut flowers.

Hybrid columbines (*A.* X *hybrida*) offer large flowers (up to 3½ inches across) in a wide range of solid colors and bicolors, on plants of various heights. The bright color combinations and intricate flower shapes are reminiscent of a jester's hat, as the name of one series, 'Harlequin', suggests. The 'Songbird' series features extra-large flowers on compact plants that look great in containers.

How to Grow. These short-lived perennials are easy to grow from seed. The seeds germinate best when they are chilled for 3 to 4 weeks at 40°F. Sow the seed in pots or trays, chill them, then set the containers outdoors for the summer. Or sow directly in the garden in a protected area in midsummer. Move the young plants to their final locations in fall or early spring. The plants also self-sow reliably where they are happy; move the seedlings in summer or early spring to where you want plants to grow. Remember that seedlings from hybrid cultivars will probably not resemble their parents; buy new hybrid seed if you want to duplicate these plants. Columbine plants are available at garden centers and through mail-order catalogs.

Columbines prefer moist, well-drained soil in full sun or partial shade. Taller cultivars may require staking. Don't deadhead unless you want to eliminate self-sown seedlings. Mature plants resent transplanting and division; grow new plants from seed. Columbines are highly susceptible to leafminers, which cause squiggly lines to appear just below the surface of the leaf. Leafminers do not kill the plant, but they do make the foliage unsightly. Remove and destroy severely affected foliage.

Uses. Columbines are lovely for borders and excellent for naturalizing in woodlands. The blooms make good cut flowers, and the seedpods make interesting additions to dried arrangements. Compact cultivars can be grown in containers.

Artemisia spp.
ar-teh-MEEZ-ee-uh.
Artemisia. Spring through fall. Zones 5 to 8.

Characteristics. Height: 1 to 3 feet. Colors: Silver foliage.

In the perennial garden, artemisias are grown mostly for their fragrant, finely cut silver foliage. The silver color blends well with many colors in the border, especially deep pinks, blues, and purples. Artemisia is also an important companion plant for white flowers in all-white color schemes.

Three types of artemisia are popular in American perennial gardens. 'Silver King' artemisia (*Artemisia ludoviciana* 'Silver King') grows 2 to 3 feet tall and has finely cut, silvery leaves. It can be quite invasive, especially in light, sandy soil. Some gardeners plant it in bottomless containers sunk in the ground to the rim to prevent it from creeping out of bounds. The spreading runners are easy to pull out, but this can disturb neighboring plants. The foliage of 'Silver King' is valuable in arrangements.

Silvermound artemisia (*A. schmidtiana* 'Silver Mound') is a low-growing type, reaching only 12 inches tall with an 18-inch spread. It has more finely cut foliage then 'Silver King' and is not invasive. It works well as an edging or in the front of the border, especially in areas with cool summers.

'Powis Castle' artemisia (*A.* X 'Powis Castle') is a hybrid of *A. absinthium* and *A. arborescens.* It is wonderfully well behaved in borders, staying where you put it and looking splendid all season, with aromatic, feathery foliage. In areas south of Zone 6, its stems tend to become woody, making it look like a gnarled, low-growing shrub. If this look doesn't appeal to you, renew the plants by cutting them back in spring and allowing new growth to come up from the ground. Farther north, plants tend to die back to the ground each winter.

How to Grow. Artemisias are usually grown from purchased plants. These three cultivars are readily available at nurseries and garden centers, and through mail-order catalogs. You can also propagate them by taking cuttings in spring.

The plants grow best in well-drained, sandy soil in full sun. They can tolerate partial shade but will grow leggy in too much shade. 'Silver King' artemisia may need staking to look neat. To encourage bushiness in all three types, pinch the plants in late spring to early summer. Use the pinched-off pieces as cuttings to propagate new plants. You can also divide 'Silver King' in spring or fall. Like many silver-leaved plants, artemisias are subject to root and foliage rot diseases, especially in areas with hot, humid summers.

Uses. These perennials are great as filler plants for borders and herb gardens. Silvermound artemisia is attractive as an edging. Artemisia foliage is excellent for cutting.

Asclepias tuberosa
as-KLEE-pee-us tew-ber-oh-suh.
Butterfly weed. Late spring to late summer. Zones 4 to 9.

○ ✳

Characteristics. Height: 1½ to 3 feet. Colors: Orange to reddish orange.

This perennial has been referred to as the "flower with

wings." Butterfly weed does appear to have fluttering wings for petals, since its sweet nectar attracts many butterflies. A tough native American wildflower, it has oblong leaves, flattened to slightly domed flower clusters, and a rounded, upright, clump-forming habit. It is easy to grow in most areas of the country and doesn't become invasive.

How to Grow. Butterfly weed thrives in full sun. It is not picky about soil, though it does not like soil that is waterlogged; if the soil is too wet, the roots will rot. The plants are generally pest- and disease-free, with the exception of problems with leaf spot or rusts. Watch for early signs, and pinch off any damaged leaves. Pinch off spent flowers to extend the bloom period.

Because butterfly weed has a long taproot, it is difficult to propagate by division. Seeds germinate readily indoors if you keep the temperature of the growing medium approximately 65° to 70°F. You can also sow the seed outdoors in the fall where you want the plants to grow. Plants are readily available through mail-order and from some garden centers.

Uses. Butterfly weed is ideal for sunny sites with dry, infertile soil. It looks great in borders and in wildflower meadows.

Aster spp.

AS-ter.

Aster. Late summer through fall. Zones 4 to 8.

Characteristics. Height: 2 to 7 feet. Colors: Blue, purple, red, pink, and white.

Asters are second only to chrysanthemums in importance in the fall garden. These easy-to-grow plants bloom prolifically at a time when color is especially welcome in the garden.

New England aster (*Aster novae-angliae*) is one of the species most often grown in American gardens. It includes 4-foot-tall cultivars, as well as some neat dwarf types that fit well in the middle of the border. 'Alma Potschke' is a well-behaved, 3-foot cultivar with intense-but-not-quite-hot-pink flowers. 'Purple Dome' offers striking, regal purple flowers on compact plants that grow 2 feet tall and 3 feet wide.

The hybrid Frikart's aster (*A. X frikartii*) includes a number of cultivars noted for their early bloom, which starts in June and extends through July, sometimes returning in the fall. 'Wonder of Staffa' offers lavender-blue flowers on 2-foot plants. 'Monch' is considered one of the best garden perennials; its 27-inch, lavender-blue flowers bloom for 4 months on 3-foot-tall plants.

One of the most dramatic asters you can grow is Tartarian aster (*A. tataricus*). It produces towering 7-foot stems that (amazingly) never need staking. The stems are topped with dome-shaped clusters of lavender-blue flowers for weeks in October, and even into November in areas with late-fall frosts. The plants look stately in the back of the border or in groups in a shrub border. The cut flowers last as long as those of any aster.

How to Grow. Asters are generally grown from purchased plants, which are readily available from nurseries and garden centers, and through mail-order catalogs.

Asters can tolerate a wide range of soil conditions but prefer good drainage. They generally grow best in full sun, although some cultivars can take light shade. Pinch New England asters twice before the fourth of July to encourage bushy growth. Tall asters, with the exception of Tartarian asters, need staking. Divide the plants every 2 to 3 years in the spring to keep them vigorous; discard the woody center and replant the younger side growth. Some cultivars are susceptible to powdery mildew; give the plants plenty of room for air circulation to help prevent a serious problem. Other than needing a little pinching and staking, asters are easy to grow and require little maintenance in the garden.

Uses. Asters are invaluable for fall color in borders and for naturalizing in wildflower meadows. Try tall cultivars as landscape accents and compact cultivars in containers. All asters make attractive, long-lasting cut flowers.

Astilbe spp.
ah-STILL-bee.
Astilbe. Early summer. Zones 3 to 8.

Characteristics. Height: 1 to 3½ feet. Colors: Pink, red, peach, purple, salmon, and white.

No perennial shade garden should be without astilbe. The feathery flower plumes are as important a feature of the June garden as columbines, bleeding hearts, and hostas. Astilbes offer attractive ferny foliage and an abundance of showy flowers. They are long-lived and easy to grow in the shade. Clip the flowers for cutting or drying, or leave them on the plants for winter interest.

Astilbe X *arendsii* is the type most often grown in

American gardens. These reliable hybrids bloom in June and July, and come in a wide range of colors and plant heights. 'Peach Blossom' grows to 2 feet and bears clear blush-pink, Christmas tree-shaped flower clusters. 'Ostrich Plume' is a bright salmon cultivar; the loose, arching plumes appear on 3½ foot-tall plants. 'Fanal' offers deep red blooms and bronze-red foliage on 2-foot plants.

A. chinensis 'Pumila' is a low-growing dwarf astilbe. It has a spreading habit and makes an ideal light-textured groundcover. The stiff, lavender-pink flower spikes bloom in July or August—later than most astilbes.

A. taquetii 'Superba' offers stiff, tight, lilac-pink flower clusters in July. The 4-foot-tall plants make a terrific landscape feature in summer, and the seedpods provide winter interest.

How to Grow. To raise your own plants, sow seed of *A. X arendsii* directly in a protected area of the garden in midsummer. Move the young plants to their final locations in fall or early spring. Plants of astilbe hybrids and cultivars are commonly available at garden centers and through mail-order catalogs.

Astilbes must have moist, rich soil. The plants can tolerate sun, but only if the soil is moist; they are usually grown as partial-shade plants. They never require staking and only need to be divided every 4 or 5 years if they become overcrowded. For propagation, divide plants in early spring. Astilbes are rarely bothered by pests and diseases, and require very little maintenance once they are established in the right place in the garden.

Uses. Astilbes are showy plants for the middle of a shaded, moist-soil border. They naturalize well in woodlands. *A. chinensis* 'Pumila' makes an attractive groundcover from spring through fall. Astilbe flowers are good for fresh arrangements and also are attractive dried.

Baptisia australis
bap-TEE-zee-uh oss-TRAL-iss.
False indigo. Early summer. Zones 3 to 8.

Characteristics. Height: 4 to 6 feet. Colors: Blue.

This perennial member of the pea family was once grown in the southeastern United States as a substitute for indigo. Now it is grown across the country for its towering spikes of deep blue, pealike flowers, which add color to the back of the perennial border in June. The shrublike plants have bluegreen, compound leaves. The foliage is attractive all season and adds a fine texture to the border when the plants are not in bloom. The flowers are followed by pealike seedpods, which you can leave on the plant for winter interest or cut for dried arrangements.

How to Grow. To raise your own plants, sow the seed in pots or trays in midsummer. Place the containers in the refrigerator for 6 weeks, then move them outdoors to sprout. Or sow seed directly in a protected area of the garden in midsummer. Move the young plants to their permanent locations in fall or early spring. Plants are also available at some garden centers and through mail order catalogs.

Like other members of the pea family, false indigo grows well in low-fertility soil. It prefers full sun but tolerates light shade. The plants are long-lived and do not like to be moved once they are established. They do not need to be divided regularly. The flower spikes generally need to be staked. Cut plants back by one-third after blooming to keep them neat.

Uses. False indigo is attractive at the back of the border or as an accent plant. The flowers are great for cutting, and the pods can be used in dried arrangements.

Begonia grandis

beh-GO-nee-uh GRAN-diss.

Hardy begonia. Late summer to fall. Zones 6 to 10.

Characteristics. Height: 2 to 3 feet. Colors: Pink or white.

Hardy begonia deserves to be grown more in American shade gardens. A sister to the familiar annual wax begonia, hardy begonia has larger green leaves and pendulous clusters of small heart-shaped pink buds that open into pink flowers. The flowers bloom from August through October. The plants are not as tightly mounded as wax begonias; instead, they are upright and spreading, like some of their tropical relatives, which are grown as houseplants. 'Alba' has white flowers.

How to Grow. Start your plantings of hardy begonia with purchased plants. They are available from some nurseries, garden centers, and mail-order catalogs. A friend with an established planting is also a good source.

Hardy begonias require rich soil that stays constantly

moist. They prefer partial or full shade and cannot tolerate the hot afternoon sun. The plants produce small bulbils along their stems, which fall to the ground and grow into new plants. Once a stand is established, the plants are maintenance-free; all you need to do is keep them from spreading where you don't want them to go. Dig up extra plants and start a new bed, or share them with friends.

Uses. Grow hardy begonia in the middle of the border, as an edging, in a woodland, or as an accent. It also looks attractive in front of a shrub border. A mass planting makes a fascinating spring-to-fall groundcover. Hardy begonia emerges relatively late in spring, making it a perfect filler for spaces where spring-flowering bulbs have gone dormant.

BELLFLOWER. See *Campanula* spp.
BLANKET FLOWER. See *Gaillardia* spp.
BLEEDING HEART. See *Dicentra* spp.
BUTTERFLY WEED. See *Asclepias tuberosa*

Campanula spp.

kam-PAN-yew-luh.
Bellflower. Summer. Zones 3 to 8.

Characteristics. Height: 8 inches to 3½ feet. Colors: Blue, violet, and white.

Several species of bellflowers are commonly grown in American gardens. They all have pretty, bell-shaped flowers in shades of blue, purple, or white, produced either singly or in clusters along spikes. Carpathian bellflower (*Campanula carpatica*) is a popular low-growing species that is covered with blue or white blooms from June to July, then sporadically until September. It tends to be short-lived in the garden, especially in areas with hot summers.

Clustered bellflower (*C. glomerata*) bears clusters of small blue flowers on 1- to 3-foot stems from June to July. The flowers are excellent for cutting and have a vase life of up to 2 weeks. The plants are short-lived in the South, lasting only 3 years in the garden.

Peachleaf bellflower (*C. persicifolia*) grows from 1 to 3 feet tall, with elegant spikes of upturned, bellshaped flowers in white, lavender, or blue. It is ideal for the middle of the border, and naturalizes well in woodlands. The flowers make beautiful, long-lasting cut flowers. Like clustered bellflower, this species tends to be short-lived in the South.

How to Grow. To raise your own plants, sow seed in a protected area of the garden in midsummer. Move the young plants to their permanent locations in fall or early spring. Plants are usually available at garden centers and through mail-order catalogs.

All bellflowers require excellent drainage. Carpathian bellflower and clustered bellflower are more tolerant of dry soil than peachleaf bellflower. The taller types prefer full sun and tolerate light shade; Carpathian bellflower prefers light shade but tolerates full sun if the soil is kept moist. Taller cultivars may require staking. To rejuvenate crowded clumps or to propagate, divide the plants in early spring. Pests and diseases are generally not a problem, though Carpathian bellflower may be bothered by slugs.

Uses. Bellflowers are reliable plants that serve many purposes in the garden. Carpathian bellflowers make attractive groundcovers, edgings, or rockgarden specimen plants. Clustered and peachleaf bellflowers are ideal for flower borders, cutting, or naturalizing in a woodland.

Centaurea montana
sen-TAR-ee-uh mon-TAN-uh.
Mountain bluet. Early summer. Zones 3 to 8.

Characteristics. Height: 2 feet. Colors: Blue.

This relative of the annual cornflower, or bachelor's buttons, bears spidery flowers that appear for several weeks in May and June. They are a gorgeous shade of deep blue with a hint of a red center. Mountain bluets make good companions for silverleaved plants, such as artemisias and lamb's ears (*Stachys byzantina*), as well as white- or pink-flowered perennials. The handsome foliage is smooth and narrow, and is attractive even without the flowers. The scaled flower buds look like large versions of those of bachelor's buttons. The plants can have a second bloom period in mid- to late summer if you cut them back after the first flush of bloom in spring.

How to Grow. To raise your own plants, sow seed directly in a protected spot in the garden in midsummer. Move the young plants to their final locations in fall or early spring. Plants are not always available at garden centers, but you can usually find them through mail-order catalogs.

Mountain bluet grows best in poor, well-drained soil in full sun or light shade. The foliage declines rather quickly after the flowers bloom, so cut it back as soon as new growth appears at the base for a second flush of leaves. The plants can spread quickly and have been called invasive, especially in the North. If you want even more plants, divide existing plants in spring or start new ones from seed. Mountain bluets are rarely bothered by pests and diseases, and require little maintenance in the garden other than the yearly haircut.

Uses. Mountain bluet is excellent for the front of the border, where it is valued for the rare, intense blue color of its flowers. The blooms are also good for cutting.

Chrysanthemum spp.

kris-AN-the-mum.

Chrysanthemum, daisy. Summer. Zones 3 to 9.

Characteristics. Height: 1 to 3½ feet. Colors: Pink, red, yellow, purple, orange, and white.

The genus Chrysanthemum includes a wide range of annual and perennial daisies for gardens and wildflower meadows. The perennial chrysanthemums most often grown in American gardens are garden mums (*C.* X *morifolium*), Shasta daisies (*C.* X *superbum*), and painted daisies (*C. coccineum*).

Garden mums are to autumn what pansies, crocuses, and daffodils are to spring. Their popularity is due to the great abundance of colorful, attractively shaped blooms, which nearly cover the foliage for many weeks. The glowing flower colors are often a perfect complement to the fiery fall foliage color of deciduous trees. There are always plenty of flowers for cutting, and they last for up to 2 weeks in the vase. Garden mums have a fresh fragrance that is pleasant but not overpowering.

Shasta daisies look like tame versions of the familiar white wildflower daisies. They come in single- and double-flowered forms. 'Starburst Hybrid', developed by Burpee, is the first hybrid Shasta daisy; it features 6-inch-wide, single blooms on 3½-foot-tall plants. 'White Knight Hybrid' is a free-flowering cultivar with 4-inch blooms. The extra-strong stems of this 2-foot-tall cultivar are tolerant of wind and rain, and never need staking.

Painted daisies, also called pyrethrum daisies, have feathery foliage. The flowers are single or double and come in shades of pink, red, lavender, and white. They are one of the prettiest chrysanthemums for cutting.

How to Grow. To raise your own plants, sow seed directly in a protected area of the garden in midsummer. Move the young plants to their permanent locations in fall or early spring. Plants are also available at garden centers and through mail-order catalogs. Most mail-order nurseries do not ship garden mums in the fall because many customers expect the plants to be blooming when they arrive. The perennials that are shipped out for fall planting are usually dormant, to minimize damage from shipping and transplant shock. When purchasing garden mums in full bloom from nurseries and garden centers, make sure you are getting hardy mums, which should survive the winter in Zones 5 to 8. Many cultivars are greenhouse-grown for fall display and may not be hardy.

All chrysanthemums prefer well-drained, moist, rich soil in full sun. Shasta daisies can grow in light shade, and painted daisies can tolerate poor soil. Taller cultivars may need staking. Divide all chrysanthemums every 2 or 3 years in spring or fall.

For a possible second flush of bloom, cut back the stems of Shasta daisies after they bloom. Pinch garden mums two or three times before mid- to late July to encourage bushiness. Make the first pinch when the plants are 6 inches tall.

Uses. There is a place in every sunny garden for chrysanthemums. These plants are terrific for beds, borders, containers, edgings, and cutting gardens. Garden mums are especially useful for fall color. Shasta and painted daisies can be naturalized in a wildflower meadow.

COLUMBINE. See *Aquilegia* spp.

Coreopsis spp.
kor-ee-OP-sis.
Coreopsis, tickseed. Summer. Zones 4 to 9.

Characteristics. Height: 1 to 2½ feet. Colors: Yellow.

These important perennials are prized for their cheerful, yellow daisylike flowers, which bloom all summer on well-behaved, easy-to-grow plants. Tickseed (*Coreopsis grandiflora*), threadleaf coreopsis (*C. verticillata*), and lanceleaf coreopsis (*C. lanceolata*) are the most popular species, because of their long periods of bloom and their reliable garden performance.

Tickseed is a bushy 1- to 2-foot-tall plant with bright golden yellow single or semidouble flowers and long, narrow leaves. 'Early Sunrise' is an excellent cultivar that won both the All-America Selections and European Fleuroselect awards for its ability to bloom the first year from seed and for its neat, uniform habit. It blooms continuously from June to August if deadheaded.

Threadleaf coreopsis has very narrow foliage, as wide as its narrow stems. The lightness of the foliage gives the plants an airy texture in the garden. The small single flowers cover the foliage from June through August. 'Moonbeam' is one of the best cultivars; in fact, it is one of the best garden perennials available today. It was selected as the Perennial Plant Association's Perennial Plant of the Year in 1992. The 15-inch plants offer exquisite, creamy primrose-yellow flowers and dark green foliage. The flower color blends well with many other colors, especially blues and purples.

Lanceleaf coreopsis is one of the most forgiving of garden plants. Its lovely, bright yellow, daisylike flowers are 1½ to 2½ inches across. The leaves are lance-shaped, and the plants have a clump-forming habit. It is hardy in Zones 5 to 9.

How to Grow. To raise your own plants, sow seed of the species directly in a protected area of the garden in midsummer. Or sow seed indoors in early spring; seed germinates best when the growing medium is kept at about 70°F. Harden off the young plants and move them to their permanent locations in fall or early spring. 'Early Sunrise' will bloom the first year from seed sown indoors about 8 weeks before the last frost date. Plants of other cultivars are available at garden centers and through mail-order catalogs.

All three kinds of coreopsis prefer well-drained soil in full sun. The plants can tolerate partial shade but bloom best in full sun. Tickseed can withstand drought; both threadleaf and lanceleaf coreopsis prefer poorer soil. In fact, too-rich soil can decrease the plants' flowering and make them too sprawling. Regular deadheading can keep tickseed in bloom for months. (If you cut lots of flowers for bouquets, there won't be as many to deadhead.) All three species appreciate a protective winter mulch north of Zone 6. Divide the plants in spring or fall for propagation or to rejuvenate old clumps.

Uses. Coreopsis is valuable for the middle or front of the border and is an ideal addition to drysoil gardens. This easy-care perennial also performs well in containers. The cut flowers are long-lasting and a welcome addition to fresh arrangements.

DAISY. See *Chrysanthemum* spp.
DAYLILY. See *Hemerocallis hybrids*

Delphinium elatum hybrids
del-FIN-ee-um el-AY-tum.
Delphinium. Summer. Zones 3 to 6.

Characteristics. Height: 3 to 7 feet. Colors: Blue, purple, pink, and white.

Delphiniums are among the most elegant of all perennials. Their stately flower spires—in regal shades of blue, purple, pink, or white—make us yearn for those perennial borders and cottage gardens we see in picture books of famous British gardens. Unfortunately, however, delphiniums are not as happy in many American gardens as they are in English gardens. Although they thrive in areas of the Pacific Northwest with cool summer nights, they are short-lived in regions with hot summers and should be treated as annuals outside of Zones 3 to 6.

Many fine cultivars are available. 'Pacific Coast' has towering 7-foot spikes of closely packed, single florets in pink, blue, and violet shades; they are magnificent but short-lived. 'Connecticut Yankee' is a 30-inch-tall, semi-dwarf, well-branched hybrid that is more heat-tolerant than other cultivars. The Blackmore and Langdon Strain tends to be longerlived and has 4- to 7-foot spikes.

How to Grow. To raise your own plants, sow the seed directly in a protected area of the garden in midsummer. Move the young plants to their permanent locations in fall or early spring. In cool areas, you can allow the plants to go dormant in summer after they flower, then pot them up and overwinter them in a coldframe. Bring them out early the following spring, divide them, then move them to their blooming locations. Plants are also available from garden centers and through mail-order catalogs for fall and spring planting.

Delphiniums require cool, moist, rich soil in full sun or light shade. They need extra watering in dry, hot weather. Taller cultivars must be staked, or the flower spikes will break in stormy weather. Cut back the flower stalks after blooming. Or, if you are growing them as annuals, pull the plants after they bloom.

Uses. Delphiniums are stunning for the back of the border, in cottage gardens, or as accent plants. They also make splendid cut flowers.

Dianthus spp.
dy-AN-thus.
Pinks. Spring or summer. Zones 3 to 9.

Characteristics. Height: 1 to 2 feet. Colors: Pink, red, salmon, and white.

This large genus of annuals, biennials, and perennials includes many fine species for the garden. All of the species share the fringed, or "pinked," edges of the flower petals; the long, narrow, green-blue or gray foliage; and the color range of pink, red, salmon, and white. The perennial species have a decided advantage in that they live longer, coming back for many years if they are happy in their location. They also have evergreen foliage.

Cottage pinks (*Dianthus plurnarius*) is named for its early use in cottage gardens—the informal, mixed plantings of flowers, vegetables, and herbs that preceded our modern flower gardens. Cottage pinks feature single red, pink, or white flowers on 18– to 24–inch stems above spreading mats of graygreen, grasslike foliage. The flowers bloom in May and June, and have a spicy fragrance. The plants live for many years but should be divided every 2 or 3 years to maintain their vitality.

The Allwood hybrids (*D.* X *allwoodii*) were developed by crossing *D. plurnarius* with *D. caryophyllus*. They are more compact and vigorous than cottage pinks. Their flowers come in shades of pink, red, and white; most are double, although single forms are available. The plants may be short-lived in areas with hot, humid summers.

How to Grow. To raise your own plants, sow seed directly in a protected area of the garden in midsummer. Move the young plants to their final locations in fall or early spring. Plants are also available at garden centers, and you can find an even wider selection through mail-order catalogs.

All pinks grow well in well-drained soil and full sun. Cottage pinks prefer slightly alkaline soil. Deadheading will encourage more continuous bloom and keep the plants looking neat. Pinks are easy to grow when they are happy and are rarely bothered by pests and diseases.

Uses. Pinks are lovely along the front of the border, as an edging, and in cottage gardens, rock gardens, and containers. They are terrific for cutting, lasting for more than a week in the vase and perfuming the room with their sweet or spicy fragrance.

Dicentra spp.
dy-SEN-truh.
Bleeding heart. Spring. Zones 3 to 7.

Characteristics. Height: 12 to 30 inches. Colors: Pink or white.

Bleeding hearts are sentimental favorites for their unique heart-shaped flowers with teardropshaped, protruding petals, which make them look as though they were bleeding. The spring-blooming flowers are arranged in rows along arching stems over deeply cut foliage.

The old-fashioned common bleeding heart (*Dicentra spectabilis*) has deep pink or white hearts. The plants grow to 2½ feet tall and spread as wide, then die back dramatically in June and disappear until the following spring. They are likely to leave a large gap in your design if you don't plan for their short season. Fill the space with a late-emerging perennial, such as hardy begonia (*Begonia grandis*), or with medium-sized annuals.

Everything about fringed bleeding heart (*D. eximia*) is smaller or lighter than common bleeding heart. It has lighter pink or white flowers on stems that are not as long and arched as those of the other species. The plants are shorter, growing only 12 inches tall, and have more finely cut foliage, in a lighter shade of green. Unlike common bleeding heart, fringed bleeding heart does not go dormant during the season. It also has one of the longest bloom periods of any garden flower—from April until September.

How to Grow. To raise your own plants, sow seed directly in a protected area of the garden in midsummer. Move the young plants to their permanent locations in fall or early spring. Plants of both species are readily available from garden centers and through mail-order catalogs.

These perennials prefer a woodland environment, with rich, moist, well-drained soil and partial or even full shade. Fringed bleeding heart may need extra watering in hot weather. Common bleeding heart usually goes dormant when hot weather arrives. Deadhead fringed bleeding heart to keep the plants looking neat and for more continuous bloom. When they are happy, both species will self-sow furiously, giving you many seedlings to expand your plantings or to share with friends and neighbors.

Uses. Bleeding hearts are perfect plants for woodland borders and for naturalizing. Fringed bleeding hearts can be used as spring-to-fall groundcovers. The flowers are good for cutting.

Echinops ritro
EK-in-ops REE-troh.
Globe thistle. Summer. Zones 4 to 9.

Characteristics. Height: 4 to 5 feet. Colors: Steel blue.

Globe thistle has spherical balls of tiny flowers that look like stars shooting out from the center. The icy blue flowers blend well with pink, silver, or white companion flowers. They bloom for 6 to 8 weeks on long, strong, stems and make perfect cut flowers for fresh or dried arrangements. The dramatic plants are rough-textured, with spiny, thistlelike foliage.

How to Grow. To raise your own plants, sow seed directly in a protected area of the garden in midsummer. Move the young plants to their permanent locations in fall or early spring. Plants are not commonly sold at garden centers but are usually available through mail-order catalogs.

Globe thistle prefers rich, well-drained soil in full sun. The plants send down deep roots and can last for many years in the garden. They are difficult to dig up and divide because of the deep roots, but these roots also tend to make the plants drought resistant. Globe thistle must be staked. To encourage a second flush of bloom on shorter stems, cut the flower stems back to the ground after bloom.

Uses. Globe thistle is useful for the middle or back of the border, or as a background plant. The flowers are good for cutting for fresh or dried bouquets.

EVENING PRIMROSE, MISSOURI. See *Oenothera missouriensis*
FALSE INDIGO. See *Baptisia australis*

Filipendula spp.
fil-ih-PEN-dew-luh.
Meadowsweet. Summer. Zones 3 to 8.

Characteristics. Height: 3 to 8 feet. Colors: Pink, purple, and white.

Meadowsweets are large, shrublike perennials with handsome foliage and clusters of tiny, astilbelike flowers. Queen-of-the-prairie (*Filipendula rubra*) can reach 6 to 8 feet tall, yet it rarely needs staking. Its fluffy, light pink flowers bloom in June above rough-textured, divided foliage. Japanese meadowsweet (*F. purpurea*) produces large, lobed leaves and fluffy clusters of deep pink flowers that mature to purple in June. It grows to a manageable 4 feet and never needs staking. Queen-of-the-meadow (*F. ulmaria*) grows 3 to 6 feet tall, with divided leaves and fluffy clusters of white flowers that bloom from June to July. 'Flore Plena' has double white flowers; 'Variegate' produces variegated leaves. 'Aurea' is a particularly striking cultivar with golden foliage. The golden color is most apparent when the plants are cut back after blooming.

How to Grow. Start with plants purchased from garden centers or through mail-order catalogs.

Meadowsweets prefer well-drained, moist soil in full sun or light shade. They do not tolerate drought well and should be watered in dry weather. Even the tallest plants normally don't need staking. Propagate by division in spring or fall. The plants are rarely bothered by pests and diseases, and are easy to maintain in the garden.

Uses. Meadowsweets are terrific for the back of the border or as accent plants. They naturalize well in moist wildflower meadows. Try cutting the flowers for fresh or dried arrangements. Or, leave the flowers to dry on the plants for winter interest.

Gaillardia spp.

guh-LAR-dee-uh.
Perennial blanket flower. Summer into fall. Zones 2 to 9.

Characteristics. Height: 1 to 3½ feet. Colors: Yellow and red.

Perennial blanket flower bears mostly single, daisylike flowers in bright combinations of red and yellow. It has an exceptionally long season of bloom—from June to October. The seed heads that follow the flowers are also attractive and add winter interest to the garden. The "hot"-colored flowers are very bright, so choose companion flowers carefully. The two most popular types of perennial blanket flower grown in American gardens are *Gaillardia aristata*, a native wildflower hardy in Zones 2 to 8, and *G.* X *grandiflora*, a hybrid species developed by crossing *G. aristata* and annual blanket flower (*G. pulchella*). *G.* X *grandiflora* is hardy in Zones 3 to 9.

How to Grow. To raise your own plants, sow seed directly in a protected area of the garden in midsummer. Move the young plants to their final locations in fall or early spring. Sometimes they bloom the first year from seed sown early indoors.

You can also start the seed indoors in late winter and set hardened-off transplants outdoors after all danger of frost has passed. Seed should germinate in 5 to 10 days at around 70°F. Gaillardias are usually available at garden centers and from mail-order catalogs.

The plants prefer well-drained, poor soil and full sun. They are tolerant of drought. Deadhead for continuous bloom. Divide the plants every 2 or 3 years in spring or fall.

Uses. Perennial blanket flowers are excellent for the middle of the border, for a cottage garden, and for naturalizing in a wildflower meadow. They are especially valuable for dry-soil areas, and are very striking when planted in large numbers. The blooms make terrific cut flowers.

GAYFEATHER. See *Liatris pycnostachya*

Geranium spp.
jer-AY-nee-um.
Hardy geranium. Early summer to fall. Zones 4 to 9.

Characteristics. Height: 12 to 24 inches. Colors: Blue, pink, lilac, purple, and white.

These understated perennials bear no resemblance to their namesake, the tender perennial zonal geranium (*Pelargonium* X *hortorum*). Hardy geraniums are low-growing plants with divided, ferny foliage and small, single or double flowers. Several species are becoming popular as gardeners are discovering these wonderful plants.

Geranium endressii features 15- to 18-inch plants with glossy green, finely cut foliage and pretty, light pink, 1-inch-wide flowers that bloom in spring and summer. The best-known cultivar is 'Wargrave Pink', which has notched, salmon-pink flowers. It performs best in cooler areas, where it blooms all summer.

G. himalayense is 12 to 18 inches tall, with blue, 2-inch-wide flowers and deeply lobed foliage. 'Plenum' has double flowers. The most popular cultivar is 'Johnson's Blue', which has a graceful, sprawling habit and more, but smaller flowers than the species.

G. sanguineum has a very long blooming season—from May to September—and is the most adaptable species. The mounded, 1-foot-tall plants produce 1– to 2–inch magenta flowers and finely-divided, starry foliage.

How to Grow. To raise your own plants, sow seed of the species directly in a protected area of the garden in midsummer. Move the young plants to their permanent locations in fall or early spring. You can find plants at well-stocked garden centers; mail-order catalogs often list a good selection.

Hardy geraniums prefer rich, well-drained, moist soil in full sun or partial shade. They are rarely bothered by pests and diseases, and are easy to care for once they are established. The plants often selfsow where they are happy. If these self-sown seedlings aren't enough, you can also propagate plants by division in spring or fall.

Uses. Hardy geraniums make a lovely, light textured, deciduous groundcover for partial shade. They are also effective in the front of the border, in a rock garden, as a woodland plant, or as an edging.

GLOBE THISTLE. See *Echinops ritro*
GOLDENROD. See *Solidago* spp.
HARDY BEGONIA. See *Begonia grandis*
HARDY GERANIUM. See *Geranium* spp.

Helianthus spp.
hee-lee-AN-thus.
Perennial sunflower. Late summer to fall. Zones 4 to 9.

Characteristics. Height: 3 to 10 feet. Colors: Yellow.

The perennial relatives of common annual sunflowers have smaller flowers and bear them in clusters. The plants can be as large as the tall, annual types, although shorter, better-behaved cultivars have been developed for garden use. Perennial sunflowers can be invasive, but the species described here are easy to control.

Swamp sunflower (*Helianthus angustifolius*) grows to 10 feet, with handsome narrow foliage and 2-inch flowers that bloom from September to November. When grown in full sun and pinched in spring, the plants can stay a manageable 7 feet. They generally need staking to avoid breaking in windy or rainy weather, although in poor soil they can be self-supporting.

Willowleaf sunflower (*H. salicifolius*) has very narrow, willowlike foliage; golden yellow daisies appear on the 6- to 8-foot stems from September to October. *H. X multiflorus* is a bushy, lower-growing, 3- to 6-foot hybrid that offers masses of sunny yellow daisies from July through September. The double flowered 'Flore Pleno' is one of the most popular cultivars, producing numerous chrysanthemum-like flowers for months.

How to Grow. To grow your own plants, sow seed directly in a protected area of the garden in midsummer. Move the young plants to their final locations in fall or early spring. Plants are usually available at garden centers and through mail-order catalogs.

Sunflowers perform best in moist soil and require

plenty of water during dry spells. As their name suggests, they need to grow in full sun. In shade they grow absurdly tall, tend to fall over and break, and bloom poorly. The plants tend to spread when they are happy; dividing them every 2 or 3 years in fall or spring will help keep them under control. Pinch them in July for shorter plants. They are remarkably free of pests and diseases, and are generally very easy to grow.

Uses. Perennial sunflowers are wonderful for bright color in late summer through autumn. Grow them at the back of the border, as a hedge or screen, as a garden accent, or in a wildflower meadow. The flowers are good for cutting for fresh bouquets.

Hemerocallis hybrids

hem-er-oh-KAL-iss.
Daylily. Summer. Zones 3 to 8.

Characteristics. Height: 1 to 4 feet. Colors: Yellow, pink, lilac, purple, red, orange, white, and bicolors.

Daylilies are nearly perfect perennials. They grow easily in all kinds of soil and weather conditions, and they offer beautiful flowers in a wide range of colors, sizes, and shapes. The narrow, arching leaves are handsome all season, and the plants are rarely bothered by pests and diseases. If you divide them every 3 or 4 years, you'll have a continuous supply of plants for your garden and for your friends and neighbors, too. In short, daylilies are very tough plants that are also very pretty.

The trumpet-shaped flowers of daylilies come in many colors, including creamy white, brassy gold to soft primrose yellow, pumpkin orange to glowing apricot, deep red to pastel pink, and lavender to deep purple. There are also many bicolors and "eyed" types. The single or double flowers can be as large as 6 inches wide or as small as 2 inches across. Each flower lasts only 1 day (the characteristic that gives the plants their common name), but each stem has many buds, so the plants can be in bloom for several weeks. Some are even repeat bloomers. If you select cultivars carefully, you can enjoy the flowers for up to 4 months.

Daylilies are often confused with true lilies, which belong to the genus *Lilium* and grow from bulbs. It's easy to tell them apart: Daylily flowers bloom on leafless stems; true lilies bloom atop stems that have short, narrow leaves all along them. Many people use the name "tiger lily" for the common roadside daylily (*Hemerocallis fulva*), even though it most correctly refers to a true lily with black-spotted orange petals and swept-back petals.

How to Grow. Unless you want to grow species daylilies, it is best to purchase plants. Many different daylilies are readily available at garden centers; for the widest selection, however, buy plants from specialty mail-order nurseries. To raise plants from seed, sow seed directly in a protected area of the garden in midsummer. Move the young plants to their final locations in fall or early spring.

Daylilies can adapt to poor, clay, or sandy soil but prefer a soil that is rich, with good drainage. The plants do best in full sun; they can tolerate partial shade but do not bloom as prolifically. Repeat bloomers flower more continuously if you remove the spent flowers. For propagation, divide the plants in fall or spring. Daylilies are rarely bothered by pests and diseases, and are among the easiest, lowest maintenance perennials you can grow. Just plant them and enjoy them!

Uses. Daylilies come in all sizes for the front, middle, and back of the border. They make excellent edgings or landscape features planted in long rows. Grow the smaller cultivars in containers. All types can be cut for fresh flowers, and some cultivars are sweetly fragrant. Daylilies are ideal for a beginning perennial gardener, since they are practically indestructible.

HOLLYHOCK. See *Alcea rosea*

Hosta hybrids
HOS-tuh.
Hosta. Summer. Zones 3 to 8.

Characteristics. Height: 3 to 36 inches (foliage). Colors: Lavender or white flowers; blue, lime green, green, and variegated foliage.

Hostas are the quintessential foliage plants for shade gardens. They send up attractive shoots in spring to accompany spring-blooming bulbs, then unfurl their leaves conveniently to hide the yellowing foliage of the bulbs after they have bloomed. The foliage forms undulating waves when planted in masses, giving a cool look to the garden.

Hosta foliage can be any shade of green, from greenish yellow to medium green, dark green, gray-green, or blue-green. Many cultivars are variegated with yellow, cream, white, or darker or lighter green edges or markings. The leaves can be long and narrow, short and broad, heart-shaped, puckered, or stiffly upright.

Some plants are miniature, growing 6 inches across and 3 to 4 inches tall; others are enormous, up to 5 feet tall. Most are somewhere in between—1 to 2 feet wide and 1 foot tall, not counting the tall flowers when they are in bloom. The larger cultivars can be very slow-growing and may not bloom for years after they are planted. Even the smaller cultivars can be slow to mature and may take 3 or 4 years to look like their catalog pictures. However, they are well worth the wait.

Hosta flowers appear on spikes for several weeks in midsummer to fall, depending on the cultivar. Some gardeners dislike the flowers and cut them off when they appear. However, many cultivars can be grown primarily for their attractive flowers. The single or double blooms may be lavender or white, in thick, stocky clusters or on tall, graceful spikes. Some are lightly fragrant and most are excellent for cutting. There are so many interesting new cultivars that collecting hostas can become an addiction! Entire books have been written about these plants, and hosta enthusiasts can rival orchid lovers for their depth of knowledge about their passion.

Because there are so many wonderful hostas, it seems unfair to mention specific ones. Some, however, stand out for their excellence or popularity. For instance, *Hosta sieboldiana* produces large, landscape-sized plants with rounded, blue-green foliage and white or lavender flowers. Cultivars of this species include 'Frances Williams', which has bluegreen leaves edged with gold; 'Golden Sunburst', with golden yellow leaves; and 'Elegans', which features steely blue leaves.

H. venusta is a dwarf species that grows 3 to 4 inches tall and 6 to 8 inches across. *H. ventricosa* has wide, dark green leaves; the popular cultivar 'Aureo-marginata' sports yellow-and-green leaves. Plantain lily (*H. plantaginea*) produces large green leaves and pretty, often sweetly fragrant, lilylike flowers; cultivars include 'Honeybells' and 'Royal Standard'.

How to Grow. Start your hosta collection with purchased plants. They are always available at garden centers and through mail-order catalogs. Specialty mail-order nurseries can provide enough interesting selections—both new and old—to keep collectors happy.

Hostas are essentially shade plants, and their inroad foliage tends to burn in full sun in warm, dry summer weather. Some cultivars are more tolerant of full sun, but all need extra watering in dry weather to keep the foliage looking fresh. Hostas prefer rich, well-drained, moist soil and can tolerate as much shade as almost any garden plant. They do not appreciate the competition for water that shallow-rooted trees such as maples, beeches, or dogwoods provide, but they can grow well under deep-rooted trees such as oaks.

Hostas seem to be the very fruit of life for slugs and snails. Check for these pests regularly (don't forget to look for them under the leaves, too), and remove and destroy any within sight. Diatomaceous earth and beer traps can help control their damage. Hostas do not die gracefully in fall, so cut them back when the foliage turns yellow. Division is an easy way to propagate hostas. Some cultivars self-sow.

Uses. Hostas are excellent foliage plants for a deciduous groundcover in shady areas and for the front or middle of a shady border. The larger cultivars make stately landscape specimen plants; lowergrowing cultivars are popular as edging plants. Hostas look great in containers in the shade, especially when they are combined with longer-blooming annuals or perennials. The flowers are good for cutting for fresh bouquets, and many have a sweet fragrance. Miniature cultivars are sometimes grown as bonsai companion plants.

INDIGO, FALSE. See *Baptista australis*

Iris spp.
EYE-riss.
Iris. Spring or summer. Zones 3 to 9.

Characteristics. Height: 6 inches to 4 feet. Colors: Blue, violet, yellow, pink, purple, apricot, deep red, bronze, white, and bicolors.

This important genus includes bulbs and perennials. They all share the familiar iris flower form, with upright or drooping "standards" and drooping "falls." The species differ in flower form and size, foliage, height, color range, bloom time, and soil requirements. With so many plants to choose from, you're sure to find at least one that is perfect for almost any site. The most popular perennial iris species include bearded iris hybrids,

Siberian iris (*Iris sibirica*), Japanese iris (*I. ensata*, also known as *I. kaempferi*), yellow flag iris (*I. pseudacorus*), and dwarf crested iris (*I. cristata*).

The bearded iris hybrids are perhaps the best known iris group. They grow from fleshy underground stems called rhizomes. They bloom from May to June, and some cultivars repeat their bloom in late summer or early fall. The flowers are characterized by the hairy "beards" on their lower petals, often in a contrasting color from the standards and falls. Bearded iris blooms are often bicolored and may have striking veins in contrasting colors. Many are fragrant. The color range is truly immense and includes every color in the rainbow. One of the prettiest shades is the glowing apricot-peach of 'Beverly Sills'.

Bearded irises vary in height from 8 inches to 3 feet, although most cultivars grow from 2 to 3 feet tall. The taller cultivars tend to have larger flowers but generally need to be staked. Medium-height cultivars are self-supporting. Bloom times vary, too; careful selection can give you a garden of bearded iris that blooms for many weeks. The upright, sword-shaped foliage is handsome, although it has a tendency to burn at the tips in the heat of summer.

Siberian iris is a vigorous perennial with long, narrow, straplike leaves. It has classic iris flowers that look more streamlined than those of bearded iris and do not have the beards. The flowers come in shades of blue, purple, pink, and white, and many have attractive veins. They bloom in May or June for about 2 weeks on 2- to 4-foot stems. The foliage always looks fresh and is more useful in the border than that of bearded iris, since it usually does not burn at the tips and is not as subject to the foliage diseases that attack bearded iris.

Japanese iris has breathtakingly beautiful flowers—perhaps the prettiest of all iris. They are large and elegant, with gently drooping standards and falls. When they are caught by breezes, they look like graceful birds in flight. Japanese irises come in shades of blue, purple, lavender, and white, and many have beautifully etched veins. They bloom in June or July for a short period—about 2 weeks. Their foliage is like that of Siberian iris, only wider. The plants grow from 2 to 3 feet tall but rarely need staking.

Yellow flag is a water-loving iris that can grow in ponds or along moist stream banks. It has big, bright yellow flowers and blooms just after the Japanese irises have finished. The plants grow over 3 feet tall and have attractive bluish-green, straplike foliage.

Dwarf crested iris is a compact wildflower that reaches only 6 to 8 inches tall. This vivid, charming plant bears blue to violet flowers; the petals are highlighted with white and yellow markings. The narrow, sword-shaped leaves grow taller than the flower stems, so the flowers bloom amid a leafy carpet. This species is hardy in Zones 4 to 9.

How to Grow. Start your iris collection with purchased plants. Plants are available at any nursery and through mail-order catalogs. There are many specialty iris mail-order nurseries.

Irises vary in their soil requirements. Bearded iris prefers rich, well-drained soil and can rot if the drainage is poor. Siberian iris also does best in rich, well-drained soil. Dwarf crested iris will grow fine in average garden soil as long as it gets adequate moisture, but good drainage is critical; waterlogged soil will cause the roots to rot. Japanese iris and yellow flag, on the other hand, can grow in wet soil, and even water. Most types grow best in full sun, but many can tolerate light shade. Dwarf crested iris can take full sun if the soil is evenly moist; otherwise, it prefers partial shade. Plant bearded irises so the rhizomes are level with the soil surface. Deadhead irises after they bloom, to keep the plants looking neat.

Bearded irises are susceptible to iris borer, a wormlike insect that bores holes in the rhizomes, causing them to rot. Divide your bearded irises every 2 or 3 years in early July and check them for borer holes; discard pieces with borers or borer damage. On the rest, cut back the foliage by half and replant the rhizomes. Divide other irises every 3 or 4 years in spring or fall, whenever they become overcrowded. Siberian irises form sturdy clumps that can be difficult to divide without a very sharp spade and a strong back.

Uses. Irises are ideal for the front, middle, or back of the border, depending on the height of the plants. Naturalize them in wildflower meadows, or plant them in masses. Japanese iris and yellow flag can be grown in water gardens and wetland areas; they are also popular in Japanese gardens. Dwarf crested iris makes an excellent seasonal groundcover and is especially good for slopes, since it thrives in well-drained soil. It is also useful as an edging plant and for spring color at the front of borders, in woodland gardens, and in rock gardens. The taller irises produce flowers that are terrific for cutting. Irises are often grouped with daylilies as the perfect perennial plants for beginners.

LADY'S MANTLE. See *Alchemilla mollis*
LAMB'S EARS. See *Stachys byzantina*

Liatris pycnostachya

lee-AT-riss pik-no-STAKE-yuh. Gayfeather,
prairie blazing star. Midsummer to fall. Zones 3 to 9.

Characteristics. Height: 2 to 5 feet. Colors: Pink to lavender. The tall, wandlike flowers of gayfeather, a native wildflower, sway gracefully in the breeze, looking as grand in the garden as they once did among tall prairie grasses across the Midwest. The flowers are unusual in that the blooms at the top of the spike open first, followed by those below. Gayfeather's long stems are covered with grasslike foliage.

How to Grow. To start your own plants, sow seed directly in a protected area of the garden in midsummer. Move the young plants to their permanent locations in fall or early spring. Plants are also available at some garden centers and through mail-order catalogs.

Give gayfeather full sun and well-drained soil that's rich in organic matter. It will not tolerate wet soil. The plants may need staking, especially in exposed, windy sites. They benefit from a good winter mulch, particularly in Zones 3 to 6, to prevent the roots from being pushed out of the ground by alternate freezing and thawing.

Uses. This plant is excellent for adding color, height, and texture to borders and meadows. It also makes a wonderful cut flower. Try planting it next to bee balm (*Monarda didyma*) and asters for a gorgeous display of pinks, reds, and lavenders.

MOUNTAIN BLUET. See *Centaurea montana*
MEADOWSWEET. See *Filipendula* spp.
MISSOURI EVENING PRIMROSE. See *Oenothera missouriensis*
MOSS PINK. See *Phlox* spp.

Oenothera missouriensis

ee-no-THEE-ruh miz-er-ee-EN-sis. Missouri evening primrose, Ozark sundrops. Summer. Zones 3 to 8.

Characteristics. Height: 9 to 12 inches. Colors: Bright yellow.

When this plant is flowering, it is like having a burst of sunlight in your garden. There are hardly any other garden plants whose color can match the dazzlingly clear, clean, and lustrous yellow of the flowers. The 3- to 4-inch blooms are borne in summer on short, hairy stems with lance-shaped leaves.

How to Grow. Missouri evening primrose needs full sun and well-drained soil. It prefers dry—even sandy, rocky, or gravelly—soil; wet conditions can lead to root rot.

The plants grow readily from seed sown directly in the garden in fall or early spring. They are also easy to divide in fall or spring. Plants are often available at garden centers and are easy to find in mail-order catalogs.

Uses. The sprawling habit of Missouri evening primrose makes it an excellent plant for raised beds and rock gardens. This cheerful, drought-tolerant perennial is especially suitable for dry-soil areas. For a beautiful combination, try planting Missouri evening primrose with Mexican hat plant (*Ratibida columnifera*), purple coneflower (*Echinacea purpurea*), and lanceleaf coreopsis (*Coreopsis lanceolata*).

ORIENTAL POPPY. See *Papaver orientale*
OZARK SUNDROPS. See *Oenothera missouriensis*

Paeonia lactiflora

pee-OH-nee-uh lak-tih-FLOR-uh.

Peony. Late spring to early summer. Zones 3 to 8.

Characteristics. Height: 2 to 4 feet. Colors: Pink, coral, yellow, red, white, and bicolors.

Peonies are among the best-loved perennials in northern gardens. They thrive in Zones 3 to 8 but perform poorly in frost-free or nearly frost-free areas. Every year, Burpee customers who have moved from cooler zones to warmer climates say they miss growing peonies more than any other garden plant.

Peonies are popular for their big, softly colored flowers. The blooms of some look like fluffy powder puffs; others resemble cabbage roses. Single, semidouble, and fully double forms are available in a wide range of colors. Many are wonderfully fragrant, and mass plantings of mixed cultivars always yield a delicious scent in the garden.

The beauty of peonies extends beyond their flowers. In spring, their emerging red leaves are as important a part of the garden as the accompanying spring bulbs.

Their spherical flower buds have a charm of their own, suspended over the foliage in anticipation of the big flowers to come. The divided foliage is handsome all summer and often takes on a glorious red color in late summer to early fall.

Gardeners often ask about the ants that are sometimes present around peony flowers and flower buds. One theory is that they are attendant ants for aphids, tiny pests that like to feed on new growth, including flower buds. But aphids may not be present while the ants are. Another theory suggests that the ants are needed to help the flowers open. But the ants aren't always present, and the blooms open well enough without their assistance. According to yet another theory, the ants are attracted to the sugary nectar that exudes from the buds and is present in the flowers. Some peony experts say they have never noticed ants around peony flowers. Whatever the reason, the ants do not harm the plants and can be easily washed off when the flowers are brought indoors after being cut.

In the proper environment, peonies are exceptionally long-lived perennials, often outliving the gardeners who planted them. They resent being moved as they age, so choose an appropriate permanent location and leave them alone. They will reward you with a lifetime of reliable performance.

How to Grow. Peonies take up to 2 years to germinate from seed, which is clearly inconvenient for even the most adventurous gardener! You're better off starting bareroot plants, which are available through many mail-order catalogs.

Most suppliers will deliver bareroot plants—with 3 to 5 "eyes" (buds)—for planting in spring or fall, although experienced gardeners agree that fall is the best time for planting. The soil should be well drained and rich, in a sunny or lightly shaded location. Prepare the soil as deeply as possible, at least 1 to 2 feet deep. Set the roots so the reddish eyes are 1 to 2 inches below the soil surface. The plants may take their time to bloom—sometimes 2 or 3 years after they are planted. However, once they start blooming, you'll forget their slow start.

Peonies benefit from support, which you can easily provide by using inconspicuous peony "hoops." The plants are heavy feeders, so scratch some bonemeal or superphosphate into the soil in spring or fall. They also need plenty of water, especially during long dry spells. Peonies are subject to botrytis, a fungal disease that kills shoots and flower buds and disfigures foliage. Cutting the plants to the ground in the fall will help prevent this problem, since the pathogen overwinters in the dead foliage.

Uses. Peonies are at their best when planted in masses as landscape features. They make wonderful herbaceous hedges with three seasons of interest. They are also splendid flowers for cutting; try them in dinner-table bouquets. (Don't forget to wash off the ants!) The cut flowers take up an astonishing amount of water, so check the water level in the vase every day.

Papaver orientale

PAH-puh-ver or-ee-en-TAL-ee.
Oriental poppy. Late spring. Zones 3 to 8.

Characteristics. Height: 2 to 4 feet. Colors: Pink, orange, red, salmon, and white.

This perennial cousin of the summer-blooming annual poppy is always a focal point when it is included in the late-spring garden. The flowers are much larger than those of their annual relatives and come in very bright, even gaudy colors, with contrasting centers and blotches in black, purple, or white. The flowers may be single, semidouble, or double. They are followed by very interesting seedpods, which make attractive additions to dried-flower arrangements. The rough-textured, hairy, fernlike foliage is a giant version of the delicate foliage of Shirley or Flanders poppy (*Papaver rhoeas*).

The plants go dormant during the summer, leaving a gap in the border that should be filled with annuals or later-blooming perennials. (Plant the annuals carefully to avoid damaging the poppy roots.) The foliage sometimes reappears in the fall.

How to Grow. To grow your own plants, sow seed directly in a protected area of the garden in midsummer. Move the young plants to their final locations in fall or early spring. To reduce the danger of transplant shock, you can also grow them in peat pots. Plants are available from garden centers.

For the widest range of colors, check out mail-order nurseries. The plants are usually shipped in pots to protect the roots.

Oriental poppies prefer well-drained, rich soil in full sun. They can tolerate summer drought when they are dormant. Like most poppies, they have long, easily damaged taproots and should not be moved once they are established. Also, avoid dividing the plants unless they become very crowded; then divide them carefully in late summer or early fall.

Uses. The brightly colored, late-spring flowers of Oriental poppies are striking in borders. Plan for companions to fill the space left when the plants go dormant. Cut the flowers for fresh bouquets; save the seedpods for interesting additions to dried arrangements.

PEONY. See *Paeonia lactiflora*

Perovskia atriplicifolia
per-OFF-skee-uh ah-trih-plih-sih-FOE-lee-uh.
Russian sage. Summer. Zones 3 to 9.

Characteristics. Height: 3 feet. Colors: Blue flowers, silver foliage.

Russian sage is gaining in popularity in American gardens for several reasons. The plants make striking landscape accents and look good the same year you plant them. Plus, they are very drought-resistant and are easy to grow and maintain. Russian sage is an excellent choice for hot, dry locations where so many other perennials burn out. Landscapers use it in one of the most difficult areas any perennial will ever have to deal with—parking lot islands surrounded by a sea of concrete. The only place this plant is not happy is in a wet, poorly drained location, or in the shade.

Russian sage has attractive foliage that persists from spring through fall and into the winter. The silvery color contrasts beautifully with both hot and cool colors in borders. The plants practically glow in the dark and can be haunting when planted near a deck or patio that is used at night. The flowers are not especially showy but add to the plants' interest for several weeks in July and August, when the perennial border often has a decidedly tired look.

How to Grow. Start with plants purchased from garden centers or through mail-order catalogs.

Russian sage prefers poor, well-drained soil in full sun; wet soil means certain death. The stems tend to become woody but will produce fresh new growth if cut back in fall or spring; they can be an interesting winter accent if you leave them until spring. Propagate by division in spring or fall or by stem cuttings in late summer. These durable, easy-to-grow plants are rarely bothered by pests or diseases and are ideal for beginners.

Uses. Russian sage is useful for the back of the border or as a landscape plant. The flowers and fragrant foliage are great for cutting for fresh arrangements. Even though the flowers are blue, Russian sage is an excellent choice for an all-white garden because of its silver foliage.

Phlox spp.
FLOKS.
Phlox. Spring or summer. Zones 3 to 8.

Characteristics. Height: 4 inches to 4 feet. Colors: Blue, pink, lilac, purple, red, salmon, and white.

There is a phlox for just about any garden use. Some species are low-growing and mat-forming, and make good groundcovers. Others are tall and narrow, and can be used in the middle or back of the border. There are also medium-sized types, which make good edging plants.

Garden phlox (*Phlox paniculata*) is the species most commonly grown in perennial borders. It grows 3 to 4 feet tall and has an exceptionally long bloom period—from July to August, sometimes even into October. The flowers appear in clusters at the top of the plants. Cultivars are available in shades of pink, red, lavender, salmon, and white, many with contrasting eyes. The plants have handsome green foliage, although the leaves are often marred by powdery mildew (a fungal disease that produces dusty white deposits). Fortunately, you can choose from several mildew-resistant cultivars, including 'David' (white), 'Eva Callum' (clear pink with a red eye), and 'Franz Schubert' (lavender with darker eyes). 'Starfire' is not particularly mildew-resistant, but it's worth growing for its exquisite, long-lasting, magenta to cherry red blooms.

Creeping phlox (*P. stolonifera*) is a shade-tolerant species that spreads by underground stems (stolons) to make a handsome woodland groundcover. The foliage is evergreen or semievergreen. Masses of light blue, lavender, or white flowers bloom in May well above the foliage on 6-inch stems. Creeping phlox is easy to grow and not susceptible to mildew. All you need to do is keep it from creeping where you don't want it to go. Wild sweet William (*P. divaricata*) is a 12- to 15-inch phlox for the front of the border or for the woodland. It has blue, pink, purple, or white flowers with slightly notched petals. The flowers practically cover the plants in April or May and are very striking when combined with spring-blooming bulbs.

Moss pinks (*P. subulata*) are grown primarily as groundcovers in full sun. They have narrow, almost grasslike, evergreen foliage and form thick mats that completely choke out weeds. They are often used for erosion control on hillsides. Moss pinks are a sight to behold in spring when they are covered with blooms, which come in magenta, coral, scarlet, light pink, white, or blue. This species is also good for rock gardens, as long as it has plenty of room.

How to Grow. Start your phlox collection with plants purchased from garden centers or through mail-order catalogs.

Garden phlox prefers well-drained, rich soil in full sun or very light shade. The plants need good air circulation to help prevent severe powdery mildew problems. They also require staking. Deadheading encourages continuous bloom. Propagate by division in spring or fall, root cuttings in early spring, or stem cuttings in summer.

Creeping phlox and wild sweet William prefer moist, rich, slightly acid woodland soil and partial shade. They are mildew-resistant and require little care in the garden. For propagation, divide the plants in fall or spring, or take cuttings in summer.

Moss pink prefers dry, well-drained, slightly acid soil

in full sun. It is resistant to mildew and is rarely troubled by other diseases or pests—just plant it and let it go. Propagate by cuttings in summer.

Uses. Garden phlox is excellent for the middle of the border and for cutting. Creeping phlox makes a good woodland groundcover. Wild sweet William is attractive at the front of the border or as an edging. Moss pink is ideal as a groundcover, for erosion control, and for rock gardens.

PINK, MOSS. See *Phlox* spp.
PINKS. See *Dianthus* spp.
PRIMROSE. See *Primula* X *polyantha*
PRAIRIE-BLAZING STAR. See *Liatris pycnostachya*

Primula X polyantha
PRIM-yew-luh pol-ee-AN-thuh.
Primrose. Spring. Zones 3 to 8.

Characteristics. Height: 10 inches. Colors: All colors, often with yellow centers.

There are many kinds of primroses, and whole books have been written about the genus. The most common garden type is *Primula* X *polyantha*. These charming plants produce rosettes of long, crinkly-edged leaves. The flower stalks rise above the foliage and are topped with clusters of small, single flowers looking out in all directions. The sweetly fragrant flowers bloom in spring, along with daffodils and tulips, and are available in any flower color you may want. The best and longest-lived cultivars are from the Barnhaven strain. The Pacific Giant strain, which is usually available in pots from florists in early spring, is short-lived in the garden and usually treated as an annual.

How to Grow. To grow your own plants, sow seed directly in a protected area of the garden in midsummer. Move the young plants to their permanent locations in fall or early spring. Plants are also available at garden centers and through mailorder catalogs. Pacific Giants strain primroses are sold in pots at nearly every florist shop in early spring.

Primroses thrive in moist, well-drained soil and light to partial shade. In hot weather, water regular ly to keep the soil from drying out. Divide crowded plants in spring. The plants require little care once they are established in the right place.

Uses. Grow primroses at the front of the border, as woodland accents, or along a stream bank. Naturalize them in moist, but well-drained locations. Primroses can also grow in pots; just be sure the soil doesn't dry out. The flowers are good for cutting and are sweetly fragrant, though never overpowering.

RUSSIAN SAGE. See *Perovskia atriplicifolia*
SAGE. See *Salvia* spp.
SNEEZEWORT. See *Achillea* spp.

Salvia spp.
SAL-vee-uh.
Salvia, sage. Summer. Zones 4 to 10.

Characteristics. Height: 18 inches to 6 feet. Colors: Blue, pink, purple, and white.

This useful genus includes many fine annual, biennial, and perennial garden plants. The three species described here stand out among the hardy perennial salvias for their reliable garden performance, long period of bloom or garden display, and particularly beautiful flowers or foliage.

Violet sage (*Salvia* X *superba*) is the best-known perennial salvia. It grows 18 to 24 inches tall, with spikes of blue, purple, or pink flowers that form waves of color from June to August. It is most effective when planted in groups of at least six or seven plants. The foliage loosely resembles that of its relative, culinary sage, and stays handsome all season. Violet sage is hardy in Zones 4 to 8. 'East Friesland' is a popular cultivar with regal, violet-purple flower spikes on compact, well-behaved, 18-inch plants. 'Amethyst' is an unforgettable mid-violet shade. 'Rose Queen' is a pink companion for the rich violet 'Blue Queen'.

S. guaranitica is a fairly recent introduction to North American gardens and a superb performer. The strong 4- to 6–foot plants bloom from July right up to the first frost in fall. They are so vigorous that they can be divided every year (or you can give them extra space so they won't have to be divided as often). 'Argentina Skies' produces heavenly flowers in a rare shade of sky blue. It is hardy to Zone 6, and should be protected with a winter mulch in that zone.

Silver sage *(S. argentea)* looks completely ent from other salvias. It is planted for its woolly, silver-gray foliage, which grows in rosettes. The leaves, which measure up to 8 inches long, are covered with fine, silky hairs and have a puckered texture. The plants reach 3 feet tall and produce spikes of yellowish white flowers in summer. The flowers tend to detract from the foliage effect, however, and can weaken the plants; many gardeners cut back the flower stems either before or just after they bloom. Because the plants are not long-lived in the garden, they may never have to be divided. Silver sage is hardy in Zones 5 to 9.

How to Grow. To grow your own plants, sow seed of the species directly in a protected area of the garden in midsummer. Move the young plants to their final locations in fall or early spring. Plants of the species and cultivars are also available at garden centers and through mail-order catalogs.

Salvias generally tolerate drought conditions but appreciate extra water during prolonged dry periods. They grow best in rich, well-drained soil in full sun, although they may take partial shade. Silver sage requires better drained soil than other salvias and should be grown in full sun. *S. guaranitica* needs staking unless you cut the plants back by half in early to midsummer; provide a protective winter mulch in Zone 6. Divide salvias in fall or spring for propagation or to rejuvenate crowded clumps.

Uses. Salvias are excellent accents for borders; use silver sage near the front and the others in the middle or back. Silver sage also looks stunning in a rock garden or in masses as a landscape feature. The flowers of violet sage and *S. guaranitica* are good for cutting; violet sage is a fine plant for drying.

Solidago spp.
sol-ih-DAY-go.
Goldenrod. Late summer. Zones 4 to 8.

Characteristics. Height: 2 to 6 feet. Colors: Yellow.

The genus Solidago includes wildflower species, many of which are native to North America. The fluffy clusters of tiny bright to deep golden yellow flowers, which appear atop stems with narrow, medium to dark green foliage, can dominate the late-summer landscape in open fields. While some of the wildflower species are too invasive for gardens, many fine, well-behaved species and cultivars are suitable for garden use.

Seaside goldenrod (*S. sempervirens*) is an excellent noninvasive species. The graceful, 4- to 6-foot plants produce bright yellow plumes from September to October. They combine beautifully with Tartarian aster (*Aster tataricus*) in the border and in bouquets of fresh-cut flowers. This species is tolerant of salty, sandy, seaside conditions. *S.* X 'Peter Pan', a hybrid goldenrod, features clusters of long, elegant, canary yellow flower plumes on 2- to 3-foot plants from July to September.

Goldenrod is often blamed for causing hay fever symptoms, but it does not deserve this reputation. The actual cause of the symptoms is ragweed, which blooms at the same time, but is not as noticeable.

How to Grow. Start with purchased plants. You can sometimes find them at garden centers, and they are usually available through mail-order catalogs. Specialty wildflower nurseries often stock the plants, too.

Goldenrods prefer well-drained soil in full sun or light shade. They are generally drought-tolerant. Cut back the taller cultivars by half in midsummer to keep them to a manageable height. Divide the plants in spring for propagation.

Uses. Goldenrods are attractive in the middle or back of the border, or massed as a landscape feature. They are perfect for naturalizing in a wildflower meadow. The flowers are good for cutting and drying; they have a wonderful, subtle fragrance.

SPIKED SPEEDWELL. See *Veronica* spp.
TICKSEED. See *Coreopsis* spp.

Stachys byzantina

STAY-kiss biz-an-TEE-nuh.
Lamb's ears. Summer. Zones 4 to 9.

Characteristics. Height: 15 inches. Colors: Purple flowers, silver foliage.

Lamb's ears are grown for their fuzzy, silver-gray, oval-shaped foliage, which has the downy texture of a lamb's ear. The silvery foliage contrasts nicely with blues, pinks, and purples, and is hauntingly beautiful when combined with white flowers in an all-white garden. The plants spread obligingly to make a striking groundcover or edging. They provide color and texture in the garden from early spring until they are killed by frost.

From June to July the plants send up flower spikes

equally as velvety as the foliage, with purple flowers. Many gardeners think the flowers detract from the foliage effect and cut them back before or after they bloom. Others appreciate the interesting texture the flowers add to the border. Some cultivars, including 'Silver Carpet', have been selected because they produce few or no flowers. 'Helene Von Stein' is an especially attractive, very vigorous cultivar with broad foliage. It seldom blooms and is less prone to rot.

How to Grow. To start your own plants, sow seed directly in a protected area of the garden in midsummer. Move the young plants to their final locations in fall or early spring. Plants are also readily available at garden centers and through mail order catalogs.

These drought-tolerant plants prefer poor, well-drained soil in full sun or light shade. Like many silver foliaged plants, lamb's ears tend to rot in hot, humid weather. Divide the plants every year to keep them vigorous and to prevent overcrowding: Dig them up in fall or spring, break them into rooted pieces 6 inches long, and replant them 6 inches apart. They will knit together quickly. You will have many plants left over; start a new colony, or share the extras with friends and neighbors.

Uses. Lamb's ears work well in the front of the border, as an edging or groundcover, or grouped in front of another perennial as a landscape feature.

STARFLOWER, BLUE. See *Amsonia tabernaemontana*
SUNDROPS, OZARK. See *Oenothera missouriensis*
SUNFLOWER. See *Helianthus* spp.
SWEET WILLIAM, WILD. See *Phlox* spp.
THISTLE, GLOBE. See *Echinops ritro*

Veronica spp.
ver-ON-ih-kuh.
Veronica, spiked speedwell. Summer. Zones 4 to 8.

Characteristics. Height: 1½ to 3 feet. Colors: Blue, pink, purple, and white.

Veronica is a large genus that includes rock garden plants, wildflowers, and lawn weeds. Several species of veronicas are ideal for the perennial garden. They have long spikes of blue, pink, purple, or white flowers that create a wonderful haze of color for weeks, or even months, during the summer. These strong plants have handsome, dark green to gray-green foliage that looks attractive all season.

Spiked speedwell (*V. spicata*) is a compact species with strong, upright plants. The flower spikes bloom in shades of blue, white, rose-pink, and purple, and last for 7 or 8 weeks in summer. 'Blue Fox' offers lavender-blue flowers and dark green, narrow foliage on 15- to 20-inch plants. 'Red Fox' is a companion to 'Blue Fox', with masses of deep rose-red flowers. 'Icicle' features icy white spires and glossy green foliage on 2-foot plants.

Longleaf veronica (*V. longifolia*) is 2 to 3 feet tall and has long, narrow leaves. Its long-lasting flower spikes are among the best of the veronicas for cutting. 'Blue Giant' is a strong, 3- to 4-foot plant with pale lavender-blue flower spikes that bloom for many weeks in summer. 'Alba' is a lower-growing, 18-inch, white-flowered cultivar.

V. X 'Sunny Border Blue' was selected as the Perennial Plant Association's Plant of the Year for 1993 for its superb garden performance. It bears thick spikes of dark blue flowers from June to August. The plants are compact and never need staking. If you can have only one veronica, this is the one to choose.

How to Grow. To grow your own plants, sow seed of the species in a protected area of the garden in midsummer. Move the young plants to their final locations in fall or early spring. Plants are also readily available at garden centers and through mail order catalogs.

Veronicas are easy to grow in rich, well-drained soil and full sun. They are rarely bothered by pests and diseases, and do not require staking. They benefit from occasional deadheading. Divide the plants in spring or fall every 3 or 4 years when they become overcrowded.

Uses. Veronicas are among the best perennials for the front or middle of the border. Tuck them into cottage gardens, or plant them in masses for an eye catching landscape feature. The spiky blooms make excellent cut flowers.

YARROW. See *Achillea* spp.

CHAPTER FIVE

BULBS

The use of bulbs is at an alltime high. We aren't just growing tulips; we are experimenting with species tulips. We have discovered that onions are not only edible, but often incredibly beautiful, too. From winter-flowering irises to fall-flowering colchicums, the wonderful world of bulbs is being rediscovered by adventurous gardeners across the country.

WHAT ARE BULBS?

Bulbous plants, which may be annual or perennial, include plants that grow from true bulbs, corms, tubers, and rhizomes. Every scholarly work on bulbs takes great pains to explain the specific differences between all of these types of "storage organs." But does it really matter if we talk about the tubers or rhizomes of calla lilies, or if we know for sure whether cyclamen grows from a bulb or a corm? Of course, you don't have to be able to recite the specific traits of true bulbs or tubers to grow gorgeous daffodils or cheerful spring crocuses. But as you gain more gardening experience, it's helpful to be familiar with the different structures. For one thing, the method for propagating each type of bulbous plant varies depending on the type of storage organ it has.

So keep in mind that not all "bulbs" in this chapter grow from true bulbs, as daffodils and tulips do. Crocuses and gladioli, for example, grow from corms. If you really want to know the specifics, check the plant portraits, which indicate what kind of storage organ the plants have.

PLANT PORTRAITS

The bulbous plants described in the following plant portraits are a sampling of some of the best for garden use. Most are relatively easy to find; a few are slightly more elusive but definitely worth the search. If you can't find the bulbs you're looking for at your local garden center, it's time to investigate the many wonderful mail-order catalogs that offer a wide variety of bulbs.

GROWING TIPS AT A GLANCE

Each of the following plant portraits includes simple symbols to highlight special features you need to know about each bulb. If you're not sure what any of the symbols mean, refer back to this key.

○   Full sun (more than 6 hours of sun a day; ideally all day)

◑   Partial sun (some direct sun, but less than 6 hours a day)

●   Shade (no direct sun)

✳   Drought-tolerant

✀   Good as a cut flower

❦   Fragrant

▼   Grows well in containers

Acidanthera bicolor
as-ih-DAN-ther-uh BY-kul-er.
Abyssinian gladiolus. Summer. Zones 7 to 10.

Characteristics. Height: 30 to 36 inches. Colors: White with purple center.

Abyssinian gladiolus (also known as *Gladiolus callianthus*) is a fascinating summer corm that is not grown nearly as much as it should be in American gardens. The light green, pleated foliage and the sweetly scented white flowers with their deep purple throats are a great addition to any garden. In ideal conditions, each stem can produce 6 to 8 wonderfully fragrant flowers. Native to southern and tropical areas of Africa, the corms are winter-hardy to about Zone 7 (6 with winter protection), but you can grow them in all areas as an annual. The flowers are produced from July to October and are relatively disease- and insect-free. The plants may flower a little too late for northeastern or upper midwestern gardens, where early frosts can nip the buds.

A variety of this species was discovered in Ethiopia in 1896. These stronger-growing, largerflowered plants are known as *Acidanthera bicolor* var. *murieliae* (or as 'Muralis'). Most of the corms sold today are this variety. When looking for Abyssinian gladioli, search spring bulb catalogs under both Acidanthera and Gladiolus; they may be listed in either spot.

How to Grow. These plants need full sun and well-drained soil; they abhor "wet feet" in the sum men Abyssinian gladiolus looks best when planted in large groups. (Fortunately, the corms are relative ly inexpensive.) Set the corms 4 to 6 inches deep and 6 to 10 inches apart after all danger of frost has passed.

In northern areas, lift the corms in the fall, brush off any clinging soil, and store them in dry peat moss in a cool, frost-free area, such as a basement. The corms multiply rapidly and need to be divided every 2 to 3 years. Otherwise, the plants produce too much foliage and too few flowers, and end up looking like tall green weeds.

Uses. Abyssinian gladioli are ideal for interplanting in a perennial bed. They make excellent cut flowers, lasting for 5 to 7 days in fresh water.

ACONITE, WINTER. See *Eranthis hyemalis*

Anemone spp.

ah-NEM-oh-nee.
Anemone, windflower. Spring. Zones 4 to 8.

Characteristics. Height: 4 to 24 inches. Colors: Pink, red, purple-blue, and white.

Anemone is a large genus consisting of bulbous plants, as well as plants commonly grown as perennials. The bulbous species flower in the spring and provide many bright colors that can be enjoyed both indoors and out. The flowers measure 1 to 3 inches across, depending on the species, and are actually made up of sepals that resemble petals. The foliage is generally fern-like and handsome; in all bulbous forms, it tends to go dormant and disappear in early summer. All of the species prefer temperate summers and are annuals in Zone 7 and south.

One of the most popular species is Grecian windflower *(A. blanda)*. It grows 6 to 9 inches tall and produces single daisylike flowers in many colors. Some of the best cultivars are 'Charmer', with deep rose flowers; 'Pink Star', which bears large, deep pink flowers; 'Radar', with reddish, white-centered flowers; and 'White Splendor', one of the hardiest cultivars.

The wonderful poppy windflower (*A. coronaria*), also known as Mediterranean windflower, is also worth mentioning. Hardy only to Zone 6, it has been admired for centuries and grown as a garden and cut flower for almost as long. The plants are not as hardy as Grecian windflowers (only as far north as Zone 7). The parsley-like foliage is attractive, and the cultivars are magnificent. The best known are the DeCaen hybrids, consisting of single flowers of mixed colors. Separate colors are also available, such as the violet-rose 'Sylphide' and the bright scarlet 'Hollandia'. The St. Brigid hybrids offer double flowers; they are usually multicolored, although they also come in solid colors. 'The Admiral', with violet blooms, and 'Mount Everest', a double white form, are just two examples. Treat this species as an annual; it is a poor perennial at best.

Other species to try include wood anemone (*A. nemorosa*) and European anemone (*A. apennina*). Both are only 6 to 9 inches tall and prefer partial shade and woodland conditions. Wood anemone is more at home in the North than the South, while European anemone, which is hardy to Zone 6, performs best in the Northwest.

How to Grow. Plant Grecian, wood, and European anemones in the fall. Set poppy windflowers out in early spring in the North; plant them in autumn in the South. To encourage sprouting, soak the tubers in warm water for about 24 hours before planting. Set them 2 to 3 inches deep in full sun in the North, or in a spot with afternoon shade in the South. Few insects bother anemones, but look out for slugs, as well as squirrels, gophers, voles, and anything else that likes to dig around. Diseases are seldom a problem.

Uses. Plant Grecian, wood, and European windflowers in large groups (at least 25 plants) and allow them to naturalize. They are terrific in rock gardens, borders, and containers. Mediterranean windflowers are wonderful as cut flowers; combine them with spring bulbs and early perennials.

Arisaema spp.
ar-iss-EE-muh. Jack-in-the-pulpit,
green dragon. Spring to summer. Zones 3 to 9.

Characteristics. Height: 1 to 3 feet. Colors: Purple, green, and white.

Compared to other bulbs, some of the plants of *Arisaema* are quite unusual. The flowers consist of two parts: a spikelike spadix, which bears either male or female flowers, and the spathe, which wraps loosely around the flowers like a large trenchcoat. The foliage of all *Arisaema* species is handsome. In fact, some gardeners find the foliage more appealing than the unusual flowers.

Two of our native species are marvelous. Jack-in-the-pulpit (*A. triphyllum*) is quite variable and may grow from 18 to 36 inches tall. It flowers in early spring through midsummer, and is hardy to Zone 3. Both the stalk of the plant and the spathe can have purple mottling on the outside. Our other common native is green dragon (*A. dracontium*). It sports a long (up to 10-inch), yellow-green spadix, which sticks out from the green spadix—weird but wonderful. Under good conditions, berries may appear on either of these species in autumn. They are bright red on Jack-in-the-pulpit and orange-red on green dragon. Both species love moisture and are often found in moist, shady woodland areas.

Of the many other species, two foreigners are very attractive. *A. candidissimum*, from China, bears a white spathe striped with pink and green. The plants are 9 to 15 inches tall. The Japanese form, *A. sikokianum*, produces a beautiful, pure white spadix surrounded by a stippled, purplish spathe. The plants can grow up to 2 feet tall but generally reach 12 to 18 inches.

How to Grow. Plant the tubers in spring or fall, at least 6 inches deep in a moist, shady location, then stand back and enjoy the show. Propagate the plants by lifting them in early fall and separating the tubers. These woodland plants prefer partial shade, and are among the few plants that tolerate heavy shade. Insects and diseases are rarely a problem.

Uses. Use the various Jack-in-the-pulpit species and green dragons in shade and woodland gardens. Ferns, hostas, and rodgersias (*Rodgersia* spp.) are good companions.

CALLA LILY. See *Zantedeschia* spp.

Begonia tuberhybrida hybrids
be-GO-nee-ah.
Tuberous begonia. Summer to fall. Zone 10.

Characteristics. Height: 12 to 18 inches. Colors: Red, pink, orange, yellow, and white.

The showy tuberous begonias add glorious color to

shady parts of the garden. Their thick, fleshy tubers produce juicy stems with hairy, heartshaped to pointed, green leaves. The upright or trailing stems also bear single or double flowers up to 4 inches across, in a range of colors and shadings. The male flowers tend to be large and showy; they are usually flanked by smaller, single female flowers.

How to Grow. Tuberous begonias need partial shade and moist but well-drained soil. Work plenty of compost into the soil before planting. Start these plants indoors in pots (plant the tubers 1 inch deep) about 4 weeks before the last frost date. Set them out when night temperatures stay above 50°F. Stake upright types. Mulch the plants well, and water during dry spells to keep the soil moist. Pinch off spent flowers to keep the blooms coming. In all but frost-free areas, lift the tubers before or just after the first frost and store indoors in a frost-free spot such as a cool basement or garage over winter.

Uses. Add tuberous begonias to lightly shaded beds and borders or container plantings. Trailing types are well suited for growing in hanging basket.

Chionodoxa spp.

ky-on-oh-DOKS-uh.
Glory-of-the-snow. Early spring. Zones 5 to 7.

Characteristics. Height: 4 to 6 inches. Colors: Blue or pink.

These early-flowering bulbs are native to Crete and Turkey. The handsome, starlike flowers are usually some shade of blue and are borne in clusters of 2 to 10 blooms. As indicated by their common name, they stay open even during snow or sleet. These tough little flowers are better suited for northern climates than southern ones, since they prefer cold winters and cool summer soils.

Chionodoxa luciliae is the most commonly sold species. It generally has blue-lavender flowers with white centers on 6-inch stems. Cultivars bearing pink or rose-colored flowers are also available. Other useful species are *C. gigantea*, which produces 1 or 2 large, upward-facing, light blue flowers; and *C. sardensis*, with numerous, clear gentian-blue flowers, each with a small white eye.

How to Grow. Plant these bulbs in the fall in well-drained soil; set them 2 to 3 inches deep and 2 to 4 inches apart. A sunny location is best, although the plants will tolerate some shade. For best performance, glory-of-the-snow requires moist conditions in both winter and spring; avoid planting it near the base of trees, since the tree roots would compete with the bulbs for water. Propagation is simple: Lift a clump of bulbs, remove the offsets, and replant.

Uses. Plant glory-of-the-snow where you can enjoy it up close, such as near a deck or patio. The bulbs naturalize particularly well; for best effect, plant them in masses of 25 or more. Or, try combining them with other early-flowering bulbs, annuals, or perennials in containers.

Convallaria majalis

kon-vuh-LAIR-ee-uh muh-JAL-iss.
Lily-of-the-valley. Spring. Zones 2 to 8.

Characteristics. Height: 4 to 8 inches. Colors: White or pink.

Bringing a handful of lily-of-the-valley flowers

indoors is like bringing in the fragrance of spring. The flowers and foliage arise from rhizomes, which are generally available from perennial growers and bulb specialists. The small white flowers are held on a many-flowered stalk just above the light green leaves. The plants are much more aggressive in the North than the South; removing unwanted lily-of-the-valley requires a pickax and shovel, and can occupy a small boy's entire weekend. In areas with hot summers, the plants are more docile and are valued more for their fragrance than their ability to cover the ground.

There is only one species, although it can be variable. The flowers are usually creamy white; *Convallaria majulis* var. *rosea* bears pink flowers. 'Fortin's Giant' has white flowers and is bigger and stouter than the species. One interesting cultivar—offered as 'Albistriata', 'Variegate', or simply 'Striate'—has yellow-and-green variegated foliage.

How to Grow. Plant the rhizomes (often referred to as "pips") 2 to 4 inches deep and 6 to 8 inches apart in spring or fall. They are happy in moist soil and struggle in hot, dry sites. The plants tolerate full sun in the North if moisture is available; partially shaded areas are best in the South. Propagate by digging a clump with your shovel, separating it, then replanting the pieces in a prepared area.

Uses. In northern gardens, lily-of-the-valley is vigorous enough to make a solid groundcover. It is especially attractive growing around rocks, along the sides of paths, or in containers. Snip a few flowers to enjoy indoors.

Crocus spp.
KRO-kus.
Crocus. Spring or fall. Zones 3 to 8.

Characteristics. Height: 3 to 6 inches. Colors: Blue, lavender, purple, yellow, and white.

How can anyone not like crocuses? They are available in a dozen colors and hues, will flower in the spring or fall, are inexpensive, and are practically foolproof. There are more than 80 species of crocus, many of which are offered by bulb specialists, as well as many commonly available hybrids.

The main group of spring-flowering crocuses available to gardeners are the Dutch hybrids, often listed as *Crocus vernus*. They bear the largest flowers and come in an assortment of colors. They are excellent, reliable, and long lived plants. 'Remembrance' has blue flowers; Jeanne d'Arc' bears white blooms; 'Pickwick' produces flowers striped in purple-blue and white. As its name suggests, 'Yellow Mammouth' bears large golden yellow blooms.

While the Dutch hybrids may be the most common, other crocuses are equally as good. Snow crocus (*C. chrysanthus*) flowers earlier than Dutch crocus and is available in many colors. The species bears golden yellow blooms in late winter. Some excellent cultivars include creamy yellow 'Advance', yellow-and-bronze 'E. P. Bowles', and straw-yellow 'Moonlight'. 'Ladykiller' is purple outside and white inside; 'White Triumphator' is white with blue markings. Another fine early-blooming species is *C. tomasinianus*, which bears lilac flowers that are paler on the outside. 'Barr's Purple' is a cultivar with large, deep purple flowers; 'Ruby Giant' has violet flowers. This species is said to be more squirrel-proof than the others.

The fall-flowering species are fabulous, since they bloom at a time when the garden is winding down. One of the best known is saffron crocus (*C. sativus*), which bears lilac flowers with long orange stigmas. The stigmas are harvested for use as a dye and as a spice. (It is estimated that more than 4,000 flowers are required to produce 1 ounce of saffron). *C. speciosus*, sometimes called showy crocus, is easy to establish and bears lavender-blue flowers in early fall. It is available in a number of selections, such as 'Atabir', which offers violet flowers, and 'Cassiope', with blue blooms.

How to Grow. Crocuses require well-drained soil and 3 to 4 hours of sun per day. Plant the corms 3 to 4 inches deep and as close together as possible. Set out the spring-flowering kinds in autumn, and the fall-flowering types as soon as they are available in mid- to late summer. Crocuses are generally problem-free, although squirrels and chipmunks dig and eat them.

Uses. Crocuses are ideal for beds, borders, and containers, as well as for naturalizing. Plant them in groups of at least 12—preferably a couple dozen—to make a good show.

DAFFODIL. See *Narcissus* hybrids

Dahlia hybrids

DAL-ee-uh.
Dahlia. Summer to fall. Zones 8 to 10.

Characteristics. Height: 1 to 5 feet. Colors: Red, pink, orange, yellow, purple, and white.

Few flowers say "summer" like the bold blooms of dahlias. These popular plants come in two basic types: compact bedding forms and tall border types. Both have upright stems and divided leaves, and grow from tuberous roots. They come in an amazing range of colors and flower forms, from single, small, daisylike blooms to huge, ruffled flowers up to 8 inches across.

How to Grow. Dahlias need well drained soil and full sun. Grow bedding types from seed started indoors 6 to 8 weeks before the last frost. Set the plants out about a week after the last frost date. To grow border dahlias, buy the roots in spring. In the North, plant them indoors in pots 2 to 3 weeks before the last frost. Set the plants out about a week after all danger of frost has passed. In milder areas, plant the roots outside around the last frost date. Dig a deep hole so that the top of the roots will be about 3 inches below the soil surface. Insert a stake at planting time; otherwise, you'll run the risk of stabbing the roots later in the season. Mulch the plants and water during dry spells. Deadhead regularly to keep the plants blooming.

In mild-winter areas, dahlias can stay in the ground all winter (give them a good winter mulch in Zone 8). In other areas, dig them in the fall, before or just after the first frost. Store the roots indoors in a frost-free area. Divide the root clumps into 2 to 4 sections before replanting in the spring. (Make sure each section has a part of the stem.)

Uses. Compact bedding dahlias are ideal for container gardens and for edging beds. Use the border types to add height and color to gardens in late summer to fall. Dahlias also make great cut flowers.

Eranthis hyemalis
er-AN-thiss hy-MAL-iss.
Winter aconite. Winter to early spring. Zones 3 to 7.

Characteristics. Height: 2 to 8 inches. Colors: Yellow.

The botanical name of this plant means "flower of spring," reflecting its tendency to bloom early in the season. Along with snowdrops (*Galanthus* spp.), winter aconites literally bloom through the snow. At the first hint of warmth, the dark green leaves begin to poke through the newly thawed soil. The bright yellow flowers are nestled on top of the leaves, on stems that grow 3 to 6 inches tall. Most bulb catalogs list only Eranthis hyemalis, but you may occasionally see others. *E. cilicica* is a little more robust than *E. hyemalis. E.* X *tubergenii*, a hybrid between the two species, is taller (up to 8 inches), with sulfur-yellow flowers.

How to Grow. Winter aconites grow best in full sun or in the shade of deciduous trees. They prefer humus-rich soil and do not perform particularly well in acid soil (below pH 5.5). Soak the tubers overnight, then plant them in fall about 1 inch deep and 3 inches apart. These plants do much better in the North than in the South, since a period with cold soil temperatures is necessary for good growth. Once planted, the tubers should not be disturbed. Where they are content, the plants will reseed themselves and form deep yellow carpets within a few years. Squirrels and other digging animals seem to enjoy the tubers; otherwise, these plants are generally pest- and disease-free.

Uses. Winter aconite is very popular not only for its ornamental value but also because it hlooms so early. For a colorful spring show, plant the tubers in masses of 25 or more under deciduous shrubs and trees, such as witch hazels (*Hamamelis* spp.). Winter aconites are also useful for containers on a patio or deck.

GLADIOLUS, ABYSSIAN. See *Acidanthera bicolor*

Gladiolus hybrids
glad-ee-OH-lus.
Gladiolus. Summer. Zones 5 to 8.

Characteristics. Height: 1 to 3 feet. Colors: Red, orange, yellow, greenish, purple, and white.

One of America's all-time favorite flowers, the gladiolus has undergone significant changes over the years. Although over 150 species have been named, nearly all of the plants in cultivation today are hybrids. Hybrid *gladioli*, commonly called glads, first appeared in 1823, and new cultivars of both small- and large-flowered forms have been selected every year. Numerous divisions of glads occur, ranging from the early-flowering *Gladiolus nanus* hybrids to the summer- and fall-flowering forms of the *G. primulinus* hybrids. The most common garden glads are the large-flowered forms, although recently there has been a resurgence of interest in dwarf and butterfly glads.

All glads, regardless of the type, are easy to grow. Their showy, colorful blooms are very popular as cut flowers. The foliage is sword-shaped and usually light green.

How to Grow. Glads need well-drained soil and full sun. Plant the corms 4 to 6 inches deep and 6 to 10 inches apart in spring after danger of frost has passed. North of Zone 7, you will need to lift the corms in the fall; place them in peat moss in a fine-mesh bag, and hang them from posts in a well-ventilated area where temperatures do not fall below 40°F, such as a slightly heated garage or basement. For propagation, you can separate the cormels (small corms clustered around the corm) when you dig the corms in fall. Or, you can separate them after flowering and plant the cormels to grow on in a prepared area. By the time you lift them in the fall, many will be of flowering size.

Glads are susceptible to all sorts of problems. Botrytis and Fusarium wilt can cause the corms to rot, while aphids, thrips, and corn borers can wreak havoc with the foliage and flowers. But don't be discouraged from trying these magnificent plants; you can help prevent problems by preparing a good planting area and starting with healthy corms from a reputable supplier.

Uses. Because they have historically been used as cut flowers, large-flowered glads are often relegated to a bed of their own or to a "cut flower" bed. However, while not the most ornamental of plants, glads deserve to be combined with other garden-worthy plants—for instance, other perennial species or small shrubs. The shorter cultivars blend well into any garden; annuals and short perennials are useful for hiding the "ankles" of the glads.

GLORY-OF-THE-SNOW. See *Chionodoxa* spp.
GREEN DRAGON. See *Arisvema* spp.
HARLEQUIN FLOWER. See *Sparaxis tricolor*

Hyacinthus orientalis

hy-uh-SIN-thus or-ee-en-TAL-iss.
Hyacinth. Spring. Zones 3 to 7.

Characteristics. Height: 12 to 18 inches. Colors: Purple-blue, pink, red, yellow, salmon, and white.

Hyacinths are among the most fragrant flowers in the plant kingdom. While Abyssinian gladiolus (*Acidanthera bicolor*) produces a subtle sweet fragrance and lily-of-the-valley (*Convallaria majulis*) brings a hint of perfume, hyacinths knock us over. For some people, they are simply overwhelming and too intense to bring into the house. Others can't get enough of the aroma.

The tubular, bell-shaped flowers are borne on spikes and emerge above the dark green leaves in early spring. They bloom for a long time, particularly if spring temperatures remain cool. Many cultivars are available, including 'Blue Jacket', 'Blue Giant', and 'Blue Magic', which has purple-blue flowers with white throats. 'Carnegie' and 'L'Innocence' offer white blooms. 'Gypsy Queen' has fabulous salmon-colored flowers. 'Pink Pearl' and 'Marconi' both produce pink blooms. Many others may be found in bulb catalogs. Some companies offer multiflora hyacinths, which produce a number of smaller spikes and can be very pretty.

How to Grow. Hyacinths require a sunny site with well-drained soil. Plant the bulbs in the fall (October in the North, November in the South), with about 4 inches of soil over the top of the bulb. In the South, set the bulbs an extra inch or two deeper to take advantage of the cooler soil temperatures. Space the bulbs about 9 inches apart. Forced pots of hyacinths may be placed in the garden after flowering is complete, but subsequent flowers will not be as large as the original.

In all but the coldest climates, treat hyacinths as 1- or 2-year plants for best results. Although the plants will bloom for 3 to 4 years, the quality of the spikes and the number of flowers per spike decline over time. Compared to the first spring's flowers, subsequent blossoms will be shorter and the flowers farther apart on the spike. Some gardeners dig the bulbs after they flower and store them at 40°F, then replant them in the fall. However, the resulting blooms seldom compare with the first year's flowers.

Hyacinths are not easy to propagate at home. Offsets form slowly, but you can encourage them by lifting the bulbs and making slices with a knife about 1 inch deep on the bottom of each bulb in the shape of a cross. Bulblets will form on the cuts.

Starting with clean, firm bulbs will prevent many of the bacterial and fungal diseases that commonly affect hyacinths. Aphids and thrips can disfigure the flowers, especially if the weather warms up. To control these pests, spray with insecticidal soap.

Uses. Hyacinths add wonderful color and scent to spring beds, borders, and container gardens. Try planting them under windows so you can enjoy the fragrance both indoors and out.

Ipheion uniflorum
IF-ee-on yow-nih-FLOR-um.
Spring starflower. Spring. Zones 5 to 9.

Characteristics. Height: 6 to 12 inches. Colors: Blue or white.

Although this bulb has been in cultivation since 1836, it is far from common in gardens today. Part of the confusion is that it constantly undergoes name changes; over time, it has been known as *Ipheion,*

Brodiaea, Milla, or *Triteleia.* By any name, this is a terrific little plant: It is easy to grow, spreads well, and is always bright and cheerful in the early-spring garden. Each plant bears a 6- to 9-inch stem tipped with a single, star-shaped, creamy white, fragrant flower with a deep blue midrib on the back. The grasslike foliage smells a little like onion when crushed. The most popular cultivar is the larger-flowered 'Wisley Blue', with deep blue blooms. 'Froyle Mill' produces rosy-purple flowers and is also very attractive.

How to Grow. Spring starflower tolerates full sun but performs best in partial shade. Plant the bulbs in the fall, about 2 inches deep and 3 to 5 inches apart. The foliage appears early in the spring, and the flowers bloom from March to early May. The bulbs produce bulblets, which, if left undisturbed, quickly fill the planting area. To propagate spring starflower, dig the plants in late spring or early summer as the foliage declines, remove the bulblets, and replant. Seed-propagated bulbs take about 2 years to reach flowering size.

Uses. While spring starflower cannot compete with brightly colored tulips or hyacinths, it provides reliably handsome flowers year after year. This cheerful flower looks best in borders or containers.

Iris spp.

EYE-riss.
Iris. Spring. Zones 5 to 8.

Characteristics. Height: 4 inches to 3 feet. Colors: Blue, purple, violet, yellow, and white.

Irises are such exceptional plants and the genus is so diverse, it is not surprising that they are among the most popular garden flowers. Bearded, Siberian, Dutch, English, Japanese, and Louisiana irises are just a few of the groups that have captured the imagination of American gardeners. The majority of garden irises grow from rhizomes and are covered in Chapter 4, Perennials; only the bulbous forms are discussed here.

Danford iris (*Iris danfordiae*) seldom grows more than 4 inches tall. The plants bear showy, bright yellow flowers in late winter and early spring. In some areas, they will bloom again the following year. In most cases, however, the bulbs have a tendency to break up into small bulblets, which do not flower the next year. For best results, treat Danford irises as annuals.

Unlike Danford iris, reticulated iris (*I. reticulata*)

reblooms dependably. The blue to purple flowers are sweetly scented and appear in February to March. The plants are about 4 to 6 inches tall and bear grasslike, blue-green leaves. Once established, these plants continue to bloom for many years. There are many cultivars, including pale blue 'Cantab', dark blue 'Harmony', violet-and-orange 'Jeannine', and sky blue-and-orange 'Joyce'.

Dutch iris hybrids have long been produced as cut flowers in Holland and elsewhere around the world, and are sold by most florists. The bulbs are winter-hardy only to Zone 7 (Zone 6 with winter protection), but they provide spectacular flowers on 2- to 3-foot stems in suitable areas. The foliage arises in the winter, and the 4-to 6-inch-wide flowers appear in March and April. The flowers can become badly damaged if late frosts occur after the buds have swollen.

How to Grow. All bulbous irises require full sun and good drainage. Plant the bulbs in the fall with 2 to 3 inches of soil above them. Thrips and aphids can be a problem if the weather warms up while the plants are in flower; to control these pests, spray with insecticidal soap. To prevent Fusarium wilt and other fungi that can cause the bulbs to rot, choose a well-drained site.

Uses. Irises are ideal for beds, borders, and containers. They also make fine additions to rock gardens. For a good show, plant Danford and reticulated irises in drifts of at least 25. Dutch irises are a little more difficult to find and also more expensive, but they are showy even in groups of 3.

JACK-IN-THE-PULPIT. See *Arisaema* spp

Lilium spp.
LIL-ee-um.
Lily. Late spring to summer. Zones 3 to 8.

Characteristics. Height: 2 to 8 feet. Colors: White, yellow, orange, red, maroon, and bicolors.

Lilies are the undisputed bulb queens of the summer garden, providing classic beauty for many months. The choice of flower colors, shapes, sizes, and heights is almost endless. There is a plethora of Asiatic and Oriental hybrids, not to mention at least a half-dozen species of these spectacular garden plants.

The terms "Asiatic" and "Oriental" refer to the ancestry

of the parents used to create the hybrids. The Asiatics generally have short, dark green leaves and upward-facing, cup-shaped flowers, which are borne near the top of the stem. They often flower earlier than the Oriental hybrids. Orange-red 'Enchantment' and yellow 'Citronella' are two well-known examples.

The Oriental types have longer leaves and larger flowers than the Asiatics. The flowers are usually downward- or outward-facing and are bowl-shaped, flat-faced, or have recurved petals. They bloom in the leaf axils on the top third of the stem, as well as at the end. Reddish, white-edged 'Star Gazer' and spotted, white 'Everest' are well-known Oriental forms. Numerous cultivars are available, and some specialist catalogs list literally hundreds.

Not to be outdone by the hybrids, a few species are also excellent additions to the garden. These include orange-flowered Henry's lily (*Lilium henryi*); the fragrant, white regal lily (*L. regale*); the white, gold-marked gold band lily (*L. auratum*); and the ubiquitous orange tiger lily (*L. tigrinum*).

How to Grow. Full sun is best, but the plants tolerate a little afternoon shade in the North and enjoy it in the South. No lilies like "wet feet," so good drainage is essential. Plant the bulbs twice as deep as they are long.

(For example, a bulb that measures 3 inches from top to bottom should be planted 6 inches deep.) The only exception is Madonna lily (*L. candidum*), which should be planted about 1 inch deep. For an extra boost, apply a little 10-10-10 fertilizer around the outside of the emerging foliage in the spring and again when the flower buds become visible. If the plants become overcrowded, lift them after they bloom and separate the various bulbs and bulblets. Bulbs that are larger than 3 inches in diameter may flower the next year; the smaller ones will take longer. It is important that you do not allow the lifted bulbs to dry out; replant them immediately.

Lilies are a favorite food for aphids, slugs, snails, and thrips, but you can keep these pests at bay by monitoring the plants carefully and simply using a spray of water from your hose to wash them off the plants. Insecticidal soaps are also effective. Some species and hybrids can carry a number of viruses, which can wipe them out in no time and infect other established lilies. Infected plants generally have foliage that is mottled with yellow and/or deformed. Buying healthy bulbs from reputable sup pliers is the best way to prevent these problems. Destroy infected plants to prevent the virus from spreading to other lilies.

Uses. Lilies suffer from the same problem as glads; the stems are not particularly attractive when the flowers are not present. (The same is true of tulips and daffodils, but their leaves disappear after flowering.) Growing lilies in groups of 3 or more makes a decent-size stand, which seems to make them look better. You can also site them to grow up through mid-sized shrubs and perennials in beds and borders. Lilies are ideal for fresh arrangements, if you can bear to cut them; many have a delightful fragrance. Try dwarf types in containers.

LILY, CALLA. See *Zantedeschia* spp.
LILY-OF-THE-VALLEY. See *Convallaria majalis*
LILY, RESURRECTION. See *Lycoris* spp.

Lycoris spp.
ly-CORE-iss.
Resurrection lily. Late summer to fall. Zones 5 to 8.

Characteristics. Height: 18 to 30 inches. Colors: Mauve or red.

Resurrection lilies are perfect for forgetful gardeners

who can't remember where anything is planted, since the flowers seem to magically arise where nothing appeared to be growing. In the winter and spring, the daffodil-like leaves cover the ground, only to disappear by late spring. Meanwhile, other perennials or annuals fill the space. Then, in late summer or early fall, the pink mauve amaryllis like flowers of the common resurrection lily (*Lycoris squamigera*) emerge on leafless flower stems. This is the hardiest species and performs well as far north as Zone 5.

Gardeners in warmer areas can also enjoy the blood red flowers of L. radiata, which emerge in early to late fall. The plants, which are hardy to Zone 7, are much shorter than *L. squamigera*, and the flowers are smaller, but their bright hue makes them stand out immediately. The foliage of *L. radiata* is also smaller and less messy as it dies back than that of the common resurrection lily. Yellow and white species are sometimes available; if you can find them, they are definitely worth a try.

How to Grow. Resurrection lilies prefer well-drained soil and full sun to light shade. Plant the bulbs as soon as they become available, which is usually in late summer or early fall. Set them 3 to 4 inches deep and 6 to

10 inches apart. *L. squamigera* spreads rapidly and requires more space than *L. radiata*. Propagate by lifting the bulbs when they get crowded, preferably when the leaves begin to die down.

Uses. Resurrection lilies are wonderful for adding an unusual accent to beds, borders, and containers at a time when many other garden plants are in decline. The blooms make excellent cut flowers, lasting for many days in fresh water.

Narcissus hybrids
nar-SIS-us.
Daffodil. Spring. Zones 3 to 9.

Characteristics. Height: 6 inches to 2 feet. Colors: Yellow, orange, and white.

Daffodils are universally popular in the United States, both with gardeners and non-gardeners alike. Even people who don't care much about gardening are likely to put a few dozen daffodils in their yard. Daffodils are easy to plant, require minimal maintenance, multiply rapidly, and are inexpensive. Combine these great features with the diversity of height, form, and color found in the genus, and it's easy to understand why even the most ardent gardener considers daffodils indispensable.

There are so many different cultivars that daffodil experts have created 10 different divisions, or groups, to categorize them all. Most of the packaged daffodils found in the retail markets are those with large "cups" and long petals on the flowers; usually, one flower is produced per stem. However, many other forms are available through garden centers and bulb outlets. For example, the petals and the cup may be the same or different colors, and the size of the individual flowers can vary greatly. Some types produce as many as 3 to 5 flowers per stem or bear double flowers. The height of the plants can also vary; some are barely 6 inches tall, while others can grow to 2 feet. The most popular cultivars include 'Unsurpassable', 'Carlton', 'Barrett Browning', 'Cheerfulness', 'Tresamble', 'February Gold', 'Pipit', 'Cragford', 'Actaea', end 'Hawera'.

How to Grow. Full sun is best, but many daffodils also do well in the dappled shade of deciduous trees. Plant the bulbs in the fall, approximately twice as deep as the height of the bulb and 6 to 9 inches apart. Fertilize the bulbs in the spring when the leaves first emerge; use a balanced fertilizer. Allow the foliage to remain until it dies down on its own. When the bulbs become too crowded, they may not flower; lift and divide them after the foliage has begun to yellow. If you start with healthy bulbs, you should have few problems. Daffodils are rarely bothered by pests or diseases.

Uses. Daffodils are perfect for beginning gardeners: You can start with a bag of daffodils from a local retail outlet, graduate to a few named cultivars from the garden center, then pore over bulb catalogs for different forms or the newest cultivars. These bulbs are also excellent for naturalizing; good bulb retailers usually sell mixtures of cultivars and forms suitable for this purpose. Daffodils make wonderful cut flowers that will last for about a week. (If you put other flowers in the same container, be sure to change the water every day.) The dwarf forms of daffodils are terrific for containers, rock gardens, or other spots where something small, but colorful, is needed in the spring.

RESURRECTION LILY. See *Lycoris* spp.

Sparaxis tricolor

spuh-RAK-sis TRY-kuh-ler. Harlequin flower, wandflower.
Spring to summer. Zones 7 to 9.

Characteristics. Height: 10 to 12 inches. Colors: Red, orange, yellow, and white.

These wonderful plants are native to South Africa, and in a land where brightly colored flowers are the norm, this is one of the brightest. The colors range from pure white to yellow, orange, and red; the flowers are often outlined in black. The plants bloom in early summer on 10- to 12-inch-tall stems above fanlike leaves.

How to Grow. Plant the corms in full sun and well-drained soil in early spring (or fall in warmer areas). Set them about 2 inches deep and 3 to 4 inches apart. Cormels form relatively slowly; separate them from the parent corms for propagation. As with glads, the corms may be stored over winter.

The main reason these plants are not more popular is that they suffer if they get too much water during the summer. They prefer to be on the dry side in summer and wet during winter. For this reason, they grow well in drier parts of the West, including Southern California. To prevent problems, be sure the soil is well drained.

Uses. Try harlequin flowers for a real show in the summer garden. For best effect, plant them in groups of at least 25. They also make a dramatic addition to both fresh arrangements and container plantings.

STARFLOWER, SPRING. See *Ipheion uniflorum*
TUBEROUS BEGONIA. See *Begonia tuberhybrida* hybrids

Tulipa spp. and hybrids
TEW-lih-puh.
Tulip. Spring. Zones 2 to 8.

Characteristics. Height: 6 to 36 inches. Colors: Red, orange, yellow, purple, pink, and white.

Tulips are an indispensable part of the garden. The Dutch have taken this native of Turkey and created spectacular palettes for the spring landscape. While *Tulipa* includes many interesting flower forms, it is the simplicity of the classic tulip that makes it such a well-loved flower.

Tulips may flower as early as March or as late as June, depending on the type you have chosen and your climate. If you are just learning about tulips, choose some single-early types, such as 'Apricot Beauty', as well as a few single-late kinds, such as 'Kingsblood'. Then, when you are ready to try some thing different, plant some Kaufmanniana or Greigii cultivars for early flowering and a few Bouquet types (for example, 'Toronto') for multiple blooms from the same bulb. Kaufmanniana types to try include 'Stresa' and 'Waterlily'; Greiggi cultivars include 'Sweet Lady' and 'Pinocchio'.

Once you have the tulip bug, you will want to try one or two of the dozen or so species tulips offered for sale. Nearly all of these are short (6 to 12 inches), and most are relatively early. Three outstanding species tulips are *T. clusiana*, with red-and-white flowers; *T. batalinii*, which offers yellow and apricot blooms; and *T. turkestanica*, a multiflowered, white tulip with an orange center.

How to Grow. Tulips thrive in full sun and well-drained soil rich in organic matter. Plant the bulbs at least 6 inches deep—8 inches is best, especially in the South. Set them close enough together to make a splash in the spring. If you buy your bulbs from a reputable outlet, insects and diseases will be minimal. Chipmunks and other rodents will eat the bulbs, unfortunately.

The tulip is botanically an annual, since the mother bulb is replaced each year by a daughter bulb. The daughter bulb must grow to sufficient size to flower the next spring. If the soil is poor, or if conditions are not to their liking, the daughter bulbs may not get large enough to flower well, or even to flower at all. Bulbs that are too small to flower often produce one large, straplike leaf and nothing else. To encourage tulips to "perennialize," especially in areas where they are not commonly long-lived, put some extra effort into preparing a loose, rich planting area. Fertilize in the fall at planting time with an appropriate bulb fertilizer. Then feed again after the bulbs flower and allow the foliage to die back on its own. Some species and cultivars are naturally more perennial than others in a given climate; Darwin Hybrid tulips, Single Late tulips, and many species tulips are among the longest-lived, but be sure to experiment with a variety of them to see which perform best in your garden.

Uses. The key to good-looking tulip plantings is generosity. Don't plant sparse, straight lines of tulip soldiers; paint the landscape with drifts of at least a dozen of each cultivar. Use a broad stroke with the tulip brush, stand back, and enjoy the scenery in the spring.

To help hide the ripening foliage, plant the bulbs to come up through annuals or perennials. Tulips also grow well in containers. Don't forget to plant a few extras for cutting, too.

WANDFLOWER. See *Sparaxis tricolor*
WINDFLOWER. See *Anemone* spp.
WINTER ACONITE. See *Eranthis hyemalis*

Zantedeschia spp.
zan-teh-DESK-ee-uh.
Calla lily. Spring to summer. Zones 7 to 10.

Characteristics. Height: 1 to 3 feet. Colors: White, reddish pink, yellow, and green.

There are few flowers as dramatic as the calla lily. The plants are related to Jack-in-the-pulpits (*Arisaema* spp.) and bear narrow flowers enveloped in a white or colorful coat, called a spathe. Callas can grow 3 feet tall and produce 6 to 12 flowers. The common calla lily (*Zantedeschia aethiopica*) is evergreen, with dark green leaves and a pure white spathe. 'Little Gem' and

'Childsiana' are dwarf selections. 'Crowborough' is supposed to be a little hardier than the species. Many of the newer species and hybrids depicted in catalogs produce deciduous mottled foliage and yellow, pink, or red spathes. One interesting selection is 'Black Magic', which sports a black throat inside the yellow spathe. Other colorful hybrids include salmon-colored 'Cameo', pink-flowered 'Pink Persuasion', and creamy yellow 'Solfatare'.

How to Grow. In its native habitat, the white-flowered common calla lily may be found growing in wet, marshy ground. In the garden, the plants tolerate normal garden soils but flourish in moist, sunny areas. The colored hybrids do not tolerate such wet conditions; site these in well-drained soil.

Plant the rhizomes about 4 inches deep and 12 to 18 inches apart. For best flowering, the plants need sun, but they appreciate afternoon shade. The greatest drawback of calla lilies is their relative lack of cold hardiness, which limits them as perennials to southern zones. In the North, you must dig them in the fall, dry them off, and store them in a cool, dry area over winter. You can also divide the rhizomes in the fall; just be sure to allow the cut ends to dry out well before storing, since soft rot can infect the rhizomes. (This problem tends to occur more in storage than in the garden.) Some leaf spotting fungi can be a problem on lower leaves; pinch off infected leaves.

Uses. Calla lilies are striking in beds, borders, and containers. They are also excellent as cut flowers.

CHAPTER SIX

ROSES

Roses are perhaps the most beloved—and the most recognizable—of all flowers. For centuries, people have found roses both captivating and mysterious, and have grown them for their stunning flowers as well as for their practical uses. Rose fruits, usually called hips, are an excellent source of vitamin C and are often used to make a delicious tea. The petals of cabbage rose (*Rosa centifolia*) are used to make rose water, which is a common ingredient in both cosmetics and food. True attar of roses (also known as oil of roses) is extracted from the petals of *R. damascena* 'Trigentipetala'. Rose petals are also sometimes candied and eaten as a sweet.

While roses clearly have practical value, it is ultimately their beautiful blooms that make them garden favorites.

In this chapter, you'll learn the secrets of planting and caring for your roses to keep them naturally healthy, vigorous, and practically problem-free. You'll also find tips for combining roses with other great garden plants—including shrubs, vines, herbs, perennials, and annuals—for season-long landscape interest.

GROWING ROSES

Rose growing should and can be fun and rewarding. The trick is to put your energy into the species and cultivars that are consistently good performers. Roses have received a bad reputation in recent years as temperamental, chemically dependent, high-maintenance plants. Of course, this is true of some roses, but not all of them deserve to be cast aside. For instance, some gardeners are discovering the virtues of the long-neglected old cultivars growing untended in cemeteries and abandoned places. There are even rose groups around the country, like the "rose rustlers" in Texas, who go to places where roses have survived, take cuttings of the plants, and grow them for garden use. Modern rose breeders are also attuned to gardeners' demands for hardy, problem-resistant roses, and are releasing many excellent new selections. These recent introductions, along with the old cultivars, give both ardent and would-be rose growers a great selection of roses to choose from.

SHOPPING FOR ROSES

Always buy roses from a reliable grower. Bargain roses for sale at a local discount store may be inexpensive, but you'll get what you pay for. It's worth paying a few dollars more to a reputable garden center or mail-order source to get a healthy, vigorous plant that's more likely to thrive in your yard.

When you buy your plants, you may have a choice between "grafted" and "own-root" roses. Many roses are sold as grafted plants, since grafting is a fast way to propagate a large quantity of similar plants. Grafted plants usually have a knob or swelling just above the roots. This area, called the graft union, is where the top part of the desired rose was joined to the roots of another. Own root roses are just that—the top and the roots are from the same plant.

If possible, buy roses that are on their own roots. That way, if the top of the plant is killed by the cold, the roots can send up new growth that will be just like the original. When the tops of grafted roses die back, the new shoots that come up from the roots will look completely different, and will probably not be what you want for your garden.

ROSE TYPES AND TERMS

With so many roses to choose from, it's sometimes hard to know where to start. To make things a little easier, roses have been divided into several groups, based on their origins and growth habits. Understanding the names for these different categories can help you choose roses that are ideal for your needs.

Below you'll find a brief overview of the main rose types. Some of the best of these are highlighted in the plant portraits in this chapter.

Albas: These disease resistant roses offer clusters of fragrant, midsummer flowers and blue-gray-green leaves on long, arching canes.

Bourbon Roses: These reblooming roses have double flowers. The shrubby plants are susceptible to black spot and powdery mildew.

Cabbage or Provence Roses: Also known as "the rose of 100 petals," these showy flowers are famous for their depiction in paintings by the Dutch masters in the 17th and 18th centuries. The double blooms are usually pink or white blushed with pink.

China Roses: *Rosa chinensis* was the first rose introduced into Europe from China. It was a popular parent for rose-breeding work, due in large part to its everblooming qualities. China roses are less hardy than the European roses and are better suited for growing in warm climates, where they tend to be long lived.

Damask Roses: Popular for their perfume, Damasks produce semidouble to double flowers on open shrubs, mainly in summer. Autumn Damasks have a prolonged blooming period.

Floribundas: This class resulted from mixing Hybrid Tea roses with Polyanthas. Floribundas are compact and bear many blossoms per stem, usually over a long period.

Gallica Roses: These compact plants produce richly colored, single to double summer flowers, which are used in medicine and to flavor confections. The plants are prone to mildew.

Grandifloras: This class of roses was developed in the 1950s. They are distinguished by large flowers and profuse bloom.

Hybrid Perpetuals: These roses are crosses between Bourbon Roses and a variety of other types of garden roses. Hybrid Perpetuals are the link between the modern and the old roses. They have many of the same characteristics as Hybrid Tea roses, but with less continuous bloom and a better perfume.

Hybrid Teas: Hybrid Teas come in a wide range of beautiful flower colors. The elegant buds and longstems make them popular as cut flowers. However, because these roses tend to require regular spraying to stay healthy, many gardeners are beginning to pass them up in favor of other roses that need less care.

Moss Roses: Moss roses are mutations of cabbage roses that were selected for their "moss"-covered, sticky buds and calyx. Otherwise, they are similar to their parents.

Noisette Roses: The first Noisette rose, 'Champney's Pink Cluster', was bred in Charleston, South Carolina, by John Champney, a rice planter. He sent the rose to nurseryman Phillip Noisette in France, who went on to develop this new class of roses. Noisette roses are known primarily for their climbing habit and showy flower clusters.

Old Roses: This general term refers to the large group of fine roses that have been garden favorites for hundreds of years, including the Albas, Damasks, and Bourbons, as well as Moss, Noisette, Provence, and Tea roses.

Polyanthas: Most Polyantha roses are small plants with abundant flowers. They are ideal for containers or small gardens and tend to have a wide range of hardiness.

Ramblers: Ramblers are known for their vigorous, sprawling habit. They tend to produce masses of blooms all at once.

Rugosa Roses: *R. rugosa* is a cold-hardy rose known for its salt tolerance, disease resistance, and showy hips. Both the species and its many cultivars and hybrids are excellent garden plants, especially for hedges.

Shrub Roses: This is a catch-all category for many of the new roses that serve as dependable landscape plants and require less pruning.

Species Roses: Species or wild roses are those types that occur naturally. There are approximately 200 such roses in existence. They often have single flowers with 5 petals. Most species roses produce attractive hips in the summer or autumn and can often be grown successfully from seed. Many of the great new shrub roses are species selections or species hybrids.

Tea Roses: It is widely believed that these roses are so named because they first arrived on tea ships from China. The long-blooming plants tend to be disease-resistant, and perform well in Zones 7 to 10.

CHOOSING THE SITE

Starting with durable, dependable plants is one part of successful rose growing; the other is choosing the right site. A minimum of 6 hours of direct sunlight per day is essential for good rose growth. If you can only choose from sites that are shaded for part of the day, a spot with morning sun and afternoon shade is preferable; the morning sunlight will dry the leaves off faster and possibly decrease disease problems.

Roses generally prefer soil that's moist but not waterlogged. Tree roots tend to dry out the soil, so avoid planting your roses near trees. You will also need a spot that is big enough for your roses to mature without being crowded. Dense, crowded growth limits air circulation around the plants and can lead to disease problems.

PREPARING THE SOIL

Roses grow best in well-prepared soil. For good root growth, work the soil deeply, loosening the top 2 feet. As you dig, add ample amounts of organic matter, such as compost or manure. (Some gardeners recommend using chicken manure, which is rich in micronutrients.) If possible, dig over an entire bed rather than just a single hole where the rose will go. This will encourage wide-spreading, healthier root growth.

Check the soil pH; it should be between 6.4 and 6.8. If your soil is too acidic, add ground limestone to raise the pH. If it is too alkaline, add sulfur or leaf compost, or both. If the pH is out of balance, nutrient deficiencies will show up later. For example, the leaves may turn yellow, or the plants may not grow as vigorously as they should.

PLANTING

The ideal time to plant roses is when they are dormant—in late fall or early spring. Many mail-order rose nurseries will ship bareroot plants (plants with just packing around the roots) in November, although this can vary by region. If bareroot roses arrive and you cannot plant them immediately, place them in a refrigerator or another cool spot. Before planting, soak the roots in a tub of water. Prune off any injured or broken roots.

Dig a generous planting hole; make it large enough to hold all of the roots in their natural position without bending them. Make a mound of soil in the middle of the hole, set the plant on top, and spread the roots around it.

Before filling in the hole, check the planting depth. The bud or crown (the point where the roots and the stem meet) should be 1 to 2 inches below the soil surface. Adjust the height of the soil mound until the plant is sitting at the right height. Tamp the soil gently, but firmly as you place it back in the hole around the roots. After planting, mound more soil around the base of the plant to give added protection during the first winter; remove the soil mound in spring.

Until the plants are well established, you'll need to water them during dry periods. A good irrigation program—including a morning rinse of the foliage and absolutely no wetting of the foliage at night—can be extremely helpful with roses. Most roses need no pruning during the first year and little or no pruning the second year.

FERTILIZING

Since roses are heavy feeders, many growers recommend a regular fertilization program. For newly planted roses, wait until after the first bloom cycle. For established roses, fertilize every 3 weeks during the blooming season. Some gardeners use a combination of organic and chemical fertilizers. Mix the fertilizer with water and then pour the mixture around the base of the plant, following the directions on the label. Good organic fertilizers for this purpose include sea kelp and dried blood. There is also a wide array of good fertilizers on the market specially formulated for roses.

To give your roses an extra boost, apply chicken manure over the area every third winter. As a winter mulch, chicken manure also provides protection against severe frost. In early spring, before new growth begins, fork the manure into the soil.

PRUNING

Rose pruning doesn't have to be a big deal; you just need to keep a few simple rules in mind. Always start by removing all dead, diseased, damaged, or crossing branches. Any further pruning depends on the growth habit of the plant and on your desired objective. Pruning should be a gradual process that includes deadheading on a regular basis and an occasional summer pruning to encourage more blooms.

Do all your pruning with high-quality pruning shears. If you prune a diseased rose, clean the shears off with rubbing alcohol before using them on another rose. Each time you prune, make the cut about ¼ inch above an outward-facing bud, and angle the cut so it slopes away from the bud. You may want to paint the cut cane ends with Elmer's wood glue or nail polish to discourage cane borers (insect pests that attack rose canes).

If possible, prune in late winter or early spring, when the roses are still dormant. Assess the winter damage and remove any dead top growth. (If you can't tell whether it's dead or not, just watch for signs of growth.) Once you've done this basic work, the remainder of your pruning tasks will depend on whether your rose blooms on new wood (the current year's growth) or old wood (last year's stems). Climbers and ramblers also need special care.

Pruning Roses That Bloom on New Wood: Roses that bloom on the current year's growth include Hybrid Teas, Floribundas, Polyanthas, Grandifloras, Hybrid Perpetuals, Miniatures, China roses, and reblooming shrub roses. These roses generally need hard pruning to produce new flowering growth.

Begin in late winter by cutting out all weak or dead growth, followed by any diseased portions of the plant. Remove any crossing branches or inwardgrowing stems.

On Floribundas, Polyanthas, Hybrid Teas, Grandifloras, and Hybrid Perpetuals, cut back the strong stems by one-quarter (for Floribundas and Polyanthas) to one-third (for Hybrid Teas, Grandifloras, and Hybrid Perpetuals).

On China roses and repeat-blooming shrub roses, thin out crowded growth, and remove one or two of the oldest canes each year. Prune the longest of the remaining canes back by no more than one-third to shape the plants, and cut all side shoots back to 6 inches. In the fall, cut off the tips of very long canes to keep them from being whipped around by the wind.

On Miniatures, remove a few of the oldest canes at the base, then trim back the remaining stems by one-quarter to one-third to shape the plant.

Pruning Roses That Bloom on Old Wood: Roses that tend to bloom on the previous year's stems include many species roses, Albas, Moss roses, and once-blooming shrub roses.

In late winter, prune out damaged or dead stems, and thin out crowded canes. Remove one or two of the oldest canes each year. Cut the remaining long new canes back by up to one-third. Prune the previous season's side shoots to 6 inches.

Pruning Climbers: Trim repeat-blooming climbers during their dormant period and once-blooming climbers immediately after flowering. The third year after planting, remove any weak, diseased, or dead wood. On repeat bloomers, also shorten the side shoots to 3 to 6 inches; on established climbers, remove one or two of the oldest (dark gray-brown) canes at the base, and train the new canes to the support.

Pruning Ramblers: Ramblers are known for their vigorous sprawling habit. Prune them immediately after flowering, since the new growth in summer will hold the next year's flower buds. To keep them in bounds, cut out all of the stems that flowered in the current year, and train the remaining unbloomed canes to the support. Or, if you really want your rambler to ramble, simply let it spread, tying it to the support as needed. Remove dead or damaged wood whenever you notice it. For more flowers, you can trim the side shoots to 6 inches in early spring.

Other Pruning Pointers: On reblooming roses, deadheading (cutting off the old, faded flowers) will promote the formation of more flowers. Cut individual flowers or an entire cluster, if appropriate.

On grafted roses, watch for sucker growth (very vigorous shoots that spring up from the roots). Remove the suckers as soon as you spot them. Scrape away the soil from the base of the sucker so you can cut it off as close to the base as possible.

PROTECTING ROSES IN WINTER

Gardeners in cold climates accept that their roses must be protected in winter. Even in milder areas, it's a good idea to devote a little time to winter protection, since rapid temperature swings can damage even normally hardy roses.

One of the simplest methods is to tie up the branches, surround the plant with chicken wire, and stuff it with leaves. Just be sure to wait until the roses have been through a hard freeze and are beginning to enter their dormant period before you try this method. Then, in early spring, you should gradually uncover the plants over a period of a few days, before they begin growing inside their cover.

In very cold regions of the United States and Canada, some gardeners protect their roses by digging a trench in front of each plant, carefully lowering the branches into the trench, then covering them with a mound of soil or mulch. Be on the lookout for animal pests, such as mice, that might chew on the canes. Uncover the plants in spring.

The following compilation is just a sampling of the many beautiful roses that are suitable as landscape plants. All of these are excellent selections.

PLANT PORTRAITS

The following compilation is just a sampling of the many beautiful roses that are suitable as landscape plants. All of these are excellent selections.

CLIMBING AND RAMBLING ROSES

Place ramblers where they can climb up an old tree stump or sprawl over something large. Train climbers on a wall or a pillar. Climbing roses have stiffer growth and a more upright habit than ram bring roses. Climbers also tend to be more repeat flowering and to have larger flowers than ramblers.

When growing climbers and ramblers, be sure the structure they are growing on is strong enough to support their growth.

Rosa 'Aloha'
Climbing Hybrid Tea.
Spring through fall. Zones 5 to 8.

Characteristics. Height: 8 to 10 feet. The flowers of 'Aloha' are large, with pink petals that are deeper pink on the back. They are extremely fragrant and excellent for cutting. The foliage is strong, leathery, dark green, and disease resistant. 'Aloha' is similar to many of the Hybrid Perpetual, roses, but its bloom is more prolific.

Cultural Notes. Good air circulation will help prevent black spot and powdery mildew. Deadhead as needed, and prune hard to encourage large flowers.

Uses. An excellent pillar rose; also ideal for a trellis.

Rosa 'America'

Climbing rose.
Spring through fall. Zones 6 to 8.

Characteristics. Height: 8 to 12 feet.

The pointed buds of 'America' open to vibrant, coral-pink blooms with a classic Hybrid Tea form. The fragrant flowers are 3 inches across, with good repeat bloom. In 1976, 'America' was the All-America Rose Selection.

Cultural Notes. Good general rose care—including regular fertilization, pruning, and dead-heading—will keep 'America' looking its best.

Uses. Train on a wall, trellis, or pillar.

Rosa 'American Pillar'

Rambler.
Late spring through early summer. Zones 6 to 8.

Characteristics. Height: 12 to 20 feet.

This vigorous, disease-free rambler blooms for a long period in late spring and summer, with large flower clusters. The individual flowers are pink with a white center and showy golden stamens. The leathery green foliage is attractive. The flowers are followed by red hips in the fall.

Cultural Notes. In humid areas, 'American Pillar' may be prone to powdery mildew. This rose grows in a wide variety of soil types and also is shade-tolerant.

Uses. Great for arbors, trellises, arches, and training up trees.

Rosa 'Blaze'

Climbing rose.
Summer through fall. Zones 5 to S.

Characteristics. Height: 7 feet.

'Braze' bears brilliant scarlet, semidouble flowers in

huge clusters. The 3-inch, cup-shaped blooms begin in June and continue through September. The handsome foliage is dark green and leathery. 'Improved Blaze' is an even better form of this already wonderful rose.

Cultural Notes. 'Blaze' is a vigorous rose with good disease resistance. It is not fussy about soil and will tolerate some shade.

Uses. Great along a fence or trained up a trellis or pillar.

Rosa 'City of York'
Large-flowered climbing rose.
Spring through early summer. Zones 5 to 8.

Characteristics. Height: 15 to 20 feet.

'City of York' is an excellent climbing rose that offers a strong spring or summer display of white-yellow flowers with showy golden stamens. The blooms are fragrant and large—3 to 4 inches across. In 1950, this rose won the American Rose Society National Gold Medal Certificate.

Cultural Notes. 'City of York' is both vigorous and disease-free. It tolerates a wide range of growing conditions.

Uses. Climbs well on trees, arbors, and trellises.

Rosa 'Golden Showers'

Large-flowered climber.
Spring through fall. Zones 6 to 8.

Characteristics. Height: 8 to 12 feet.

'Golden Showers' is one of the most popular climbers. This easy-to-manage, free-flowering rose has lovely, 3- to 4-inch, lemon yellow blooms with a mild lemon fragrance. The shiny, dark green foliage is very attractive.

Cultural Notes. 'Golden Showers' needs good air circulation to prevent black spot. The thorns are fairly substantial, so it is best to keep the plants away from pathways.

Uses. Train to climb a pillar or to cover a wall.

Rosa 'New Dawn'

Large-flowered climber.
Spring through fall. Zones 5 to 8.

Characteristics. Height: 14 to 18 feet.

'New Dawn' was the world's first patented plant. Its abundant, pale pink flowers are fragrant and reliably disease-resistant. The attractive foliage is a shiny, medium green. 'New Dawn' is considered to be the everblooming form of 'Dr. W. Van Fleet', and the two roses are sometimes confused.

Cultural Notes. 'New Dawn' can take hard pruning, if necessary, and still bloom well. It can grow up through trees, although it will bloom less when grown in shade.

Uses. The perfect rose for a large trellis or arbor.

Rosa 'Seven Sisters'
Rambler, Hybrid Multiflora.
Summer. Zones 5 to 8.

Characteristics. Height: 15 to 20 feet.

The flowers of 'Seven Sisters' are much larger than those of its close relative, multiflora rose (*R. multiflora*). This once-blooming rambler has distinctive, fragrant flowers that change color as they age, from carmine-purple to mauve, fading to pale pink and cream. Its name is derived from the many different colors in each cluster of flowers. The foliage is dark green and coarse, on rather stiff stems.

Cultural Notes. This is not a picky rose; it tolerates poor soil and shade, and needs no special care.

Uses. Site 'Seven Sisters' to cover a large trellis or old tree stump. It also makes a great addition to a cottage garden.

Rosa 'Sombreuil'
Climbing Tea rose.
Spring through fall. Zones 7 to 9.

Characteristics. Height: 8 to 12 feet.

'Sombreuil' is an exquisite rose. Its perfect white blooms have large, full, textured, well-formed petals. The dark, leathery foliage blends well into the garden.

Cultural Notes. This disease-free plant requires no pruning. Deadhead throughout the growing season to encourage continuous blooming.

Uses. Ideal for a cottage garden, since it blends well with antique flowers; train it as a fan on a wall or as a shrub. Grow as a pillar or along a fence.

Rosa 'White Dawn'
Large-flowered climber.
Spring through fall. Zones 5 to 8.

Characteristics. Height: 15 feet.
'White Dawn' has clusters of medium-size, double white flowers that resemble gardenias. It is a vigorous climber with a strong fragrance. The foliage is shiny and attractive.

Cultural Notes. This rose is similar to 'New Dawn' except that the flowers are white. It is reliably free of insect and disease problems.

Uses. Suited to a large trellis, tree, or arbor.

MINIATURE AND PATIO ROSES
Miniature roses are small versions of larger roses. Most are everblooming and range in height from 8 to 24 inches. Many are susceptible to fungal diseases. They are excellent in containers, as borders, or in rock gardens. More recently, the patio roses have become popular for growing on terraces or balconies. Both miniature and patio roses grow best on their own roots, rather than as grafts.

Rosa 'Gourmet Popcorn'

Miniature.

Spring through fall. Zones 6 to 8.

Characteristics. Height: 2 feet.

'Gourmet Popcorn' has beautiful buds that open to fragrant white flowers with yellow centers.

Cultural Notes. This rose is generally insect and disease-free. Be sure to deadhead as needed.

Uses. Works well in a large container or as an accent plant in a border.

Rosa 'Green Ice'

Miniature.

Summer through fall. Zones 6 to 8.

Characteristics. Height: 8 to 10 inches. 'Green Ice' is a fascinating miniature with a wonderful bushy growth habit. Its sprawling canes are covered with slightly fragrant, whitish pink blooms that change to light green as they age. The high-centered flowers resemble those of a Hybrid Tea.

Cultural Notes. 'Green Ice' is one of the most reliable miniatures. It tends to be disease-free and winter-hardy. Prune back any dead tips in the spring.

Uses. Ideal when grown in a border, hanging basket, or container.

Rosa 'Red Cascade'
Climbing or Weeping Miniature.
Summer through fall. Zones 6 to 8.

Characteristics. Height: 8 to 12 inches.

The well-formed, strong-red, cupped flowers of 'Red Cascade' are showy but have little fragrance. The plant produces long canes that spread up to 3 feet, with dark green, semiglossy foliage.

Cultural Notes. 'Red Cascade' is susceptible to powdery mildew in warm, humid areas.

Uses. Superb in a hanging basket or on a low trellis.

Rosa 'Sunblaze'
Miniature Floribunda, Patio rose.
Spring through fall. Zones 6 to 8.

Characteristics. Height: 12 to 16 inches.

'Sunblaze' bears clusters of 1½ inch, fully double, orange red flowers. The blooms are slightly fragrant. The abundant foliage is dark green with a matte finish. This rose has a dense, bushy growth habit.

Cultural Notes. Cut off old flowers to encourage continuous bloom.

Uses. Excellent in containers and borders, or as an edging.

SHRUB ROSES

Shrub roses come from diverse backgrounds, but they share the ability to blend into many different landscapes. These excellent plants are generally easy to care for and problem-free.

Rosa 'Agnes'

Hybrid Rugosa, Shrub rose.
Spring through summer. Zones 5 to 8.

Characteristics. Height: 5 to 6 feet.

The flowers of 'Agnes' are pale amber-yellow, which is very unusual for a Rugosa. The double blooms have a deep center and are extremely fragrant. The leaves are a dull light green and coarse in texture.

Cultural Notes. 'Agnes' is a tough, disease-resistant rose. It is extremely thorny and relatively vigorous. Once it establishes itself, it will bloom repeatedly throughout the season.

Uses. Great as a hedge or in the back of a border.

POLYANTHAS AND FLORIBUNDAS

Polyanthas are noted for their continuous bloom and many flowered clusters. They have a bushy habit and tend to be quite hardy. Floribundas are the result of crossing the carefree Polyanthas with the larger-flowered Hybrid Tea roses. They have a more open habit than the Polyanthas and tend to be healthier and a little smaller than the Hybrid Teas. Floribundas are also sometimes called Cluster-Flowered Roses.

Rosa 'Country Dancer'

Shrub rose.
Spring through fall. Zones 4 to 8.

Characteristics. Height: 3 to 4 feet.

The large flowers of 'Country Dancer' are rose-red, double, and fragrant. The foliage is large, dark green, and leathery. This bushy plant has a compact, upright habit and it is an also an excellent repeat bloomer.

Cultural Notes. 'Country Dancer' is a tough, hardy, low-maintenance rose. Trim the shoot tips back a little in spring, and it should bloom profusely most of the growing season. Deadhead as needed.

Uses. Attractive when used in a cottage garden or flower bedor border, where it can be planted alone or in a mass.

Rosa 'The Fairy'

Polyantha.
Spring through fall. Zones 4 to 8.

Characteristics. Height: 3 feet.

'The Fairy' is easy to recognize by its characteristic

clusters of dainty pink buds, which are borne in charming bouquets. 'The Fairy' also makes a wonderful "standard" or "tree" rose. Left untrained, it has a rounded, free-flowing, mounded shape that allows it to blend well in gardens. The flowers are very double and have little or no fragrance. The small green leaves are shiny and attractive.

Cultural Notes. 'The Fairy' is a hardy and disease-resistant rose. In hot summers, it may stop flowering for a period; otherwise, it is a generous bloomer.

Uses. A fine small border accent, specimen, or container plant.

OLD GARDEN ROSES

'Old garden" refers to any rose that was grown before the development of the first Hybrid Tea in 867 or that belongs to one of the categories of roses that is considered "old" (such as the Albas, Damasks, and Gallicas). Most old roses from Europe bloom for several weeks in spring and are known for their distinctive rose fragrance, unique flower forms, and many petals. Old roses from China are very different; they bloom continuously throughout the growing season and tend to be less fragrant and less hardy. They are some of the best shrubs for warm regions because they do not require a dormant period in order to bloom.

Rosa chinensis 'Mutabilis'
China.
Spring through fall. Zones 6 to 9.

Characteristics. Height: 4 to 8 feet.

Often called "the butterfly rose," 'Mutabilis' has exquisite, silky flowers that flutter above the foliage. The flowers are single and cup-shaped and have petals that range from yellow or orange to red or crimson. The blooms are set off by the strikingly beautiful, reddish leaves on maroon stems. The foliage and flowers, which appear from summer into fall, change color as they mature—an outstanding feature of this rose. 'Mutabilis' has also been sold as 'Tipo Ideale'.

Cultural Notes. 'Mutabilis' is generally healthy and trouble free. For best results, look for plants that have been grown on their own roots, rather than from grafts.

Uses. An extraordinary shrub for the border; it can also be trained up a pillar in warmer climates.

Rosa damascena 'Semperflorens'

Autumn Damask.
Summer through fall. Zones 5 to 8.

Characteristics. Height: 6 to 8 feet.

Commonly called "the four seasons rose," this plant is important in the long history of roses. Unlike most other Damask roses, it flowers again after its primary flush of bloom in late spring. Its blooms are medium pink, very double, and intensely fragrant. The foliage is rather gray, downy, and soft.

Cultural Notes. This rose is occasionally susceptible to disease problems but is generally a strong grower. Deadhead to keep the plant blooming in summer and fall. Although it does repeat bloom, it produces only scattered flowers after its big show in spring.

Uses. A tall shrub that is suitable for training up a trellis or fence, or use it as a specimen in an herb garden.

Rosa 'Souvenir de la Malmaison'
Bourbon.
Spring through fall. Zones 6 to 9.

Characteristics. Height: 4 feet.

'Souvenir de la Malmaison' is a well known rose that is often referred to as the "queen of beauty and fragrance." The large, double, quartered flowers are a blend of cream, flesh, and rose tones and have an intense, spicy fragrance. The leaves are large and dark green in color. The plants tend to rebloom more than other Bourbon roses.

At its best, 'Souvenir de la Malmaison' is considered the finest of all the Bourbon roses. At its worst, it is dreadful—the flowers often turn into a soggy brown mess after a rain.

Cultural Notes. Keep the plants deadheaded, especially after a rain.

Uses. Suited to a small garden or container.

SPECIES ROSES

There are many fine species roses to choose from. These plants are suitable for a natural garden or as large mounded shrubs.

Rosa carolina
Species rose.
Summer. Zones 4 to 9.

Characteristics. Height: 3 to 5 feet.

Commonly called pasture rose, *R. carolina* bears fragrant, single, dark pink flowers up to 2 inches across in July or August, followed by small red hips. The slender stems have narrow prickles and dark green, slightly glossy foliage. The variety alba bears white flowers; the variety grandiflora has larger leaves than the species. 'Plena' produces double flowers and is a repeat bloomer when grown under ideal conditions.

Cultural Notes. Pasture rose can grow in some shade. It produces many suckers.

Uses. Excellent for a native plant collection, habitat planting, or any natural area.

Rosa X *harisonii*

Hybrid Foetida.
Spring. Zones 5 to 8.

Characteristics. Height: 8 feet.

This once-blooming rose, which is commonly called "Harison's Yellow," has bright lemon yellow flowers and is valued for its ability to survive with no care. It is said to have been discovered on a farm in Manhattan in the 1830s and, because it was so popular, it travelled west with the settlers—the origin of the "yellow rose of Texas."

Cultural Notes. This rose needs no special care. It will grow well in poor soil.

Uses. Great for neglected areas such as roadsides, or as an informal hedge.

HYBRID TEAS

For many people, Hybrid Tea roses symbolize the classic rose. The flowers are exquisite, but the plants themselves are usually less appealing. For best bloom, Hybrid Tea roses need hard pruning, since they flower on new wood. They require regular fertilizing, pruning, deadheading, spraying for insects and diseases, and winter protection.

Rosa 'Apricot Nectar'

Hybrid Tea.
Spring through fall. Zones 5 to 8.

Characteristics. Height: 6 feet.

The flowers of 'Apricot Nectar' are apricot colored and as large as 5 inches across, with slightly ruf fled petals that have a tea rose fragrance. This constantly blooming, bushy, sturdy plant has large, dark green foliage. 'Apricot Nectar' was an All-America Rose Selections in 1966.

Cultural Notes. Like other Hybrid Tea roses, 'Apricot Nectar' needs regular care to stay healthy and vigorous.

Uses. Attractive in a rose garden or a border.

Rosa 'Mister Lincoln'

Hybrid Tea.
Spring through fall. Zones 6 to 8.

Characteristics. Height: 6 feet.

'Mister Lincoln' is considered the best red rose in its class. Its rich, deep red buds open to velvety petals and classic Hybrid Tea flowers that do not fade in intensity.

The incredibly fragrant flowers bloom atop long stems. The large leaves are a glossy dark green.

Cultural Notes. 'Mister Lincoln' is one of the most reliable Hybrid Tea roses. It needs well-prepared, rich soil and benefits from regular fertilization and pruning.

Uses. Great in a rose garden or as an accent plant.

GRANDIFLORAS

These roses are known for producing large, clustered flowers on long stems. They were created as bedding plants, although they can grow to 6 feet tall. Their flowers open more quickly than those of Hybrid Teas and are exceptionally colorful. Like the Hybrid Teas, they need severe pruning to produce large blossoms. Most Grandiflora roses are susceptible to a broad range of pests.

Rosa 'Love'

Grandiflora.
Spring through fall. Zones 6 to 8.

Characteristics. Height: 3 feet.
'Love' is a unique, shapely flower with scarlet-red

petals that are silvery white on the back. This upright plant is known as a good exhibition rose.

Cultural Notes. 'Love' tends to be one of the tougher Grandifloras. Give it good general rose care. If you want few, but larger flowers, pinch off the smaller side buds to leave one main flower bud per stem.

Uses. Attractive in a rose or flower garden.

Rosa 'Queen Elizabeth'.
Grandiflora.
Spring through fall. Zones 6 to 8.

Characteristics. Height: 5 feet.

This outstanding rose has received a great deal of attention, and with good reason. It has clusters of long, high-centered buds that open to clear pink flowers. The plant is vigorous and upright, with rye, dark green leaves.

Cultural Notes. This rose needs a little pampering to perform well; fertilize, prune, and mulch regularly.

Uses. Suitable for a rose or flower garden.

CHAPTER SEVEN

VEGETABLES

Few things can compare with the satisfaction of picking and eating garden-fresh produce. The rich taste of a sun-warmed, vine-ripened tomato or the crisp snap of a just-picked snow pea are just two examples of the many joys awaiting the home vegetable gardener.

VEGETABLE-GROWING BASICS

No matter where you live, you can grow at least a few vegetable crops. Cold-climate gardeners succeed easily with cool-weather vegetables such as peas, broccoli, and cabbage; southern gardeners grow heat-loving melons, okra, and sweet potatoes to perfection. With a little extra planning, such as late-season plantings for cool-weather crops in the South and indoor seed-starting for long-season crops in the North, gardeners in nearly all areas can have luck with a wide range of vegetables.

You don't have to have a lot of room to grow vegetables, either. Even some of the most space hungry crops, such as squash and cucumbers, are now available in compact bush forms. If you don't have room for a separate vegetable garden, try planting vegetables in flower borders. Or, grow them in containers on a deck or balcony, or in sunny window.

The real key to successful vegetable gardening giving your crops plenty of light. A site that gets sun is ideal; at least 6 hours a day is okay. So crops, such as beets, can get by on as little as 4 hours of sun, but most will grow poorly in too much shade.

When choosing a site, you should also consider convenience. If you have a choice of spots, site the garden fairly near the house, to make harvesting and maintenance easier. It's also handy to have a water source nearby, so you don't have to lug water buckets or haul hoses a long distance during dry spells.

Loose, rich soil is also important for good crop growth. When you prepare the soil, dig or till the top 8 inches or so (at least 1 foot for carrots and other root crops), and work in plenty of compost or other organic matter.

PLANT PORTRAITS

The following plant portraits include those vegetables that are most commonly grown in home gardens, along with a few others that deserve to be be more widely grown. Unlike most of the other entries in this book, these plants are listed by their common name rather than their botanical name. Most, if not all, seed companies list vegetables by their common ame, and few gardeners ever have occasion to use the botanical names.

GROWING TIPS AT A GLANCE

The following plant portraits includes simple symbols to highlight special features you need to know about each vegetable. If you're not sure what any of the symbols mean, refer back to this key.

○   Full sun (more than 6 hours of sun a day; ideally all day)

◐   Partial sun (some direct sun, but less than 6 hours a day)

❇   Cool-weather crop

✳   Warm-weather crop

▼   Grows well in containers

Artichoke, Globe
Aster family. Perennial.

Characteristics. Height: 5 feet.

Globe artichokes are grown for their thistlelike flower buds, which consist of layers of tender bud scales that are peeled off at the table as they are eaten. The tender hearts, found at the center of the buds, are delicious in salads or stuffed with meat, fish, or vegetables and served cold.

These plants are limited in their growing range, preferring damp weather, cool summer temperatures, and mild winters. They are grown commercially in coastal areas of northern California.

Globe artichokes are perennials and can survive for 5 or 6 years in mild-winter areas. Adventurous northern gardeners can grow them as annuals by starting the seed early indoors and harvesting in the fall, or raising the plants in large tubs and moving them to a protected area for the winter. 'Green Globe' is the most popular cultivar for the home garden.

How to Grow. If you are growing globe artichokes as perennials, keep them separate from annual vegetables so they won't be in the way as you turn the soil for spring or fall planting. The large plants are heavy feeders and love moist, welldrained soil enriched with plenty of manure or other organic matter.

Grow globe artichokes from seed or roots. Sow seed early indoors, 6 to 8 weeks before the last frost in spring. Transplant hardened-off seedlings outside after the danger of heavy frost has passed. Or set roots in the garden in early spring, after the danger of heavy frost has passed, with the buds just above the soil line. Allow at least 4 to 6 feet between the plants.

While artichokes cannot survive cold winters, a thick layer of loose winter mulch may be enough to protect the plants in areas with moderate winters. The bud scales tend to become tough in hot weather; gardeners in warmer regions can improve their chances of success by providing plenty of water when temperatures rise.

The plants are sometimes attacked by aphids or slugs. Spray with insecticidal soap to control aphids; handpick slugs or lure them away with beer traps. Cut the stems to the ground in the fall to discourage overwintering pests. In areas with moderately cool winters, leave 10 to 15 inches of the stalks above ground for the winter, and mulch the roots heavily in the fall.

How to Harvest.. Pick the flower buds when they are about the size of an orange. Cut them off with 1 to 2 inches of the stem attached.

Uses. Serve cooked bud scales and hearts hot or cold, with a sauce for dipping. The plants themselves are dramatic-looking and can serve as landscape features. If you lose track of time or go away on vacation when the buds are ready to harvest, they will bloom into 6-inch, blue, thistlelike flowers that are good for drying.

Asparagus
Lily family. Perennial.

Characteristics. Height: 4 to 6 feet.

Asparagus is probably the longest-lived vegetable in the garden. A well-sited, well-maintained asparagus patch can be productive for 20 years or more. This crop is grown for its tender shoots, or spears, which emerge in the warm temperatures of late spring and early summer. If they are not harvested, they develop into bushy plants with ferny foliage. In fall, they take on an attractive golden color.

Asparagus produces male and female plants. Mature female plants are pollinated by male plants when they bloom, and produce beautiful red berries in the fall. The fruit contains seed, which self-sows to produce many seedlings. This is a disadvantage, since the seedlings can crowd out older plants, and seed production weakens the female plants. Research has been underway for many years to develop asparagus strains that produce predominantly male plants. 'Jersey Giant' is one of the more popular cultivars that produce mostly male plants.

Because the plants need a dormant period triggered by the first frost in fall, they do not perform well in frost-free areas. Cultivars are being bred that are more tolerant of mild winters, including 'UC 157', a predominantly male cultivar that is resistant to Fusarium wilt disease.

How to Grow. Asparagus prefers rich, welldrained, slightly acid soil in full sun or light shade. Choose a location apart from your annual vegetables so the soil won't be disturbed every year. The more care you give to soil preparation before you plant asparagus, the better it will produce and the longer it will live.

You can grow asparagus from seed or from 1- or 2-year-old roots. Your choice will depend on how long you're willing to wait for your first crop. (The roots should be 3 years old before you start harvesting.) First-year spears are about as thick as the lead in a pencil, second-year spears are as thick as a pencil, and third-year and older spears are as thick as a finger.

To plant asparagus, dig a trench 12 inches wide and 15 inches deep for each row, and space the rows 4 feet apart. Mound up 8 to 9 inches of soil at the bottom of the trench.

If you're starting with roots, soak them overnight before planting, so they can take up water more easily. Set the crowns 18 inches apart on the mounds, and spread the roots out as evenly as possible. Then cover them with only 2 inches of soil.

If you're starting with seed, scatter it on top of the mounds. Cover it with ½ inch of soil, and keep the soil moist until the seed germinates.

As the stalks grow up, carefully mound the soil around them throughout the summer, so that by fall the soil level is even. (Be very gentle with the seedlings.) The patch needs plenty of water the first year, especially if you are planting roots. Since the roots will be as many as 6 inches below the soil surface by the end of the summer, the water must penetrate at least 8 inches deep each time you irrigate. Once the plants are established, they are more tolerant of dry conditions. Allow the foliage to die back in the fall before cutting it to the ground. That way, the plants can store plenty of energy for next year's crop.

Weeding is especially important in an asparagus bed, since you won't be cultivating the soil each year; a summer mulch can help keep weeds to a minimum. Plants are susceptible to rust and asparagus beetles; sometimes Fusarium wilt can also be a problem. Look for disease-resistant cultivars, and handpick pests as you spot them.

How to Harvest. To enable your plants to get a vigorous start, wait to begin harvesting from seedgrown plants until the third spring after sowing; wait until the second spring after planting 1-year roots, and the first spring after planting 2-year roots. During the first harvest season, pick for only 2 weeks. The second harvest season, pick for 3 weeks; the third season, pick for 4 weeks. Fully mature plants can be harvested for 4 to 6 weeks, until the stalks become progressively thinner. Harvest only spears that are thicker than a pencil. Cut them just above the soil level when they are 6 to 8 inches tall.

White asparagus is considered even more of a delicacy than green asparagus, and it's fairly easy to produce: Simply pile another 8 to 10 inches of soil over the bed. When the spears push through, remove the soil and harvest them at ground level, just as you would with green asparagus. The soil protects the stalks from the sun, preventing them from developing their green color. Do not try to grow white asparagus until your patch is at least 4 years old.

Uses. Asparagus does not retain its freshness for more than a day or two, so enjoy your harvest as soon as possible. This vegetable is delicious boiled or steamed, served with a sauce or by itself. The ferny plants add a light texture to the garden. The foliage with berries can be picked for fresh flower arrangements.

Bean
Bean family. Annual.

Characteristics. Height: 20 inches for bush beans; 5 to 8 feet for pole beans.

There is probably more diversity among beans than any other garden vegetable. Whole cookbooks—and whole gardens—have been devoted exclusively to beans. Some beans are grown for the pods and seeds; others are grown for the seeds only. They come in shades of green, yellow, purple, and red, and some have spots, stripes, speckles, or black "eyes." The pods can be short or long, round or flat, broad or narrow, on bushy or vining plants. In short, there's a bean for everyone and every sunny garden.

Snap beans, also known as string beans, are the familiar crisp green beans that snap when you bend them. They are eaten whole, with their ends snipped off. The bushy or vining plants can have yellow, purple, or green pods. (The yellow-podded types are also called wax beans.) 'Romano' is a popular, flat podded pole bean. 'Rome II' is a bush version of 'Romano'. Snap beans are great raw (served with dips or in salads), steamed, or boiled. Most types freeze well after they are blanched. Bush types are usually ready for harvesting 45 to 60 days after sowing, while pole cultivars take from 60 to 80 days.

Filet beans, also called haricots verts, are long, narrow, and crunchy, and usually grow on bush-type plants. They are produced in great numbers starting about 45 to 55 days after sowing and should be her vested every day for continuous production. Pick them when they are about 4 to 6 inches long and about ⅛ inch wide, before the pods begin to swell. 'Triomphe de Farcy' is a popular heirloom cultivar that has green pods with faint purple stripes.

Lima beans, also called butter beans, are consid ered shell beans because the seeds are removed from the shell, which is then discarded. There are both bush and pole cultivars. The pods and beans vary in size: Baby lima pods are 2½ to 3 inches long, with 3 or 4 small beans in each, while the large "potato" type limes are 3 to 6 inches long, with 3 to 5 large beans inside. 'Florida Speckled' has buff-colored beans splashed with maroon. Lima beans generally require warmer temperatures than snap beans. The bush types mature in 70 to 80 days, the pole types in 75 to 90 days. Lima beans are usually cooked and can be combined with corn to make succotash.

How to Grow. Beans require full sun and well-drained, rich soil. These warm-season crops cannot tolerate any frost and grow slowly in cool temperatures. Like other members of the pea family, beans act as a host for beneficial bacteria that live on their roots. These bacteria take nitrogen from the air and convert it to a form that the plants can use. If you are planting beans in a new spot, you may need to add an inoculant (readily available from seed companies) to the seed to make sure the right bacteria are present. Once you have grown beans in that spot, the bacteria can survive in the soil for several years until the next planting.

Sow seed directly in the garden in late spring or early summer, after all danger of frost has passed and the soil is warm. Plant seed of bush cultivars 2 to 3 inches apart, cover it with 1 inch of soil, and keep it, moist until seedlings appear. Thin the seedlings to about 6 inches apart when they are large enough to handle.

Vining types need some kind of support, such as poles (spaced 2 or 3 feet apart) or a fence or trellis. Sow the seed 2 to 3 inches apart around each pole or along the fence or trellis. Cover the seed with 1 inch of soil and keep the soil moist until seedlings appear. When the seedlings are large enough to handle, thin them to 5 or 6 plants per pole or 6 to 10 inches apart along the fence or trellis.

The plants may stop producing pods temporarily in hot summer weather, since temperatures over 80°F can kill the pollen before the flowers are pollinated. When temperatures become cooler, the plants should resume production.

Beans are susceptible to a variety of problems, including root rot diseases, anthracnose, bacterial diseases, and bean beetles. Check with your local Cooperative Extension office to find out which problems are most common in your area, and look for cultivars that are resistant to those problems. Planting beans in a different part of the garden each year can help prevent soil-borne root rot diseases. Avoid working around bean plants when they are wet to prevent the spread of diseases.

How to Harvest. Pick snap beans when the pods are firm and crisp, and the seeds are still small or undeveloped. Hold the stem with one hand and pull off the pod with the other to avoid breaking the branch of the plant. Harvest constantly, or the pods will become tough and stringy. Regular harvesting also keeps the plants more productive.

Harvest shell beans when the pods are firm, plump, and fully mature, after they change color but before the beans dry out completely. Harvest dry beans after the pods dry on the plants. You can pull up the whole plant and hang it upside down to dry the pods more fully. When the pods split open, shell the beans and store them in tight-lidded jars in a cool, dry location.

Uses. There are as many uses for beans as there are types of beans. Enjoy snap beans raw in dips and salads, or serve them cooked. Limas and other shell beans are shelled and cooked. Shell and dried beans can be baked. Mung beans are grown for sprouts, which are tasty in salads and stir-fried dishes.

Beans are excellent crops for children to raise, because the seed is easy to handle and the plants grow quickly.

Beet

Goosefoot family. Biennial grown as an annual.

Characteristics. Height: 8 inches.

Beets are a cool-season crop grown for their fleshy, round, oblong, or cylindrical roots and their leafy tops. Both plant parts are highly nutritious; together, they are rich in carotene, potassium, calcium, iron, and vitamins A, B_1, B_2, and C. 'Detroit Dark Red, Medium Top' is a popular cultivar with perfectly round, dark red roots that grow to 3 inches across. 'Little Ball' is a gourmet baby beet that can be served whole.

The red roots of traditional beets are well known for their habit of "bleeding" all over kitchen counters and sinks, as well as other ingredients. Golden and white cultivars, such as 'Burpee's Golden', do not have this problem.

How to Grow. Beets appreciate loose, friable, deeply worked soil that's been enriched with organic matter. They cannot tolerate very acidic soil, so add lime to your growing beds the fall before planting.

This vegetable prefers cool temperatures and can be planted as both spring and fall crops. (In areas with frost-free winters, you can also plant beets as winter crops.) Sow the seed directly in the garden in early spring, as soon as you can work the soil. Sow again in midsummer for a fall crop. Or plant successive crops every 3 weeks for a continuous harvest. The seed you plant is actually a dried fruit—a cluster of 3 or 4 seeds—so try not to plant too thickly. Plant the seed in rows spaced 8 inches apart. Thin the plants to 2 to 3 inches apart when they are 2 to 3 inches tall.

Beets tolerate both cold and hot temperatures but may produce seed stalks in prolonged temperatures below 50°F. If your beet roots have bitter black spots on them, there may be a boron deficiency in the soil. You can have your soil tested to verify this. If it is a problem, amend the soil as recommended on the test results.

How to Harvest. Pick beet greens when they are 4 to 6 inches long. The roots are usually best when they are less than 2 inches in diameter. Fall-harvested beets can be stored at 33° to 35°F and in 95 percent humidity. (Do not allow them to freeze in storage.) You can also can or pickle the roots.

Uses. Cook beet greens as you would spinach. The roots are delicious baked, grilled, or boiled. Add them to salads, make them into borscht, or serve them as a side dish.

Broccoli
Cabbage family. Annual.

Characteristics. Height: 2 to 3 feet.

Broccoli is one of the most nutritious garden vegetables you can grow. It is high in vitamins A and C, and is an excellent source of fiber. While some people have been known to publicly denounce broccoli, many more prize it for its exceptional flavor, whether cooked or eaten raw. This crop is gaining in popularity, and more than half of all vegetable home gardeners in this country now grow it.

Broccoli is grown for its edible flower buds and foliage. Cultivars are available with different maturity dates, so if you choose carefully, you can enjoy broccoli fresh from the garden for months. 'Green Comet' is an early-maturing All-America Selections winner with big central heads up to 7 inches across, followed by many side shoots. It matures in 55 days after transplanting. Purple-headed cultivars are also available and are sometimes offered as a purple cauliflower. 'Romanesco' is an old-fashioned Italian type with chartreuse-colored central heads that appear to spiral out from the center. It has a long maturity period of 75 days.

How to Grow. Broccoli is a slow-growing, cool-season crop that grows best in a rich, well-drained soil in full sun. Start seed indoors 4 weeks before the last frost in spring. The seedlings need a great deal of light and can grow tall and leggy if they don't receive enough. To be on the safe side, have plant lights available as a back-up if you plan to grow the seedlings in a sunny window; just a day or two of cloudy weather after they sprout can cause them to skyrocket on spindly stems. If you don't have the time or space to start the seed early, you can purchase bedding plants, which are often available at garden centers.

Transplant hardened-off seedlings to the garden after the last hard frost. Plant them slightly deeper than they were growing previously, with the soil almost up to the lowest leaves. Set the seedlings 1 to 2 feet apart in rows spaced 2 feet apart.

For a fall crop, sow the seed directly in the garden in midsummer, 3 months before the first fall frost. Plant the seeds 1 inch apart in the rows and thin to 1 to 2 feet apart when the seedlings are large enough to handle. The plants can tolerate a light frost in the fall.

Broccoli plants need lots of water for vigorous, steady growth. Water regularly and mulch the plants to keep the soil moist.

This crop is susceptible to flea beetles, aphids, cabbageworms, and cabbage loopers. To keep pests out, protect the developing plants with floating row cover. To prevent problems with diseases such as black rot, black leg, and wilt, avoid planting broccoli or its relatives in the same spot each year.

How to Harvest. Pick broccoli when the heads have tight, firm buds. Cut off the central head with 6 inches of stem attached. After the central head has been cut, most cultivars will produce many smaller side heads, which can also be harvested. Enjoy broccoli heads fresh, store them in the refrigerator for a week or so, or freeze them.

If you don't harvest the heads at the right time, they will become looser and the yellow petals will begin to show. If you see yellow, the heads may be past their peak; pull the plants out for the compost pile, or let them bloom to have the flowers, which are edible.

Uses. This versatile vegetable can be eaten raw or cooked. Try it in salads, as a side dish, or in soups, casseroles, stir-fries, or stews. Broccoli makes a tasty stuffing for baked potatoes, too. You can also eat the foliage, either raw or cooked as greens. For a special taste treat, try peeling the thick stems and chopping and adding them to salads. They have a sweet, nutty taste. Even the yellow flowers, if allowed to bloom, can be used in salads or as a garnish.

Cabbage
Cabbage family. Biennial grown as an annual.

Characteristics. Height: 18 to 20 inches.

Cabbage is one of the most popular and versatile vegetables grown in home gardens. It is rich in vitamins A, C, and K, as well as essential minerals. And homegrown cabbage has a sweet flavor that store-bought cabbage just doesn't seem to have.

Cultivars are red or green, with smooth or savoyed (wrinkled) edges and flat, round, or pointed heads.

Early-, mid-, and late-season cultivars are available, so cabbage devotees can harvest cabbage throughout much of the summer into fall.

'Early Jersey Wakefield' is a popular, yellow-resistant heirloom cultivar with compact, pointed heads that are ready to harvest 63 to 65 days after transplanting. 'Danish Roundhead' is another heirloom, valued for its large heads, which mature in 105 days after transplanting. It should be planted as a fall crop.

Chinese cabbage has a mild, sweet flavor and crinkled leaves on elongated heads. It is usually grown as a fall crop, although 'Two Seasons Hybrid' has been developed for both spring and fall crops. Pak choi is a related crop grown for its leafstalks, which are tasty raw or cooked in Oriental dishes.

How to Grow. Cabbage prefers full sun or light shade and well-drained soil enriched with organic matter. It is a cool-season crop and does not tolerate hot temperatures. Start spring crops early to give the plants a chance to mature before hot weather. Sow seed indoors 5 to 6 weeks before the last frost in spring. Transplant hardened-off seedlings outside after danger of heavy frost has passed. Or plant seedlings purchased from a local garden center after danger of heavy frost. Direct-sow fall crops in midsummer. Set plants 12 to 18 inches apart in rows spaced 2 feet apart.

Cabbage plants benefit from rapid, uninterrupted growth, which is aided by 1 to 1½ inches of water every week, plus liberal applications of compost or 10-10-10 fertilizer. They are susceptible to the same diseases and pests as their relatives, so avoid planting any cabbage family crops in the same spot 2 years in a row. Floating row covers can protect the developing plants from many pests.

How to Harvest. Gather cabbage heads when they are firm. Cut the stem at soil level and remove the outer leaves, or leave several inches of stem and leaves in the garden. After the central head is harvested, smaller heads may develop near the base of the leaves. Harvest Chinese cabbage when the leaves are loose and 10 inches tall, or wait until they form heads. Fall-harvested cabbage heads can last for several months if you store them at 40°F and in high humidity.

Uses. Serve cabbage cooked or raw, in combination with other vegetables or with meat dishes; it can be stir-fried, steamed, boiled, sauteed, or baked. Or shred it for cole slew or sauerkraut.

CANTALOUPE. See *Melon*

Carrot

Carrot family. Biennial grown as an annual.

Characteristics. Height: 12 inches.

Carrots are grown for their sweet-tasting, bright orange roots, which are high in vitamin A. While the large cultivars require loose, deep, sandy soil for good root development, gardeners with heavy clay soil can have success with shorter cultivars, some of which grow no deeper than 2 or 3 inches. These short-rooted types also grow well in containers.

Carrot roots develop inner and outer cores as they mature. The outer core tastes sweeter and contains more vitamins and minerals, while the inner core tends to be tougher in texture. The best-quality carrots have small inner cores and large outer cores.

The roots vary in length from 1½ to 9 inches. They can be long and narrow or short and rounded; they can taper toward the tip or be cylindrical. 'Thumbelina' is an All-America Selections winner with round, golf ball-size roots that can be eaten whole. 'Little Finger' is a delicious gourmet type that grows 3½ inches long and

⅝ inch wide, with a small inner core. 'Imperator' grows 8 to 9 inches long; the slender roots are only 1½ inches wide.

How to Grow. Carrots require a sunny location with well-drained soil that is free of stones and has been worked at least as deep as the length of the cultivar's roots. (If the roots reach a hard-packed layer or stones, they will either stop growing or split apart.) This cool-season crop tolerates light frost. Sow seed directly in the garden in early spring, after danger of heavy frost has passed. Sow again at 2-week intervals for a continuous supply, or just make one large repeat sowing in midsummer for a fall crop. Space the rows 6 inches apart. Water regularly to keep the soil moist while the seeds are sprouting, which can take up to 2 weeks. Thin the seedlings to 3 inches apart when they are large enough to handle.

The tops of the roots will turn green if they are exposed to sunlight. To prevent green "shoulders," feed and water the plants regularly; this will promote rapid growth of the foliage, which can shade the tops from the sun. You can also heap soil around the roots about 40 days after sowing.

Carrots are bothered by few pests and diseases, with the exception of root nematodes, which are microscopic worms that can severely disfigure the roots. If the roots are stunted and hairy-looking, you may want to have your soil tested for nematodes. You can prevent the buildup of these pests by planting your carrots in different parts of the garden each year.

Shallow watering can also damage the roots. Remember that each time you irrigate, the water must soak in slightly deeper than the length of the roots.

How to Harvest. You can begin to harvest carrots at thinning time. The harvested thinnings make great snacks right in the garden. Leave the rest of the carrots in the ground until you are ready; to use them. They are easier to harvest if you soak the bed with water before you begin pulling. Gently grab the tops and twist them as you pull the roots up. If there are still some carrots left in the fall, you can leave them in the ground after the first frost, but in cold climates you'll need to pull them up before the ground freezes. Store them in a root cellar or other cool, humid area until you are ready to use them. In mild areas, you can leave carrots in the ground and harvest them all winter long.

Uses. Raw carrots, especially the smaller cultivars, make great in-the-garden snacks. They are important ingredients for salads, either shredded or sliced, and can be used for dipping. You can also cook them in various ways, including steaming, boiling, baking, glazing, or sauteing in olive oil. Carrots are ideal in soups and stews, and as garnishes for meat dishes. They make a terrific curry soup, which can be served hot or cold. The young tops can be used to flavor soups. If you allow carrots to overwinter, they produce pretty flowers that look like Queen-Anne's-lace.

Cauliflower
Cabbage family. Annual.

Characteristics. Height: 2½ feet.

Cauliflower is the most challenging member of the cabbage family to grow. When gardeners are successful, the plants produce delicious heads of creamy white flower parts called "curds." When they are not successful, the heads can turn yellow, or the curds can fall apart or become "riccy." The secret to success is to maintain continuous, rapid growth in cool temperatures.

The cultivars differ in their maturity dates, resistance to diseases, and ability to maintain their quality when frozen. 'Early White Hybrid' is an excellent 52-day cultivar with 9-inch heads that do not tend to become loose and "ricey."

How to Grow. Cauliflower needs full sun and rich, well-drained soil. Start seed indoors 4 weeks before the last frost, and give the seedlings plenty of light to keep them compact. Transplant hardened-off seedlings to the garden after danger of a heavy frost. Sow fall crops directly in the garden in mid-summer. Set transplants or thin seedlings to stand 2 feet apart in rows spaced 30 inches apart.

Too much heat will prevent cauliflower heads from forming, and too much cold will slow them down. It is important to water and fertilize regularly to encourage continuous growth, as any interruption will delay the production of heads. Cauliflower is susceptible to the same pests and diseases as other cabbage family crops, including black rot and cabbageworms. To prevent the buildup of diseases, avoid planting cabbage family relatives in the same spot 2 years in a row. Floating row covers can protect developing plants from pests.

Cauliflower must be shielded from the sun to maintain its white color. Some cultivars have long leaves that grow close to the heads, offering "selfblanching" protection. If your cultivar is not selfblanching, you'll have to do it yourself, by tying the foliage over the heads: When the heads are 2 to 3 inches across, tie the foliage over them with rubber bands, or hold them with one or two clothespins. (Clothespins are easier to move as the heads grow larger.)

How to Harvest. This crop is ready to harvest when the heads are the appropriate size for the cultivar, and the curds are held tightly together. Cut the heads off the main stem, leaving 1 to 2 inches of stem on each head. Use the heads as soon as possible after harvesting, or freeze them for future use.

Uses. Cauliflower can be served raw or cooked. Raw curds are great for snacks or dipping, or in salads. Cauliflower is also good stir-fried, sauteed, steamed, boiled, or baked, alone or combined with meats or other vegetables. It is especially delicious in a cauliflower curry dish with Indian spices and yogurt.

Corn

Grass family. Annual.

Characteristics. Height: 4 to 9 feet.

Eating fresh sweet corn is one of the greatest delights of summer. Nothing can match the flavor of the luscious, succulent, sweet kernels of corn on the cob, fresh-picked from the garden. Although the plants take up a great deal of room and yield as little as an average of 2 ears per plant, anyone who has ever tasted fresh sweet corn from his or her own garden knows that growing this wonderful crop is well worth it.

Most corn plants look like giant blades of grass and grow from 4 to 9 feet tall. Sweet corn cultivars can be yellow, white, or bicolored (with both yellow and white kernels). Sweet corn has been the subject of much hybridizing in the seed industry, and recent breakthroughs in breeding programs have led to the sugary-enhancer hybrids and the super-Arisaema sweet hybrids.

The super-sweet cultivars can be up to 4 times as sweet as other types of sweet corn. They do not even have to be cooked or amended in any way to taste as delicious as standard cultivars smothered in butter and salt.

The sugary-enhancer hybrids can stay sweet much longer than earlier cultivars. Most corn has a small window of ripeness—usually just 2 or 3 days—before the sugar turns to starch and the corn tastes stale. The sugary enhancer hybrids stay sweet up to 2 weeks after picking. This means you do not have to harvest your entire crop as soon as it ripens in order to avoid starchy, overripe corn.

The part of corn that we eat is the kernel, or seed. The immature seeds swell when the female flowers, or silks, are fertilized by pollen carried by the wind from the male flowers, or tassels. The silks must be pollinated by the same corn cultivar, or the kernels will be uneven in size and quality. For good pollination, plant your corn in blocks at least 4 rows wide. If you want to plant more than one cultivar, separate them by at least 400 yards to prevent cross pollination, or choose cultivars that mature at least a month apart. (One advantage of choosing the sugary-enhancer hybrids is that they do not need to be isolated from other sweet corn cultivars.)

Dry conditions can stunt corn growth. Under severe stress, the plants may tassel when the stalks are only 2 to 3 feet tall, before the silks are produced. If the pollen dies before the silks appear, the corn will not have a chance to be pollinated. To prevent this problem, mulch the plants and water regularly.

Pests and diseases generally aren't too serious in corn patches. If you see ugly gray, swollen masses that open to release what looks like black soot, your corn has corn smut, a fungal disease. Smut can appear on the foliage, the silks, and the kernels. When it gets in the kernels, it can make them swell to immense irregular shapes. Smut is not toxic and is even harvested as a delicacy in some cultures, but affected plant parts should be removed before the spores are released. Corn earworms can also be a problem. They enter the ears through the silks and feed on the upper kernels. Once they are in the ears they cannot be controlled, but they do not usually cause severe damage; break off and discard the damaged tips after harvest.

How to Harvest. The ears are ready to harvest about 17 or 18 days after the silks appear. The kernels of sweet corn should be milky when you pierce them with your fingernail. If they are thick and creamy, they are over-ripe; if they are watery, they are not ready yet. There are obvious drawbacks to this method of determining ripeness, and it should only be used when you are learning what a ripe ear feels like. If you open the husk before the ear is ripe, put a paper bag over it to protect it from birds and insects. Harvest by snapping the ear off the stalk with a quick, twisting motion. Store standard cultivars in the refrigerator for up to 3 days; you can refrigerate the super-sweet and sugary-enhancer hybrids for up to 2 weeks. Harvest popcorn and ornamental corn when the husks and plants are dry.

Uses. It's hard to resist snacking on fresh-picked sweet corn right in the garden. If you manage to get some to the kitchen, boil the husked ears lightly and eat the kernels right off the cob. Or cut the kernels off the ears, steam them, and enjoy them alone or added to other vegetable dishes. Corn can be combined with lima beans to make succotash. It can also be used in stuffings, and makes great fritters, breads, and puddings. Pop popcorn for a nutritious snack. Use ornamental corn for autumn decorations.

Cucumber

Squash family. Annual.

Characteristics. Height: 2 to 4 feet for bush types; up to 9 feet for vining types.

Cucumbers are vine or crops grown for their green fruits, which have a refreshing, mild, cool flavor. Standard cucumbers have straight, narrow fruits with spiny, waxy skins that range from medium to dark green. Most cultivars grow on vines, which should be supported with trellises. Bush cultivars are also available; they take only one-third as much space as vining types and can even be grown in containers. 'Bush Champion' produces prolific crops of straight, slender, bright green fruits up to 11 inches long on bush-type plants. Pickling cultivars—both vining and bush-type—produce shorter, plumper fruits with lighter skins for fresh eating or for pickles.

Many other types of cucumbers make interesting additions to the vegetable garden. For instance, Oriental cucumbers are long and curved, with a rough texture. They are good for slicing and adding to salads or for making into pickles. Armenian cucumbers, also called snake or serpent cucumbers, grow 3 feet long. They have thin skins and a sweet flavor that is never bitter. "Burpless" cucumbers lack the gene that makes some cucumbers bitter and difficult for many people to digest. They taste sweet and do not need to be peeled before you eat them. Lemon cucumbers are bright yellow and look like their namesake. They do not taste like lemons, however, but are sweet and crisp.

Cucumbers produce male and female flowers on the same plant. The male flowers pollinate the female flowers, which in turn produce the fruit. Many newer cultivars produce only female flowers and are called "gynoecious." They bear considerably more fruit per plant than other cucumbers. However, they still need some male flowers to produce the pollen, so seeds of a standard cultivar are included in packets of gynoecious cucumber seeds. The seeds are not always marked, so if you don't want to plant all the seeds in the packet, you'll need to distinguish the pollinator from the other seeds. The pollinator seeds tend to be a little larger and plumper than the gynoecious seeds. (Under stress, the female plants may also produce male flowers.)

How to Grow. This warm-season crop prefers rich, warm, well drained soil in full sun. In areas with short summers, you can start the seed indoors about 4 weeks before the last frost date and transplant the hardened-off seedlings to the garden after all danger of frost. In areas with long summers, sow seed in the garden after all danger of frost has passed. Sow the seed of vining types 1 inch deep in rows spaced 3 to 4 feet apart, and thin the seedlings to 12 inches apart when they are large enough to handle. Or plant the seed in "hills"—groups of 3 plants with 2 to 3 feet between groups. Plant bush types in containers, or 12 inches apart in rows spaced 2 to 3 feet apart.

Provide a trellis for vining types to climb; otherwise, they will produce curved fruits. Cucumbers tend to be shallow-rooted and need extra water in dry weather. They can stop growing if they become too dry but will usually start growing again when conditions improve. Mulching the soil can help keep the roots evenly moist.

Cucumber flowers are pollinated by bees, which must visit the blooms many times before enough pollen is transferred to produce full-size, straight fruits. If the flowers are not properly pollinated, the fruits can be distorted, or the plants may produce no fruit at all. Bees tend to be less active in cloudy: weather and in gardens where pesticides are used. If your bees aren't doing their job, you can pollinate the flowers yourself: On a cloudy day or early in the the morning, simply remove the male flower and rub it on the female flower. (The female flowers have a tiny fruit behind them, which will eventually swell into a cucumber.) Contrary to popular opinion, cucumbers do not cross-pollinate with melons, and bitter cucumbers are not produced by other vine crops growing in the vicinity.

Cucumbers are susceptible to a number of pests and diseases common to squash family members, including anthracnose, powdery or downy mildew, cucumber mosaic virus, aphids, cucumber beetles (which spread bacterial wilt disease), and vine borers. Many cultivars have been selected for resistance to these problems. Check with your local Cooperative Extension Service office for recommended cultivars for your area. Avoid planting squash family crops in the same spot 2 years in a row.

How to Harvest. Pick cucumbers at any stage of growth, but before they become larger than the cultivar should grow. The more you harvest, the morel the plants will produce; pick the fruits daily, or at least every other day, when the plants are at peak production.

Uses. Slice standard types for salads, chop or grate them to add a cool taste to dips, or combine them with yogurt and Indian spices to make raita. They can also be sauteed, stir-fried, added to, casseroles, or made into a terrific soup that can be served hot or cold. Pickling types are good for pickling or eating fresh.

GLOBE ARTICHOKE. See *Artichoke, Globe*
HONEYDEW. See *Melon*
HOT PEPPER. See *Pepper*

Eggplant
Tomato family. Annual.

Characteristics. Height: 2 to 3 feet.

Eggplant is a close relative of tomatoes and peppers. It produces beautiful fruit with a luscious, succulent texture and mild flavor. The fruit can be egg shaped or long and cylindrical, with glossy purple, lavender, pink, yellow, or white skin. The deep purple-fruited heirloom 'Black Beauty' was introduced by Burpee in 1902 and is still popular.

Eggplants vary in size from miniature, thumbsize fruits to large, oval shaped fruits. Italian types are long and slender, growing to 10 inches long and 2½ inches wide. Japanese types are narrower and can reach 12 inches long and 2 inches wide. Most eggglants form bushy plants that grow 2 to 3 feet tall, although miniature cultivars are available; they grow just 12 inches tall and are perfect for patio containers.

How to Grow. Eggplant thrives in warm, rich, well-drained soil in full sun. This warm-season crop cannot tolerate any frost. It takes a long time to mature, so start the seed indoors 10 to 12 weeks before the last frost in spring. Transfer the seedlings to individual containers when they are 2 inches tall. Transplant hardened-off seedlings to the garden after all danger of frost. Set the plants 12 inches apart in rows spaced 30 inches apart.

The plants are fairly tolerant of dry conditions once they are established, but they appreciate extra water in prolonged dry weather. They do not normally require support.

Eggplants are susceptible to the same pests and diseases that attack tomatoes. Common pests include flea beetles, aphids, Colorado potato beetles, and Japanese beetles; use floating row covers to protect the plants. To prevent diseases, grow resistant cultivars and plant in a different site each year.

How to Harvest. You can harvest the fruits at any stage of maturity, from gourmet baby eggplants to full-size fruits. For regular-size fruits, pick them when they are 4 to 5 inches long, while the skin is still glossy. When the skin turns dull, the fruit is probably overripe. Use a sharp knife or pruning shears to cut the fruits, leaving 1 inch of stem attached. Eggplants do not keep well, so eat them as soon as possible after harvesting.

Uses. Eggplant can serve as a vegetable substitute for meat in many cooked dishes, soups, and stews. Try it stir-fried, deep-fried, sauteed, baked, or stuffed. It is an important ingredient in many Middle Eastern dishes, such as baba ganoush. For a taste treat, prepare eggplant curry with Indian spices and yogurt. The miniature cultivars are great stuffed and served whole as hors d'oeuvres.

Garlic

Onion family. Perennial.

Characteristics. Height: 1 to 2 feet.

Garlic is grown for its large bulbs, which are made up of sections, or "cloves," and have a unique, tangy flavor. This onion family member is nutritious as well as delicious, and is believed to help lower blood pressure.

Garlic is grown not from seed but rather from the cloves. The larger the clove, the larger the bulb it will produce. Elephant garlic produces extra-large cloves in enormous bulbs measuring 2 to 3 inches long and 4 inches wide. Its flavor is milder than that of standard garlic.

How to Grow. Garlic plants require deep, friable, well-drained soil in full sun. Dig plenty of organic matter into the soil before planting. In the South, plant garlic cloves in the fall for a spring crop. In the North, plant in early spring for a fall crop. Elephant garlic is usually planted in the fall in both the North (with winter protection) and the South. Plant the cloves with the pointed side up. Set them 1 inch deep and 4 inches apart in rows spaced 1 to 2 feet apart.

Give the plants extra water during dry periods; otherwise, the bulbs may be stunted. They have the same pest and disease problems as onions, including thrips and root maggots. Rotate planting sites each year to prevent the buildup of soil-borne problems.

How to Harvest. Gather garlic when the foliage dies back. Carefully dig the bulbs with a pitchfork, and allow them to cure in a warm, dry place for a week. Store the cured bulbs in a cool, dry place. You can leave the stalks on the plants and braid them.

Uses. Garlic is useful as a seasoning. Roasted cloves have less bite than raw cloves and may be eaten as a snack or side dish. Garlic foliage has a milder flavor than the bulbs. Harvest and chop leaves and add them to salads, dips, or garlic bread. Don't harvest too many leaaves from a single plant, though, because it will reduce bulb size. The blooms make attractive cut flowers.

Lettuce

Aster family. Annual.

Characteristics. Height: 9 to 15 inches.

Lettuce is one of the easiest vegetables to grow. It thrives in full sun or partial shade, in the garden or in containers. It also grows quickly, and pests and diseases are usually not a problem. Lettuce foliage can be sweet or slightly bitter; it may be bright red, yellowish white, or light to deep green, with smooth, curled, frilled, or deeply lobed edges. Lettuce is an important source of fiber and is high in vitamins A and C, as well as calcium. Some cultivars are also high in iron.

There are four major types of garden lettuce. Iceberg, or crisphead, lettuce is the closest to the round heads of pale green salad lettuce found in supermarkets. The foliage is thin and crisp, and the heads are firm and round. The leaves blanch to a creamy white in the middle. Their maturity season is relatively long—80 to 90 days from seed. Burpee introduced one of the most popular cultivars, 'Iceberg', in 1894.

Butterhead, or bibb, lettuce forms looser, softer heads than crisphead types, and the foliage has a more delicate flavor. Butterhead types are also more heat-tolerant, and their foliage is more easily bruised. The inner leaves are a creamy yellow, and the outer leaves are medium to dark green. Butterhead lettuce matures in 45 to 75 days. It is higher in iron than other types of lettuce. 'Buttercrunch' is an All-America Selections winner that has a luscious, buttery texture and tolerates high temperatures.

Cos, or romaine, lettuce has an upright habit and long, loose leaves. The outer leaves are green and the inner leaves are creamy white. Romaine lettuce matures in 65 to 70 days. It is the most nutritious type of lettuce, as well as the most shade-tolerant. 'Parris Island Cos' is a classic cultivar with thick, crisp leaves that tolerate high temperatures.

Leaf, or loosehead lettuce, does not form heads. Its leaves can be curly, deeply lobed, serrated, or savoyed (wrinkled). Some cultivars are bright red and look attractive in containers or window boxes. 'Oak Leaf' has deeply cut foliage that resembles the leaves of a white oak tree. 'Black-Seeded Simpson' was introduced by Burpee in 1879 and is still popular today. It has light green, frilly leaves. 'Red Salad Bowl' has deeply cut burgundy leaves and is heat-resistant. Looseleaf types mature in 45 to 50 days and are more tolerant of high temperatures than other types.

How to Grow. Lettuce prefers rich, well-drained soil in full sun or light shade. It is a cool-season vegetable that "bolts," or forms flowers and seeds, in high temperatures. The leaf edges also burn in hot weather. Once lettuce bolts, the leaves turn bitter.

Sow seed directly in the garden in early spring, after danger of a heavy frost. For a fall crop in the North, sow in late summer, after the worst of the summer heat is over. (Lettuce will not germinate in high temperatures.) You can start the seeds indoors if conditions there are cooler; transplant the seedlings when outside temperatures cool down. For a winter crop in the South, sow in the fall. Space the rows 12 to 18 inches apart. Thin the plants or set the transplants to stand 4 to 6 inches apart for leaf types, 6 to 8 inches apart for romaine and butterhead types, and 10 to 12 inches apart for crisphead types.

Keep plants well watered during dry periods to promote rapid, uninterrupted growth. Lettuce does not have many pest and disease problems, although slugs and cabbageworms may be troublesome; handpick these pests. Lettuce is shallow-rooted, so avoid disturbing the soil around the plants when weeding.

How to Harvest. Pick crisphead types when the heads are firm. Harvest loosehead types anytime the leaves are large enough to use. Harvest romaine and butterhead types when they have formed heads and the leaves are a good size. Cut the heads below the crown. On leaf types, you can just pick a few leaves at a time, if you like.

Uses. Lettuce is the classic ingredient in salads. It adds crispness to sandwiches and can be used as a garnish, braised, or added to soups. Many of the loosehead cultivars are decorative in the garden.

Melon
Squash family. Annual.

Characteristics. Height: 1 to 2 feet; vines spread to 9 feet or more.

Melons—including cantaloupes, winter melons, and watermelons—are popular garden crops that grow on vining plants, which can spread out over the garden or be trained up a trellis or other support.

Cantaloupes are a delight both to taste and to smell. The fragrance of ripe cantaloupe is second only to quince in sheer ambrosial quality. In fact, cantaloupes are also called muskmelons (for their delicious, musky fragrance), and one of the most popular cultivars is 'Ambrosia'. The flavor of the extra-sweet, juicy flesh is never a disappointment, and the skin has a special beauty of its own: finely textured, intricately netted, and the color of dried grass with a hint of green, with evenly spaced ridges that look like the latitude lines on a world globe. The plants are vining, although bush types, such as 'Sweet Bush Hybrid' and 'Honeybush', are also available.

Winter melons are so called because they have a longer season of maturity. They generally have smooth skin and lack the aroma of cantaloupe. Honeydews have pale green flesh; crenshaws have salmon-pink flesh. Exotic melons, such as 'Early Silver Line', can have bright yellow skin and crisp white flesh. 'Sunrise' has canary yellow skin and sweet white flesh.

Watermelons are practically symbolic of summertime. Their refreshing, vivid red flesh is a common sight at summer barbecues, especially on the Fourth of July and Labor Day. The fruits are large—from 12-pound "ice box" types to giant, 200-pound monsters. Some cultivars have beautiful lemon yellow flesh and a slightly milder flavor. The large black seeds are considered by some to be the one drawback of watermelons, since they are difficult to dispose of discreetly. "Seedless" cultivars have been developed, including 'Redball Seedless', which may have a few small, edible white seeds. Watermelons generally take a long time to mature, although faster-maturing cultivars are available for northern gardens. Bush types are also available, including 'Bush Sugar Baby'.

How to Grow. All melons are warm-season crops that prefer rich, warm soil in full sun. In long-season areas, sow the seed directly in the garden after all danger of frost. In areas with shorter seasons, sow the seed indoors 3 to 4 weeks before the last frost date; transplant hardened-off seedlings to the garden after the danger of frost has passed. Sow the seeds 1 to 1½ inches deep, and thin the seedlings or set the transplants to stand 1 foot apart. Grow melons in rows spaced 3 to 4 feet apart or in "hills," with groups of 2 plants every 3 feet or 3 plants every 4 feet. You can also train melons on a fence or trellis, as long as it is strong enough to support the weight of the fruit.

Melons have the same cultural requirements as cucumbers. They appreciate ample water during dry periods and a side-dressing of 5-10-5 fertilizer after they begin to vine. They are normally pollinated by bees, but you can also hand-pollinate the flowers as you would for cucumbers, if fruits aren't forming. Long spells of cloudy weather occasionally cause the fruit to taste bitter. Melons are subject to the same pests and diseases as cucumbers, so avoid planting these and other squash family members in the same place 2 years in a row.

How to Harvest. All melons should be allowed to ripen on the vine. Cantaloupes have a delicious aroma when they are mature. The fruit color changes from green to yellow or tan, and the fruit generally breaks away (or "slips") easily from the vine with only slight pressure. (Some cultivars do not exhibit this "full slip" quality; cut them off the vine when they have the right aroma and the blossom end is soft.) Winter melons are ready when they turn the appropriate color and the blossom end is soft. The undersides of watermelons turn from white to yellow when they are ready to harvest, and the tendrils closest to the fruit turn brown and dry up. The skin becomes dull and hard, and the fruit should make a dull "thudding" sound when tapped.

Uses. Melons make delicious, refreshing snacks in hot summer weather. Serve them as breakfast foods, as a side dish for lunch, or as a dessert for dinner. Cut them into cubes or scoop them with a melon bailer for fruit salads. Watermelon rinds can be pickled.

Onion
Onion family. Biennial grown as an annual.

Characteristics. Height: 10 inches.

No kitchen would be complete without onions for flavoring a wide variety of cooked or raw dishes, including salads, stuffings, soups, stews, and omelettes. Use them on sandwiches, for onion rings, add them to casseroles, or cooked as a side dish. Indeed, it is difficult to think of a meal in which onions would be out of place.

Onions vary in size from large, 4-inch-wide, globe-shaped bulbs to small "pearl" types measuring less than

1 inch in diameter. They can be white, yellow, or red, and globe-shaped, oval, flattened, or shaped like a lemon. Green onions, or scallions, can be either harvested as immature onions or grown from cultivars that do not produce bulbs. 'Walla Walla Sweet' produces 4-inch, flattened globe-shaped bulbs with sweet, yellow flesh. 'Granex', the popular Vidalia onion from southern Georgia, produces large, flat bulbs with yellow skin and mild white flesh. 'Crystal Wax Pickling PRR', a pearl-type onion, produces creamy white, round, ½ to ¾-inch onions that are perfect for pickling.

The formation of onion bulbs is triggered by day length. Long-day cultivars form bulbs when the day length is more than 13 hours; they are best suited for northern gardens. Short-day cultivars form bulbs when the day is less than 13 hours long; they are suitable for growing in the South.

How to Grow. Because onions are grown for their underground bulbs, they require deep, well-drained soil free of stones and enriched with organic matter. They also need full sun. You can grow onions from seed, plants, or sets.

Seeds take from 100 to 300 days to mature. Start them indoors 8 to 10 weeks before the last frost in spring. Make sure the seedlings receive plenty of sunlight, and supplement a sunny windowsill with plant lights to offset cloudy weather. Transplant hardened-off seedlings outside after the danger of heavy frost has passed. Set the plants 2 to 3 inches apart in rows spaced 12 to 16 inches apart.

Onion plants are available for spring or fall planting. In the North, set them out in early spring as soon as you can work the soil; in the South, plant them in the fall for a spring harvest. Set them 1 to 1½ inches deep and 3 inches apart.

Onion sets are small, dry onions that have already begun to form bulbs. They produce full-size onions in about 85 days. In the North, plant them as soon as you can work the soil, in the South, plant them in the fall.

Onions are heavy feeders and appreciate a scattering of 10-10-10 fertilizer twice during the season. They do not compete well with weeds for water and nutrients in the soil, so weed regularly. These vegetables can be grown successfully in containers. To prevent the buildup of diseases and pests, avoid planting onions and other onion family members in the same place 2 years in a row.

How to Harvest. Pick green onions when the plants are 6 to 8 inches tall. For bulbous onions, gently bend the tops over when about one-quarter of the tops have already fallen over and turned yellow naturally. Avoid nicking or breaking the bulbs, or diseases and insects may enter the wounds. After a few days, pull the bulbs and cover them with the foliage to prevent sunburn. Allow them to dry in the garden for up to a week, then cure them indoors in a warm, dry place with good air circulation for 2 to 3 weeks. After curing them cut off the foliage, leaving 1 inch above the top of the bulb. Place the bulbs in mesh onion bags or old panty hose and store them in a cool, dry location.

Uses. Onions can be sliced into rings or chopped into small pieces and used as a garnish, condiment, or salad ingredient. Raw or sautéed onions make a tasty topping for sandwiches or hamburgers. The larger cultivars can be used to make deep-fried onion rings, and the smaller pearl types may be creamed and served as a side dish. You can also pickle onions. Add scallions to salads, soups, or stir-fried dishes. Onion foliage is also edible, as are the flowers (before they become dry).

Pea

Bean family. Annual.

○ ❄ ▼

Characteristics. Height: 18 inches to 8 feet or more for vining types.

Only home gardeners and their lucky friends really know how delicious homegrown garden peas can be. Peas lose their freshness soon after harvest, so store-bought peas are never as fresh and sweet as homegrown ones. Peas are produced on either bushy plants or vines. They can adapt well to life in containers. Three types that are commonly grown in American gardens are garden peas, edible-podded peas, and snap peas.

Garden, or English, peas are harvested after the seeds mature and are shelled from their inedible pods. The pods range from 3 to 4½ inches long and contain 7 to 12 peas. The seeds can be small and tender, as in the French 'Petit Provencal', or large, like those of 'Burpeeana Early'.

Edible-podded peas—generally known as snow, sugar, or China peas—are grown for their crunchy, succulent, flat pods, which contain immature peas. If you don't harvest them early enough, you can shell them and prepare them as you would garden peas. They may be stir-fried, steamed, or eaten fresh, and are frequently included in Oriental dishes.

Snap peas are a fairly recent development in pea breeding. They are harvested when the seeds are mature and when the pods are thick and fleshy. The peas are sweet and crunchy and can be eaten raw or cooked. The pods are also edible. Snap peas freeze well but are not recommended for canning. 'Sugar Snap' is one of the most popular cultivars and has the distinction of being a Number-One All-Time All-America Selections vegetable winner.

How to Grow. These cool-season vegetables prefer rich, well-drained soil in full sun. In the North, you can plant them as early as St. Patrick's Day, if the weather is fairly warm. (If the soil is too cold, the seeds will take a long time to germinate and can rot in the soil.) In the South, grow peas as a winter crop. Bush cultivars are self-supporting; vining cultivars climb by tendrils, so put a trellis in place before planting. To encourage earlier germination, soak the seed overnight before planting. Sow the seeds 2 inches deep in rows spaced 18 inches apart. Thin the seedlings to 8 to 10 inches apart when they are large enough to handle.

Peas may need extra water under dry conditions, but they often mature before dry weather sets in. They do not perform well in overly wet conditions, and the seeds can rot in wet soil before they germinate. The plants do not normally require fertilizer. However, as with beans and other legumes, certain bacteria must be present in the soil for the peas to grow vigorously, so coat untreated seed with an inoculant (readily available from seed companies). After you have grown peas once, the bacteria can survive in the soil.

This crop is susceptible to various diseases and pests, but disease-resistant cultivars are available. Check with your local Cooperative Extension Service office to find out which problems are common in your area and which cultivars perform best.

How to Harvest. Pick garden peas when the pods are well filled but not dry or faded in color. For the freshest peas, pick as close to mealtime as possible. Pull the pods from the plants with care to avoid damaging the plants. The peas do not all ripen at the same time and may require several harvests. Freeze extras before the end of the harvest season.

Edible-podded peas are ready to harvest when the pods are 3 to 5 inches long (depending on the cultivar) and before the peas inside mature. They are usually ready about a week after the flowers bloom. Edible-podded peas must be picked frequently, or they will become over-ripe. If they swell too much, harvest and shell them as you would garden peas.

Pick snap peas when they are plump and the full size for the cultivar.

Uses. Shell garden peas, then steam or boil them; enjoy them alone, or combine them with other vegetables as a side dish. Many cultivars are good for freezing. Edible-podded peas can be stirfried, steamed, boiled, sautéed, or eaten raw. Steam snap peas, or use them for dips or stir-fries.

Pepper
Tomato family. Annual.

Characteristics. Height: 2 to 2½ feet.

Whole seed companies, cookbooks, and gardens are devoted to peppers, and pepper fanciers can be among the most fanatical of vegetable gardeners.

There is a wide range of types to choose from, including sweet and hot peppers in red, green, yellow, purple, lilac, and orange. These popular vegetables also come in many shapes, sizes, flavors, and maturity dates. Many are pretty enough to grow in the flower garden, and the fruits make attractive table decorations before they are eaten. All peppers are rich in vitamin C and carotene, and are a good source of fiber.

Sweet bell peppers are blocky in shape, with thick walls that make them good for stuffing. They can be elongated or nearly cube shaped. They may be huge (up to 6 inches long and 5 inches across) or tiny (just 2 inches long and 1¾ inches across). Green peppers are actually red, yellow, or purple peppers that are harvested before they turn their characteristic color.

Hot peppers can be bell-shaped, round like cherry tomatoes, or long and slender. They may be red or green and have varying degrees of heat. 'Habanero' is a blocky, extra-super hot type. Cayenne types are long, slim, and slightly curved; they grow from 2 to 12 inches long. Chili types are long and slim and grow about 3 inches long. All-America Selections winner 'Mexi Bell Hybrid' is the first hot bell-shaped pepper.

How to Grow. Peppers prefer rich, well-drained soil in full sun. Start seed indoors 8 to 10 weeks before the last frost in spring. Set the plants outside in the garden after all danger of frost has passed and the weather is warm. Space the plants 18 inches apart in rows spaced 2 feet apart. They are also easy to grow in containers.

Peppers need 1½ inches of water every week. They appreciate watering in dry periods and an extra feeding with 5-10-5 fertilizer as the fruits begin to form. Peppers are subject to the same pests and diseases as tomatoes and eggplants. To prevent the buildup of diseases, avoid planting peppers and other tomato family crops in the same place 2 years in a row. To prevent the spread of tobacco mosaic virus, smokers should avoid handling the plants.

How to Harvest. Pick the fruits when they are the proper size and color for the cultivar. Break or cut off the fruit with a bit of stem attached. Hot peppers can be dried and strung together for handy kitchen use.

Uses. Enjoy raw sweet peppers in salads, for dipping, as a crunchy hors d'oeuvre, or sliced and added to sandwiches. They can also be grilled, sautéed, stir-fried, roasted, stuffed and baked, or added to soups, stews, and sauces. Use hot types carefully to spice up many dishes. Hot peppers can also be pickled. Always use rubber gloves when preparing hot peppers, as they can burn cuts on your hands. Be especially careful not to touch your face when handling hot peppers; the hottest types will cause severe burning in your eyes and nose.

Potato

Tomato family. Annual.

Characteristics. Height: 18 to 24 inches.

The potato is one of the most important staple foods in our diet. It is rich in vitamins B and C, potassium, protein, complex carbohydrates, and fiber. Potatoes can be prepared so many ways that you can eat them every day for a year and not grow tired of them. They have a delicious flavor of their own, yet they also blend well with herbs, spices, sauces, and stronger-flavored vegetables and meats. When you grow potatoes at home, you get the added treat of harvesting fresh new potatoes in mid-summer.

Many kinds of potatoes are available, including standard white-fleshed baking types and heirloom types with blue, yellow, pink, or white flesh. Potatoes can be round, elongated, oval-shaped, or narrow "fingerling" types that can be 2 to 5 inches in length. They can have red or tan skins. 'Yukon Gold' has a light yellow skin and golden yellow flesh that tastes as though it has been smothered in butter. 'Kennebec' is a popular all-purpose, white-fleshed potato that is resistant to late blight. 'Red Pontiac' is a red-skinned cultivar that performs well in heavy soil.

How to Grow. Potatoes are thickened underground stems called tubers. For good tuber development, potatoes require deep, loose, well-drained soil that is free of stones. They also need full sun for the tops of the plants to grow well. Seed companies and garden centers sell "seed potatoes"—tubers with buds (called "eyes")—for planting in spring. Always purchase certified disease-free tubers to avoid disease problems. (Don't buy grocery-store potatoes for planting; they are chemically treated to prevent sprouting.) Plant the tubers as soon as you receive them, after danger of heavy frost in spring in the North, and in fall through February in the South. Either plant the tubers whole, or cut them into pieces with 2 or 3 "eyes" each and spread them out in a well-ventilated place to dry for 24 hours before planting. Plant them with the eyes up, 2 to 3 inches deep and 10 to 12 inches apart in rows spaced 2 feet apart.

The tops of the developing tubers should not be exposed to sunlight, or they will turn green. (Green patches on potato tubers are poisonous and should be discarded.) When the plants are about 5 to 6 inches tall, begin to heap soil around the base of the stems, or surround the plants with a thick layer of mulch. Potatoes need regular watering throughout the season. If their growth slows due to dry weather and then starts again in wet weather, the tubers can form knobs. The tubers can also develop cavities inside when the plants don't have a consistent supply of water.

Potatoes are subject to various pests and diseases. Plant only certified disease-free stock to prevent serious potato diseases. To avoid the buildup of soil-borne diseases, avoid planting potatoes and other tomato family members in the same spot 2 years in a row. One of the worst pests of potatoes is the Colorado potato beetle, a small orange-and-white-striped insect. Many gardeners plant their potatoes as early as possible so that the plants are a fairly good size before the beetles are a problem. (Vigorous plants are better able to survive an attack.) Covering plants with floating row covers can also protect them from pests.

How to Harvest. For "new" potatoes, harvest about 10 weeks after planting. When potato blossoms appear, it is a sign that the frist new potatoes are ready for harvest, simply feel around in the soil with your fingers for the small tubers. Try not to damage the roots of the plant or you may reduce the main harvest.

Harvest mature potatoes after the tops die back and before the first frost. Dig carefully to avoid damaging the tubers. After harvesting mature potatoes, store them in a dark, dry place for a week at 65° to 70°F. Then store them at 35° to 40°F at fairly high humidity. Some cultivars store better than others; if you know you will be storing your potatoes, choose suitable cultivars. Potatoes do not freeze well.

Uses. The culinary uses of potatoes are limited only by your imagination. They can be boiled, baked, roasted, deep-fried, grilled, sautéed, stir-fried, braised, glazed, mashed, creamed, or scalloped. Enjoy them as a soup or side dish; stuff them, make them into a soufflé, or combine them with other vegetables or meats in soups, stews, breads, or casseroles. They can also be made into potato chips, potato pancakes, or hash browns.

Pumpkin
Squash family. Annual.

Characteristics. Height: 1 to 2 feet; vines spread to 10 feet or more.

A front doorstep decorated with pumpkins—combined with chrysanthemums and ornamental corn—is as symbolic of the fall season as holiday greens are of the Christmas season. But pumpkins are also prized for their delicious, coarse-grained flesh, which can be used to make pies, breads, muffins, and soups. The seeds make great snacks when they are roasted. One cultivar, 'Triple Treat', is named for the three main uses of pumpkins: carving, pies, and seed.

Pumpkins are actually winter squashes and are produced on spreading vines. The fruits vary in size from miniature 'Jack Be Little' pumpkins, which grow 3 inches across and 2 inches high, to 'Atlantic Giant', which can weigh over 700 pounds but usually ranges from 300 to 400 pounds. Pumpkins can be round or oblong, with black or tan stems. The outer skin is traditionally orange, but the cultivar 'Lumina' has white skin.

When choosing a cultivar to grow, think of what you want to do with your pumpkins. If you want to carve jack-o'-lanterns, choose a round cultivar about 10 to 12 inches across, such as 'Jack-o'-Lantern'. If you want to cook pies, choose a sweet cultivar, such as 'Small Sugar'. Choose 'Prizewinner Hybrid' if you want to win a prize for growing the largest pumpkin. If you do not have a huge garden, choose 'Bushkin', which produces 10-pound fruits on 6-foot vines.

How to Grow. This warm-season crop needs space, plenty of sun, and well-drained, fertile soil. If the fruit will not be very heavy, you can train the vines on a trellis to save space. Large-fruited cultivars need lots of room to ramble. In long-season areas, plant the seed directly in the garden after all danger of frost, when the weather is warm. In short-summer areas, choose a fast-maturing cultivar and plant the seed outdoors, or start plants indoors 3 to 4 weeks before the last frost date and transplant the seedlings to the garden after all danger of frost. Sow the seed 2 inches deep. Thin the seedlings or space the transplants so that you have groups of 3 plants every 5 to 10 feet. Bush types can grow closer together, with 1 plant every 3 feet.

Pumpkins need plenty of water and fertilizer through their long growing season. Like their close relatives, cucumbers and melons, they produce male and female flowers on the same plant. You can hand-pollinate the flowers as you would for cucumbers if the bees aren't doing their job. If you are trying to grow extra-large pumpkins, allow only one fruit per plant to mature. To prevent the buildup of diseases, avoid planting pumpkins and other squash family crops in the same spot 2 years in a row.

How to Harvest. Pumpkins are ready to harvest when the rinds are hard and the proper shade of orange or white for the cultivar. Sometimes the vines are killed by light frost before the pumpkins are harvested; cut the fruits from the vines—with 3 to 4 inches of stem attached—before they are damaged by heavy frost. Pumpkins can be stored for weeks or months in a warm, dry place at 50° to 60°F.

Uses. Use the flesh for baked pies, soups, casseroles, muffins, or bread. Or cook pumpkin as you would winter squash, and serve as a side dish. Roast the seeds for a tasty snack. The flowers are also edible and can be dipped in batter and deep-fried, stir-fried, or sautéed. Pumpkins are important autumn decorations: Leave them unadorned, paint them, or carve them for jack-o'-lanterns.

SCALLION. See *Onion*
SNAP BEAN. See *Bean*
SNAP PEA. See *Pea*
SNOW PEA. See *Pea*

Spinach

Goosefoot family. Annual.

Characteristics. Height: 10 to 12 inches.

Almost anyone can learn to enjoy this cool-season green—even people jaded by childhood experiences when they were forced to consume overcooked, unadorned, boiled spinach. You can sneak spinach into quiches, pancakes, crepes, and omelettes. It is valued by cooks for its distinctive, slightly bitter flavor, which blends well with both stronger and weaker flavors in cooked and raw dishes. It is also rich in vitamin A and iron. Gardeners like spinach because it is quick and easy to grow for a spring or fall crop.

Spinach has thick, succulent, glossy green leaves that may be savoyed (wrinkled) or semi-savoyed. 'Avon Hybrid' is prized for its heat tolerance and its large, succulent, semi-savoyed leaves. 'Bloomsdale Long-Standing' produces heavy crops of very savoyed, dark green leaves on upright, heat-resistant plants. 'Melody Hybrid' is an All-America Selections winner that is resistant to downy mildew and mosaic virus.

New Zealand spinach is often grown as a warm-weather substitute for spinach. Although it is not really a spinach, it produces succulent, brittle green leaves that can be used raw as a salad green, or as a cooked green.

How to Grow. This crop prefers a rich, well-drained soil in full sun or light shade. For a spring crop, sow seed in spring, after danger of heavy frost; for a fall crop, sow in midsummer. In the South, plant in fall for a winter crop. Space the rows 12 inches apart. Thin the plants to 4 inches apart when they are large enough to handle.

Spinach is shallow-rooted and requires 1 to 1½ inches of rain each week for continuous, rapid growth. It does not have many serious pest and disease problems, although cabbageworms, aphids, and leafminers are common. Choose disease-resistant cultivars to prevent problems with specific diseases in your area. Protect the plants with floating row covers to keep pests off the plants.

How to Harvest. Cut the entire spinach plant to the ground when it has 3 to 5 leaves, or just harvest the outer leaves as needed when they are 3 inches long. When the weather turns warm and a seed stalk begins to develop, harvest the whole plant right away.

Uses. Spinach makes a delicious raw green salad and an attractive garnish. It can also be boiled, steamed, sautéed, stir-fried, or creamed. Add it to tomatoes in a tomato and cheese loaf, or combine it with mushrooms and cheese in pancakes. Spinach is commonly used in omelettes, quiches, and souffles.

Squash
Squash family. Annual.

Characteristics. Height: 2½ feet; vines spread to 10 feet or more.

Squash is a warm-season crop related to cucumbers, melons, and pumpkins. It is grown for its fruit, which forms on vining, semivining, or bush-type plants. There are two basic types of squash: summer squash and winter squash.

Summer squash is grown for its immature fruit, which is harvested at any stage of growth in summer, before frost kills the vines. The kinds of summer squash range from long, slender zucchini and butterstick types to flat pattypan types with scalloped edges. The fruits can be yellow or various shades of green; some have silver stripes. Crookneck summer squash has a bulbous, elongated shape with a hooked, gooseneck end. Summer squash grows on bush or vining plants.

Winter squash is grown for its hard-shelled fruit, which matures in the fall, often after frost kills the vines. The fruits vary from acorn-shaped to butternut types (with a distinctive elongated shape that widens at the base) to pumpkin-shaped, in various colors. The warty or smooth skins may be metallic blue, green and yellow, orange, tan, or white; many are striped or spotted. Vegetable spaghetti squash has an oblong shape with a yellow rind. It is grown for the stringy fibers inside, which can be used as a substitute for spaghetti. Winter squash usually grows on vining plants.

Gourds are similar to winter squash but are grown for ornamental purposes. They also vary widely in their shapes and colors. Loofas are grown for their fibrous flesh, which is dried and used to make bath sponges.

How to Grow. All squash prefer full sun and well-drained soil that is rich in organic matter. Sow seed outdoors after all danger of frost has passed and the weather is warm. Sow seed 2 inches deep, in groups of 4 seeds. For vining types, space the groups 5 feet apart in rows spaced 8 feet apart; thin the seedlings to leave 2 or 3 in each group. For semivining types, space the groups 4 feet apart in rows spaced 6 feet apart. Thin bush types to stand 30 inches apart in rows spaced 3 feet apart.

Squash plants appreciate extra water in dry weather. You can use a trellis to support vining types, as long as it is sturdy enough to hold the weight of the fruit. The plants are susceptible to the same pests and diseases as cucumbers and pumpkins. Choose disease-resistant cultivars, and avoid planting squash family crops in the same spot 2 years in a row, to prevent the buildup of diseases.

How to Harvest. Pick summer squash fruits when they are immature and still tender, at whatever size you wish. To get the fruit at peak quality, harvest daily or every other day by cutting it from the plants with a sharp knife. The plants are extremely prolific, and you will have plenty of squash to share with friends, neighbors, relatives, and passersby! Use the fruits as soon as possible after harvest.

Harvest winter squash after the shells harden. Cut the fruits from the vines with 1 or 2 inches of stem attached, then cure them for a week in a warm, dry location with good air circulation. Store them in a cool, dry place at 50° to 55°F for use throughout the winter.

Uses. Harvest summer squash as a gourmet mini-vegetable, then stuff it and serve it as hors d'oeuvres. Larger summer squash can be sliced and sauteed, steamed, boiled, grilled, stuffed, or baked in casseroles. You can also use it to make soup, zucchini bread, fritters, or corn bread. Use winter squash to make pumpkin pie, or bake it and serve it as a delicious side dish. It can also be made into soup or added to casseroles, as well as baked meat and vegetable dishes. Try marinating the cubed or sliced flesh in soy sauce and ginger before grilling, steaming, or stir-frying. The flowers of all squash types are edible and can be stir-fried, breaded and deep-fried, or stuffed with cheese.

STRING BEAN. See *Bean*
SUGAR PEA. See *Pea*
SWEET BELL PEPPER. See *Pepper*
SWEET CORN. See *Corn*

Tomato

Tomato family. Annual.

Characteristics. Height: 12 inches to 4 feet or more.

The tomato is America's favorite garden vegetable. There are many reasons for tomatoes' popularity, but probably the most important is flavor. Anyone who has ever tasted a homegrown tomato and compared it with one purchased at the supermarket knows there's a real difference. While this is true of many vegetables, it is especially the case with tomatoes.

Tomatoes are among the most important and versatile foods we eat. They are used to make many products and dishes we consume on a regular basis, from soups and sauces to condiments and salads. Cultivars have been developed especially for the commercial market to improve their yields, uniformity, shippability, and shelf life. Because of the longer period between harvest and consumption for commercially grown tomatoes, they are generally harvested green and then ripened artificially by exposure to ethylene gas. The flavor of these tomatoes just can't compare with those grown in the home garden and vine ripened in the sun.

The tomato cultivars available to home gardeners are rarely available in supermarkets. There is a tomato for every gardener and for every garden.

Tomato plants range from large, sprawling vines to dwarf bush plants that grow only 12 inches tall.

Cultivars have been developed for hanging baskets, window boxes, and patio containers. Tomato fruits range from small, cherry types to big, juicy beefsteak types that can weigh over 7 pounds! Plum tomatoes are pear shaped and are often used to make paste, sauces, and ketchup. Tomato fruits can be red, pink, orange, or yellow, and some cultivars have stripes.

Some tomatoes have been bred for resistance to various diseases and pests. The letters "V", "F", "N", and "T" refer to Verticillium, Fusarium, nematodes, and tobacco mosaic virus, respectively. Cultivars that have these letters in their names or descriptions are resistant to these diseases or pests.

Tomato cultivars have been bred to produce from as early as 54 days after transplanting to as late as 90 days, allowing you to harvest tomatoes from early summer to the first frost in autumn. Some cultivars bear fruit continuously; others produce their crops all at once. Some cultivars are hybrids, while others are open-pollinated. Many heirloom cultivars with unusual shapes, colors, or flavors are becoming available.

Tomatoes are classified as determinate or indeterminate. Determinate plants grow to a specific height and produce a crop all at once. They are the best type for gardeners who need large numbers of tomatoes at one time to can or process into soups or sauces. Indeterminate types keep producing smaller numbers of tomatoes continually throughout the season until frost kills the vines. These are a good choice for gardeners who want to be able to run into the garden now and then to pick a tomato or two for salads or sandwiches.

How to Grow. Tomatoes need full sun and warm, rich, well-drained soil. These warm-season plants cannot tolerate any frost. They take a fairly long time to mature, so start the seed indoors 6 to 8 weeks before the last frost in spring. Transfer the seedlings to individual containers when they are 2 inches tall.

Set supports up before you move the plants to the garden. You can train tomatoes on stakes, over A-frame supports, on a trellis or fence, or in circular tomato cages. Transplant hardened-off seedlings to the garden after all danger of frost. Set the plants 18 inches apart in rows spaced 3 feet apart.

The plants need 1 inch of water every week. Water container plants when they are partially dry, but not wilted; they may need watering every day. All tomatoes appreciate a scattering of 5-10-5 fertilizer in midsummer. If you are training the plants to trellises or stakes, prune the developing plants to keep one or two strong stems. Every week, remove the side shoots that develop from where each leaf meets the main stem.

In general, tomatoes will stop producing fruit when temperatures drop below 50°F or rise above 90°F, although some cultivars are more tolerant of these temperature extremes than others. In hot, dry weather, plants may drop their flowers or fruit, but when conditions improve, they generally recover fully. When the weather is very dry and then very wet, tomatoes are liable to produce cracked fruit, because the fruit grows too quickly when the wet weather arrives; some cultivars are more resistant to cracking than others. Tomatoes can also develop "green shoulders," which occur when they ripen unevenly; cultivars differ in their resistance to this problem.

Sometimes the blossom end of the tomato develops a tough, black leathery patch—a sign of blossom end rot.

This common problem is caused by a calcium deficiency in the soil, or by uneven watering. If your soil is deficient in calcium, add lime in the fall for next year's crop. Try to keep the watering schedule as consistent as possible.

Tomatoes may be scalded by the sun in too-hot temperatures, when the fruit is not shaded from the direct sun. The fruit needs warmth—not light—to ripen, so you can cover the developing tomatoes with the leaves to shield them. Do not plant tomatoes near black walnut trees; the plants are susceptible to a toxin exuded by the roots of the tree, which causes "walnut wilt." The plants may grow well for many weeks, but one day they will wilt dramatically and never recover.

The most common tomato pests and diseases are Verticillium and Fusarium wilt, nematodes, and tobacco mosaic virus. There are no cures for any of these, so choose resistant cultivars. To prevent the buildup of soil-borne diseases, avoid planting tomato family crops in the same spot 2 years in a row.

How to Harvest. Pick tomatoes when they are as ripe as possible—they should be fully colored and firm. When you know there will be a frost, pick all the almost-ripe tomatoes you can, and ripen them in brown bags or spread on newspapers at room temperature. Many cultivars will store for months. ('Long-Keeper' stores for at least 5 or 6 months. Every year, customers write to Burpee to report that they managed to keep 'Long-Keeper' fruits from one crop to the next!) Store only sound fruit, at 50° to 60°F.

Uses. The foliage of tomatoes is toxic and should not be eaten. The fruit, however, is another matter! Tomatoes are enjoyed in many cooked dishes as a flavoring. Use them to make soups, sauces, stews, ketchup, paste, juice, quiche, and pies. Add them to curries, casseroles, and chutney. They can be stuffed, stewed, pickled, preserved, canned, or made into relish. Slice them raw for sandwiches and salads. Cherry tomatoes make great in-the-garden snacks.

WATERMELON. See *Melon*
ZUCCHINI. See *Squash*

CHAPTER EIGHT

HERBS

When you think of herbs what comes to mind? There's a whole world of exciting and versatile herbs out there just waiting for you to try. Whether you grow herbs for cooking, healing, crafts, or just enjoying in the garden, they are sure to bring you lots of satisfaction.

WHAT ARE HERBS?

Loosely defined, herbs are plants that are of use to humans. (This does not include vegetables, or plants that we just grow for ornament.) These plants may be valued for their flavor, fragrance, medicinal qualities, or insecticidal properties. Some herbs have economic or industrial use (for example, as a source of fiber, rubber, or oil); other herbs provide coloring material for dyes. Spices are plants that are used like herbs but are from tropical or sub-tropical regions.

WHY GROW HERBS?

Vegetables give us a useful yield. Flowers beautify our yards. Herbs give us the best of both worlds; not only can they be used in a multitude of ways, but many also have attractive leaves or flowers and are good garden plants in their own right.

HERBS FOR COOKING

It has long been known that herbs improve and enhance the flavor of food. The trick, however, is having a handy supply of fresh herbs at your disposal. With a home herb garden, you can dash outside and snip a few chives or mint leaves to add just the right touch to any dish. And if the luxury of having a steady supply of fresh herbs isn't enough, you can grow extra and preserve their flavors any number of ways, including drying, freezing, or making vinegars, sauces, and jams. Growing a wide variety of herbs will encourage you to experiment with different flavors and uses, making boring meals a thing of the past.

HERBS FOR HEALING

Herbs have been valued for their medicinal properties for thousands of years. Today, they are still used to alleviate various physical ailments. For example, a cup of mint tea can be a soothing way to settle an upset stomach; a cup of chamomile tea can be just the thing to help you unwind after a stressful day at work. New discoveries are emerging that validate the immense value of herbs in medicine. To be on the safe side, it's best to use herbs under a doctor's supervision; some can be extremely toxic if ingested accidentally or in large doses. You also need to be careful if you're pregnant, nursing, or taking medications for other ailments.

HERBS FOR FRAGRANCE

Often, just the scent of herbs is enough to refresh even the most harried gardener. In fact, the natural essences of many herbs are used for healing and relaxation in a technique known as aromatherapy.

You can enjoy the scents from your own plants simply by brushing the leaves to release their aroma. Grow them where they are within easy reach—for instance, in a planter on a deck, in a raised bed by a door, or along a path to the driveway. Many of these aromatic herbs keep their fragrance when dried, so you can preserve their scent for winter enjoyment in potpourris, wreaths, arrangements, and a variety other crafts.

HERBS FOR BEDS AND BORDERS

While herbs are traditionally grown together in a separate herb garden, many of these great plants are showy enough for the flower garden. The leafy green rosettes of parsley, for instance, make an attractive—and edible—edging. The flowers of lavender, calamint, and anise hyssop look lovely with other perennials and annuals. Rose geranium makes an elegant container specimen. And low-growing herbs, such as creeping thyme and sweet woodruff, are marvelous as groundcovers. Mixing herbs with flowers in beds and planters is a great way to save space if your garden area is limited.

HERB-GROWING BASICS

Herbs can grow successfully just about anywhere in the United States. If you want to grow the widest possible range of herbs, you'll need to take into account the special needs of the particular plants. In the North, for instance, you may need to grow tender herbs in pots and bring them indoors in winter, or give them special protection outdoors. In the hot, dry West, moisture-loving herbs will need supplemental watering to survive a drought. If easy maintenance is more your style, you can choose herbs that are naturally suited to your climate's conditions so you won't have to worry about watering or winter protection.

Good soil conditions are essential for growing herbs successfully. In general, the soil should be loose and light, with some organic matter and moderate fertility. A too-rich soil will produce weak herbs that are prone to disease problems. The pH should be approximately 6.5, although most herbs will grow in soil that is slightly acidic or slightly alkaline.

To grow healthy, productive herbs, you must also provide them with adequate light. Most herbs thrive in full sun (at least 6 hours of sun a day; more is generally better). In too much shade, sun lovers tend to be spindly and unproductive. Your choice of herbs is somewhat more limited for shady areas, but there are some—parsley, peppermint, and sweet cicely, for example—that grow well in light shade.

Water is most important while new plants are getting established. Once the plants have taken hold, watering is usually only necessary in times of extreme drought. To avoid disease problems, water in the morning. Unless you are trying to encourage growth, there is no need to add fertilizer. If you do choose to fertilize, try an organic fertilizer such as kelp or fish emulsion.

For best results, prune your herbs throughout the growing season; regular pruning will produce fuller, more compact plants. Cut back woody perennials—such as thymes, lavender, and savory—in spring and then as needed through the summer. Annuals benefit from pinching, which encourages branching and produces fuller plants. Just pinch out the stem tips with your fingers, or snip them with scissors to shape the plants. Use the pinched tips for cooking or as cuttings for starting more plants.

Herbs tend to be fairly pest-resistant, but aphids, whiteflies, mites, and other common pests may occasionally attack the plants. If you can, remove the pests by handpicking them (if they're large) or by pinching off infested plant parts. If you're not planning to harvest within a week or so, you can also use soap sprays. However, avoid spraying anything on herbs you plan to eat.

HARVESTING HERBS

For best flavor, harvest your herbs just as they are about to bloom; very young or end-of-the-season herbs tend to have less flavor. Cut your herbs in the morning, after the dew has dried and before the sun is too bright. If you plan to harvest a large quantity, select a cloudy day; otherwise, the herbs may wilt or lose some of their flavor as you cut and prepare them.

If you like to use fresh herbs, simply pick a few leaves or sprigs here and there as needed throughout the season. If you want to harvest a lot at one time for drying, leave some of the foliage so the plant can continue to grow. Use sharp scissors or garden shears to snip off the parts you want to harvest. On bushy herbs, you can take the tips; on clumping herbs, such as parsley, just cut off the outer leaves. As you harvest, place the herbs in a water-filled container to keep them from wilting.

Use the herbs right away, or store them in the refrigerator. To keep them from drying out, leave them in a container of water or wrapped in moistened paper towels in a plastic bag.

PLANT PORTRAITS

The following plant portraits are a sampling of some of the best annual, biennial, and perennial herbs you can grow. Some are popular for cooking; others are great for crafts. All of these herbs are attractive and productive. Most are easy to grow from seed or are commonly found at local garden centers.

GROWING TIPS AT A GLANCE

Each of the following plant portraits includes simple symbols to highlight special features you need to know about each herb. If you're not sure what any of the symbols mean, refer back to this key.

○ Full sun (more than 6 hours of sun a day; ideally all day)

◐ Partial sun (some direct sun, but less than 6 hours a day)

● Shade (no direct sun)

❉ Prefers cool temperatures

✀ Good as a cut flower

❀ Good as a dried flower or foliage

▼ Grows well in containers

Anise hyssop

Agastache foeniculum. ag-ah-STAH-chee fee-NI-yow-lum.
Summer. Zones 5 to 9 feet.

Characteristics. Height: 3 feet. Spread: 1½ to 2 feet. This large, showy herb has prolific purple flower spikes and looks equally at home in flower, herb, and vegetable gardens. Both the leaves and flowers have a pungent licorice scent. There is a white-flowered form known as 'Alba'. Korean anise hyssop (*Agastache rugosa*) is a related species with pinkish flowers and slightly scalloped leaves.

How to Grow. Anise hyssop prefers rich, moist soil in a sunny location. Start with purchased plants, or grow it from seed sown indoors or out in spring. This herb tends to be a short-lived perennial, but it will reseed in locations where it is happy.

Uses. Use the anise-flavored leaves and flowers as a seasoning or to make a pleasant-tasting tea. The flowers attract many interesting insects, including honeybees. They also look wonderful in fresh or dried arrangements.

Basil

Ocimum basilicum. OH-sih-mum bah-SIL-ih-kum.
Summer. Tender annual.

○

Characteristics. Height: 2 feet. Spread: 1 foot.

Basil lovers have a marvelous variety of flavors to choose from. One of the best loved is sweet basil (Ocimum basilicum), a bushy, upright plant with broad, smooth, shiny green leaves. The cultivar Napoletano has large wrinkled leaves. Lemon basil (*O. basilicum* 'Citriodorum') is a sturdy grower with delightful lemony basil flavor. 'Cinnamon' is also used in cooking or for its fragrance. 'Purple Ruffles', a Burpee introduction, is an All-America Selections winner; the beautiful, crinkly, rich purple leaves make it a terrific bedding plant. 'Dark Opal' has smooth, dark purple leaves that are especially striking when combined with gray foliage. 'Minimum' has a compact habit and forms a delightful little rounded shape. It is ideal for a container or as a low hedge.

How to Grow. Basil needs full sun and evenly moist—but not wet—soil. Sow seed indoors 6 to 8 weeks before the last frost date. Set hardened-off seedlings into the garden after all danger of frost has passed. To promote branching, pinch the shoot tips when the plants are 4 to 6 inches tall. To encourage the production of more leaves, pinch off the flower eads as they form.

Uses. Basil is considered the premiere culinary herb. Use the fresh leaves to make pesto or as a seasoning for fresh or cooked tomatoes. Basil is also a great flavoring for oils and vinegars. The bushy plants, especially the purple-leaved types, look great in the flower garden.

Caraway
Carum carvi. KARE-um KAR-vee.
Summer. Zones 3 to 8.
○

Characteristics. Height: 2 feet. Spread: 1 foot.

This biennial herb produces ferny green leaves during its first growing season. The second year, it bears flat clusters of white flowers that resemble those of Queen-Anne's-lace. Once the flowers set seed, the plants die.

How to Grow. Caraway thrives in full sun and rich, moist soil. It resents transplanting, so start plants from seed sown directly in the garden in fall or spring. It normally reseeds readily; thin out the seedlings as needed.

Uses. Caraway seeds are most often used to flavor bread, cakes, and cheeses. The seeds are also eaten to aid digestion. Enjoy the fresh leaves with vegetables; cook the root as a vegetable. Grow caraway in an herb garden, with vegetables or in a border.

CATMINT. See *Catnip*

Catnip

Nepeta spp. NEP-eh-tuh.
Early summer. Zones 3 to 9.

Characteristics. Height: 2 to 3 feet. Spread: 2 feet.

Several species of Nepeta are grown in herb and flower gardens. Catnip (*N. cataria*) is not especially ornamental, but it is the species used primarily for catnip tea and to excite cats. This tall, coarse herb has gray-green leaves and small white flowers. Lemon-scented catnip (*N. cataria* 'Citriodora') combines the flavor of catnip with that of lemon. The more ornamental members of the genus are generally known as catmints. This group includes *N. X faassenii* 'Blue Wonder', which is shorter than catnip (18 inches tall) and produces large, deep blue flowers. *N. mussinii* 'Dropmore' grows to 1 foot tall and bears prolific, deep blue-lavender flowers that last well over a month. It has a loose, sprawling habit and will self-seed in the garden.

How to Grow. Place both catnip and catmint in a sunny to lightly shaded location with good drainage. Start with purchased plants, or sow seed of catnip indoors or out in spring. (Cultivars of catmint are best grown from purchased plants.) In areas with high humidity, the plants are susceptible to fungal problems. To improve air circulation around the plants, cut them back by about one-half after the first flush of bloom. Cutting them back will also encourage another flush of bloom in late summer. Divide the plants every 2 or 3 years to keep them vigorous and to prevent them from spreading too much.

Uses. Grow catnip for your feline friends, or use it yourself for a soothing tea. Catmints are marvelous as edgings for perennial beds and borders, as groundcovers under roses, or cascading over the edge of containers.

Chamomile

Chamaemelum nobilis, Matricaria recutita.

kam-ee-MEL-um no-BILL-iss, mah-trih-KARE-ee-ah reh-cue-TEE-tah. Spring. Zones 4 to 8.

○

Characteristics. Height: Roman chamomile, 4 to 12 inches; German chamomile, 2 to 3 feet. Spread: 1 foot.

Roman chamomile (*Chamaemelum nobilis*) is a creeping perennial herb with lacy leaves. Its delicious apple-like scent is most noticeable in the flowering tips and young leaves. The flowers are small white daisies.

The plant commonly known as German chamomile is actually an annual, *Matricaria recutita.* Also known as sweet false chamomile, German chamomile looks similar to Roman chamomile, but is more upright and has a pineapple-like flavor and fragrance. It comes up in early spring, then sets seed and dies in late spring.

How to Grow. Both types of chamomile prefer full sun and dry soil. Start with purchased plants, or sow seed indoors or out in the fall. To encourage the plants of Roman chamomile to spread outward, mow off the flowers. For propagation, divide Roman chamomile;

German chamomile tends to reseed readily.

Uses. The flowers of both types of chamomile make a soothing tea. Roman chamomile grows well in cracks and crevices, between stones in a walkway, or in a wall. Grow German chamomile in any open, sunny site in the herb garden.

Chives

Allium schoenoprasm. AL-ee-um skee-noh-PRAZ-um.
Mid-spring. Zones 3 to 10.

Characteristics. Height: 12 inches. Spread: 10 inches. Chives produce clumps of upright, hollow leaves and showy pink-lavender flowers. They are distinguished by their onion flavor. When interplanted with other garden plants, chives can repel insect pests; they are excellent companions for roses. This herb is also a good choice for growing in containers indoors or out.

How to Grow. Chives grow best in full sun and rich, moist, well-drained soil. Sow seed indoors or out in spring. Cut the clumps to the ground after blooming to encourage the production of new leaves. Divide the clumps every 3 to 4 years to keep them vigorous.

Uses. Harvest the leaves by clipping them back to 1 inch above the ground; new leaves will emerge. Add fresh leaves to salads, soups, cream cheese, butter, or sandwiches. Sprinkle the florets on salads. The leaves and flowers make a flavorful vinegar. Try adding the pink-lavender blooms to a white vinegar—they will give it a light onion flavor and a beautiful pink color.

CILANTRO. See *Coriander*

Coriander

Coriandrum sativum. kore-ee-AN-drum sat-EE-vum.
Late spring. Tender annual.

Characteristics. Height: 2 feet. Spread: 1 foot. Coriander is a short-lived annual. The green, parsleylike leaves are known as cilantro and are used in Mexican and Asian cuisine. The flowering stem is topped with a flat cluster of white to pink flowers. 'Long Standing' is slow to go to flower, so it produces more leaves from a single sowing than the species.

How to Grow. Coriander likes good garden loam in full sun. Grow from seed sown directly in the garden once the danger of heavy frost has passed. Sow seed every 3 weeks during the growing season to ensure a steady supply.

Uses. Harvest the leaves before the flower stem has developed. Harvest the seeds once they start turning from green to gray-brown. The leaves do not dry well, so use them fresh; the taste is better than the smell. The ripe seeds are an important ingredient in curry. They are also used as a pickling spice or sugar-coated and eaten as a candy. Grow coriander with herbs and vegetables in the garden or in a container.

CORSICAN MINT. See *Mint*

Dill
Anethum graveolens. an-EE-thum grav-ee-OH-lenz.
Spring to summer. Tender annual.

Characteristics. Height: 3 feet. Spread: 2 feet. Dill has handsome, feathery, blue-green foliage topped with clusters of delicate golden flowers. The plants prefer cool weather and quickly go to seed during the heat of summer. Once they begin going to flower, they stop producing foliage. 'Bouquet' is considered one of the best dill cultivars for flavor. 'Dukat' is a tall (4-foot) cultivar that was selected for its high yields of foliage and seeds. 'Fernleaf' is perhaps the best cultivar. This Burpee selection, which won the All-America Selections Award, has many fine qualities. Compared to the species, it is slower-growing and less apt to bolt quickly, and it has a more compact growth habit (to 18 inches). 'Fernleaf' is a great dill for growing in containers. Dill will reseed in spots where it is happy.

How to Grow. Choose a site with full sun and moist, fertile soil. Sow seed directly in the garden in early spring. Make successive sowings every few weeks as space permits until the weather heats up.

Removing the flowers as they appear can help prolong leaf production for a short time. Pinching off spent flowers can also prevent prolific self-sowing. At the end of the season, let some plants go to seed to provide a crop next year.

Uses. The fresh, young leaves are a popular flavoring for fish, poultry, seafood, eggs, soups, salads, sauces, and new potatoes. Use the seeds for pickling; enjoy the blooms as cut flowers. Grow dill in herb or vegetable gardens.

Fennel

Foeniculum vulgare. fee-NIK-yew-lum vul-GAR-ee.
Summer. Zones 4 to 10.

Characteristics. Height: 5 feet. Spread. 2 to 3 feet.

Fennel—with its feathery foliage, wonderful flavor, and many uses—is a favorite among herb gardeners. Sweet fennel (*Foeniculum vulgare*) is a short-lived, lacy-leaved perennial; the yellow flower clusters can be used in fresh cut arrangements. Bronze fennel (*F. vulgare* 'Rubrum') has gorgeous purplebronze leaves and combines beautifully with bulbs, such as Madonna lily (*Lilium candidum*). It is a welcome addition to both perennial borders and herb gardens.

The vegetable fennel, commonly known as finocchio or Florence fennel (*F. vulgare* var. *dulce*), is grown as an annual. In autumn, it produces a delicious bulbous base that is eaten raw or cooked.

How to Grow. Fennels prefer well-drained loam in

full sun. Sow seed outdoors after the last frost date. As a perennial, sweet fennel is short-lived, but it will reseed abundantly.

Uses. Enjoy the young leaves as a garnish and flavoring for soups, salads, and fish. Use the tasty seeds crushed or whole in sausage and other meats, as well as to make a refreshing tea with a warm, sweet, anise flavor. Fennel's lacy texture makes it a valuable garden plant.

FRENCH TARRAGON. See *Tarragon, French*
GERMAN CHAMOMILE. See *Chamomile*
HYSSOP, ANISE. See *Anise Hyssop*

Lavender
Lavandula spp. luh-VAN-dew-luh.
Late spring. Zones 5 to 9.

Characteristics. Height: 12 to 24 inches. Spread: 12 to 30 inches.

The handsome gray foliage of lavenders gives them year-round interest. The flower colors range from dark blue to light lavender and even white. Many new cultivars of English lavender (*Lavandula angustifolia*) have been introduced recently. 'Lady' is an exciting new Burpee introduction that can be grown from seed and will bloom the same year. It is compact, reaching only 10 inches high and 12 inches wide, and bears blue flowers. 'Munstead' is distinguished by green leaves and dark violet buds that open into dark violet-blue flowers; it grows 15 to 30 inches tall. 'Hidcote', perhaps the most frequently grown cultivar, is known for its dark purple flowers, small silver leaves, and compact, slow-growing habit.

Most promising of the new lavender groups are the *L. X intermedia* cultivars. These plants, commonly called lavandins, are the result of crosses between *L. angustifolia* and *L. latifolia.*

Their advantages include superior fragrance, wider gray or gray-green leaves, and longer flowering spikes. Lavandins bloom in mid-season and are hardy to 0°F. 'Grosso' is perhaps the most stunning of all, with large flowers on spikes over 2 feet high. It makes an outstanding addition to perennial borders, rose gardens, and containers.

How to Grow. Lavenders need full sun and average to dry, well-drained soil. Start with purchased plants, or sow seed outdoors in the fall or indoors in the spring. Trim the plants in early spring to keep them compact. To encourage repeat flowering, cut back the flowers after they bloom. To propagate, dig up rooted stems, or take cuttings in summer.

Uses. Lavender leaves and flowers are valued for their fragrance. Use them fresh or dried to make a soothing tea; add the dried parts to potpourris. Lavenders are excellent plants for a border, container, or rock garden; they also make a great low hedge.

Lemon grass
Cymbopogon citratus. sim-boh-POH-gon sit-RAH-tus.
Summer. Zones 10 to 11.

Characteristics. Height: 5 feet. Spread: 3 feet.

Lemon grass is a robust grass that forms dense clumps of long, thin, pointed leaves. It rarely flowers. It is also sometimes called fevergrass and West Indians Lemon.

How to Grow. This herb will grow in a variety of soil types, but is most vigorous with plenty of moisture and full sun. In Zones 9 and north, keep lemon grass in a pot so you can bring it indoors over winter. In summer, set the pots out in a protected location. Or plant lemon grass directly in the garden after the last frost and just pot up a small piece in the fall to over-winter indoors. To harvest the leaves, snip them and use them fresh anytime during the summer. Leaves can also be harvested and dried for winter use; for best flavor, dry them quickly.

Uses. The leaves of lemon grass make a delicious herbal tea. The tender inner portion on the base is used in Thai food to make lemon grass soup and to season chicken. This herb has a relaxing effect when added to bathwater. The lovely grassy texture adds interest to the garden and to container plantings.

Marjoram, Sweet
Origanum majorana. oh-rig-AH-num mah-jer-AH-nuh.
Summer. Zones 9 to 10.

Characteristics. Height: 1 foot. Spread: 1 foot. Sweet marjoram has pungent, gray leaves that are satiny in texture. The bloom clusters consist of handsome, green petal-like bracts with small white flowers. The plants grow as perennials in the warmest climates; in Zones 9 and north, grow them as annuals.

Several other marjoram relatives are also popular herbs. *Origanum* X *majoricum,* commonly known as hardy marjoram or Italian oregano, is a sterile hybrid, probably between *O. vulgare* subsp. *virens* and *O. majorana.* It possesses the flavor of marjoram and some of the hardiness of oregano. 'Compact Greek' has a smaller habit and exceptionally beautiful, velvety gray leaves.

How to Grow. A sunny spot with good drainage and slightly acid soil is ideal for sweet marjoram. Sow seed indoors about 6 weeks before the last frost date; set hardened-off plants into the garden after the danger of frost has passed. Pinch or harvest from the plants frequently throughout the season to encourage bushy, upright growth. Propagate from seed.

Uses. The warm, sweet flavor of marjoram makes it one of the best culinary herbs. Try it in vinegars, salads, and sauces; add it to dishes with meat, fish, pasta, or mushrooms. Marjoram is attractive in the garden and makes a good edging or rock garden plant.

Mint

Mentha spp. MEN-thuh.
Late spring to summer. Zones 4 to 9.

Characteristics. Height: 15 inches to 2 feet. Spread: 2 feet or more.

A variety of mints make excellent additions to herb gardens. Peppermint (*Mentha* X *piperita*) is noted for its dark, purplish stems and the strong minty fragrance of all of its above-ground parts. There are many cultivars, including 'Todd Mitcham', with an especially intense peppermint flavor, and 'Chocolate Mint', which supposedly has a slight chocolate taste.

Spearmint (*M. spicata*) is perhaps the best loved of all the mints. This herb bears lavender flowers in late spring; the leaves are dark green and sharply pointed. Curly mint (*M. spicata* 'Crispata') is an especially decorative selection with distinctive, crinkled, rounded, bright green leaves. Red mint (*M.* X *gracilis*) is a close relative, with red-tinged leaves and a mild spearmint flavor. It is considered the best culinary mint for use with rice, salads, or fruit desserts.

English pennyroyal (*M. pulegium*) is a low-growing mint that looks superb as a groundcover in the spaces between stepping-stones or planted in a hanging basket. Hardy to Zone 7 (6 with protection), it is a valuable companion plant for repelling insects. As a dry herb, it is used to make herbal flea collars and insect-repellent sachets.

Corsican mint (*M. requienii*) is another low-growing species with tiny leaves that smell like crème de menthe. It makes a fine shade-loving groundcover.

Both apple mint (*M. suaveolens*) and white-leaved pineapple mint (*M. suaveolens* var. *variegata*) bear leaves with a fruity fragrance.

How to Grow. Most mints thrive in full sun or partial shade with evenly moist, rich soil; Corsican mint prefers a shady site. Start with purchased plants; pinch a leaf before buying a plant to make sure you get one with good fragrance. In the right spot, mints can spread rapidly. To control the spread of these enthusiastic colonizers, grow them in a pot, contain them with metal edging, or plant them in a bottomless container sunk into the soil. Another option is to plant mints in an out-of-the-way spot where their spreading isn't a problem. To encourage a flush of new growth, cut the stems back to the ground after the plants flower. To propagate, divide the plants in spring or fall.

Uses. Fresh or dried, spearmint, peppermint, and apple mint leaves make a healthful and delicious tea. Add the fresh leaves and flowers to salads and desserts. Pennyroyal and Corsican mint are usually grown as ornamental plants. Include mints in herb gardens, container plantings, and children's gardens.

Oregano
Origanum spp. oh-rig-AH-num.
Summer. Zones 5 to 9.

Characteristics. Height: 18 inches. Spread: 24 inches.

The most commonly grown of this group of herbs is Greek mountain oregano (*Origanum vulgare* subsp. *hirtum*, formerly known as *O. heracleoticum*). It has dark green leaves, hairy stems, and white to lavender flowers. Wild oregano (*O. vulgare* subsp. *vulgare*) is an invasive plant with attractive purple flowers that are great for drying. Unlike its culinary relative, wild oregano produces leaves that are flavorless and have no value in cooking. 'Compactum Nanum' is a very dwarf form of this oregano and is often used as a low border plant. Another cultivar, 'Aureum' has golden leaves and is very decorative. *O. onites* is considered an oregano, despite its common name, pot marjoram. It has an upright habit and leaves that are a paler green than other oreganos; its flavor has a real bite. Pot marjoram makes an attractive container plant.

How to Grow. All oreganos need full sun and average, well-drained soil. Seeds tend to produce plants with varying flavor, so it's generally best to start with purchased plants. (Pinch a leaf before you buy a plant, to make sure it has a good aroma.) Pinch or harvest from the plants frequently to keep them bushy. Once you find an oregano with a flavor you really like, propagate it by division in spring or cuttings in summer.

Uses. Greek mountain oregano is one of the best hardy oreganos for cooking, and it has one of the strongest flavors, too. Grow it in a children's garden, a "pizza" garden (with tomatoes, onions, and peppers), or in a container.

Parsley

Petroselinum crispum. peh-troh-seh-LY-num KRIS-pum.
Summer. Zones 4 to 9.

Characteristics. Height: 15 to 24 inches. Spread: 18 inches.

Parsley has many fine ornamental qualities. The dark green leaves have a beautiful, ferny appearance, and they grow in mounded clumps that look especially attractive along a border. Although this herb is actually a biennial, it is normally grown as an annual. Once parsley flowers, the flavor of the leaves deteriorates, and the plants die after they set seed.

There are many kinds of parsley to choose from. They vary in the curl of the leaves and in the shade of green. The curly types are classified as *Petroselinum crispum* var. *crispum.* The most commonly grown flat-leaf type is Italian parsley (*P. crispum* var. *neapolitanum*).

How to Grow. Give parsley full sun to light shade and rich, deeply dug soil that has ample moissure. Sow seed outdoors in spring (it can take sever al weeks to germinate), or start with young purchased plants. To increase leaf production, fertilize several times during the growing season, and remove any flowering stalks that appear. If you let one or two plants go to seed, parsley will often self sow.

Uses. Parsley leaves are rich in vitamins and minerals. Harvest the outer leaves by cutting them at the base of the leafstalk. They are delicious in salads and make an excellent accent for vegetables and potatoes. Chewing on a fresh leaf can freshen your breath. Parsley is superb as a border plant or as an underplanting for roses. Try it in a container, or grow it in the vegetable garden.

PENNYROLL, ENGLISH. See *Mint*
PEPPERMINT. See *Mint*

Rosemary

Rosmarinus officinalis. rose-mah-RINE-us oh-fish-in-AL iss.
Late winter to early spring. Zones 7 to 10.

Characteristics. Height: 2 to 6 feet. Spread: 2 to 6 feet. Rosemary is a classic culinary herb with short, needlelike leaves that have a pungent aroma and taste. The plants can grow to be large shrubs in warm climates; elsewhere, you'll need to bring them indoors over winter. Small blue flowers bloom along the stems in late winter to spring. 'Arp' is a hardier cultivar that can survive outdoors in Zone 6 with a loose winter mulch. 'Prostrate' is a creeping form of rosemary.

How to Grow. Rosemary thrives in average, well-drained soil and full sun. Sow seed of the species indoors in spring. (Fresh seed works best; old seed may germinate poorly.) Plants of the species and cultivars are commonly available for purchase from garden centers in spring. Propagate by cuttings in summer. In cold-winter areas, grow rosemary in pots so you can bring it indoors for the winter.

Uses. The fresh, frozen, or dried leaves are great for seasoning poultry, beef, fish, lamb, and pork; chop them before adding them to food. Sprinkle the fresh flowers over salads. Shrubby rosemary plants look great in the garden and in container plantings.

RUSSIAN CHAMOMILE. See *Chamomile*

Sage

Salvia spp. SAL-vee-uh.
Late spring. Zones 5 to 8.

○

Characteristics. Height: 2 feet. Spread: 3 feet.

Sage is a shrubby herb with a distinctive rounded shape and a striking leaf texture. It has long been a symbol of wisdom, as well as a valuable addition to herb gardens. Ornamental forms of culinary sage (*Salvia officinalis*) bring great color to the garden. 'Icterina' has gold-and-green variegated leaves. 'Purpurea' (also known as 'Purpurascens') bears purple foliage. 'Tricolor' is variegated with cream, purple, gray, and white. Pineapple sage (*S. elegans*) is a tender plant with a pineapple flavor; the leaves and flowers add a refreshing touch to desserts. The bright red fall flowers are also ornamental, and they attract hummingbirds. Clary sage (*S. sclarea*) behaves like a biennial. It forms a rosette of large serrated leaves, which are topped with billowing clusters of lilac flowers.

How to Grow. These herbs must have full sun and well-drained soil. Sow seeds of the species indoors or out in spring; start with plants of the cultivars. Prune established plants back by one-half to two-thirds in early spring if they are getting too large or leggy. In humid areas, sage is susceptible to fungal diseases. If the leaves or branches start to die, remove them, and the plant may recover. If removing the leaves or branches does not solve the problem, start with a new plant in a different site. If mites are a problem, treat the plants with a soap spray. In frost-prone areas, bring pineapple sage inside for the winter. Clary sage often reseeds; propagate others by cuttings in summer.

Uses. Sage leaf tea is useful in treating colds and for aiding digestion. Try the leaves as a flavoring in breads and stuffing or with meats or vegetables. The large size, attractive mounding habit, and 1 textural leaves of the plants make them highly ornamental in the garden. Use them as a corner accent, or mix them with perennials, annuals, and other herbs in a cottage garden.

SPEARMINT. See *Mint*
SWEET BASIL. See *Basil*

Sweet bay

Laurus nobilis. LORE-us no-BILL-iss.
Early spring. Zones 9 to 11.

Characteristics. Height: 15 feet. Spread: 4 feet. Sweet bay is an aromatic evergreen tree with sturdy, flavorful green leaves and an elegant shape. It is a slow grower and can last many years in a container. Golden bay (*Laurus nobilis* 'Aurea') has golden leaves and requires some shade to prevent the leaves from burning. Willow-leaf bay (*L. nobilis* 'Angustifolia') has narrower leaves than the species.

How to Grow. Plant sweet bay in full sun to light shade and rich, moist, well-drained soil. Choose a site protected from winds. In Zones 8 and north, grow the plants in containers; bring them indoors over winter and put them outside during the warmer months. Sweet bay is frost-tolerant and has been known to die back to the roots and still come back. Start with purchased plants. Bay trees are susceptible to scale insects, which can be treated with horticultural oil. For smaller, pot-grown specimens, use a Q-tip dipped in alcohol to control scale insects. Sweet bay can be difficult to propagate; try taking cuttings from soft, new growth.

Uses. Use the dry leaves to flavor soups and stews and sauces. (Remove them before serving.) You can also use the leaves to make herbal wreaths or add them to bathwater to relieve aching limbs. Bay makes an excellent topiary or is an especially attractive container plant.

SWEET MARJORAM. See *Marjoram, sweet*

Tarragon, French
Artemisia dracunculus. ar-teh-MEEZ-ee-uh
drah-KUNK-yew-lus. Summer. Zones 6 to 8.

Characteristics. Height: 2 feet. Spread: 1 foot.

French tarragon is prized as a culinary herb for its delicate anise flavor. True French tarragon can only be grown from root or stem cuttings or from division. (Although the plants sometimes bloom, they almost never set seed.) Russian tarragon, which is sometimes sold as tarragon or French tarragon, is weedy and has no value in cooking. It is seed-grown. When you buy plants, always pinch a leaf to make sure the ones you are buying have the anise flavor of true French tarragon.

How to Grow. French tarragon prefers full sun to light shade and well-drained soil enriched with organic matter. Start with purchased plants. Pinch the shoots when they are 4 to 6 inches tall to encourage branching. For best growth, remove the flowers as they appear. Divide the plants every 3 years in spring or fall. You can grow French tarragon indoors in winter, just pot young divisions or plants in late summer and cut the foliage back to just above the soil.

Uses. Use the fresh leaves to enhance fish and chicken dishes, sauces, and salads. French tarragon also makes a superb vinegar. The plant has no special ornamental qualities other than its bright green foliage.

Thyme, Common
Thymus vulgaris. TY-mus vul-GAIR-iss.
Summer. Zones 5 to 9.
○

Characteristics. Height: 1 foot. Spread: 1 foot. Common thyme is a small herb with an upright growth habit and gray-green leaves that are highly aromatic. There are many variations of thyme to choose from. They have been confused in the trade because of their ability to cross with one another. Be careful when shopping for thymes—pinch the leaves to make sure you get the fragrance you want. 'French' is distinguished by its superior flavor and narrow gray leaves; 'English' has flatter, greener leaves. Both are upright in habit. 'Orange Balsam' features a wonderful orange-spice fragrance and attractive, dark green leaves; the plant thrives in rock gardens.

Lemon thyme (*Thymus* X *citriodorus*) has a number of marvelous cultivars. 'Aureus', commonly known as golden thyme, doubles as a culinary herb and an outstanding ornamental with attractive golden foliage. 'Silver Posie' has silver-edged leaves. It is similar to silver thyme (*T. vulgaris* 'Argenteus'), which is highly ornamental and a bit less hardy (to Zone 6).

How to Grow. Thymes need full sun and well-drained soil. Sow seed of common thyme indoors or out in the spring; start with purchased plants of cultivars. The life span of thyme plants averages about 5 to 6 years. If you notice that the plants are beginning to deteriorate, you can take cuttings and start new

ones, or prune the existing plants back hard to rejuvenate them.

Uses. This classic herb is traditionally added to many
meat and vegetable dishes. It makes a great low, evergreen hedge or rock garden or border plant.

CHAPTER NINE

GROUNDCOVERS

There's something about a lush, finely clipped lawn—an open, friendly space that invites you to play, stroll, or just lounge around. The downside of lawns is all the maintenance they need—regular mowing, plus edging, watering, fertilizing, and pest control. And sometimes, no matter how hard you try, there are areas where grass just won't thrive—under trees, in wet spots, or on dry slopes, for instance—and you are left with ugly bare patches. Fortunately, there is an easy and attractive solution to all of these problems: groundcovers!

WHAT ARE GROUNDCOVERS?

Groundcovers are plants that spread out to form a living carpet over the soil. The term is usually used for low-growing, creeping plants that are no more than 1 or 2 feet tall. Lawn grasses can technically be considered groundcovers, since they are short and they spread to cover the soil. In most cases, though, "groundcovers" refers to creeping nonlawn plants, including perennials, herbs, sprawling vines, and even low shrubs. In low-maintenance areas, low-growing weeds such as ground ivy and English daisies can serve as groundcovers. Even moss can make a marvelous groundcover in shady areas.

GARDENING WITH GROUNDCOVERS

Like all other garden plants, groundcovers grow best when you match their needs to the conditions you have to offer. For a hot, sunny site, stick with drought-tolerant species, such as creeping juniper (*Juniperus horizontalis*). For more sheltered spots, plant shade

lovers such as epimediums (*Epimedium* spp.) and dead
nettle (*Lamium maculatum*). By matching the plants
to the site, you'll end up with a planting that is naturally healthy and vigorous without a lot of fussing on
your part.

Keep in mind that some groundcovers are evergreen,
while others are deciduous (that is, they die back to the
ground each winter). Lady's-mantle (*Alchemilla mollis*),
lamb's ears (*Stachys byzantina*), and other deciduous
groundcovers tend to be very showy during the growing
season, and they can work fine for discouraging weeds.
During the winter, however, you'll be left with bare soil,
which doesn't look especially attractive. For spots where
you really need year-round interest, stick with English
ivy and other evergreen plants.

Plant Portraits

The following portraits highlight some of the best
groundcovers for home gardens. Some are evergreen;
others are deciduous. They may have showy flowers,
attractive leaves, or both. You can buy all of these
groundcovers from retail sources—either mail-order catalogs or local nurseries and garden centers.

GROWING TIPS AT A GLANCE

Each of the following plant portraits includes simple symbols to highlight special features you need to know about each groundcover. If you're not sure what any of the symbols mean, refer back to this key.

○ Full sun (more than 6 hours of sun a day; ideally all day)

◑ Partial sun (some direct sun, but less than 6 hours a day)

● Shade (no direct sun)

✳ Drought-resistant

❦ Fragrant

AARON'S-BEARD. See *Hypericum calycinum*

Ajuga spp.

ah-JEW-guh.
Ajuga, bugleweed. Spring. Zones 3 to 9.

Characteristics. Height: 6 inches. Spread: 18 inches. Ajuga, also commonly known as bugleweed, is a fast-spreading, semi-evergreen or evergreen groundcover. It forms dense carpets of flat or crinkled leaves that are accented by spikes of blue, pink, or white flowers in spring. The most common species is *Ajuga replans*, which comes in a variety of attractive leaf forms. There are several cultivars with bronze-colored leaves, most notably 'Bronze Beauty'. The leaves of 'Burgundy Glow' are pink edged with cream; new growth is burgundy-colored. 'Multi-color' (also known as 'Rainbow') has shiny leaves with a mixture of colors, including pink, cream, and bronze. 'Silver Beauty' produces lovely gray-ish leaves with white around the edges. 'Catlin's Giant' has taller flower spikes (to 8 inches) and large, bronze-green foliage. *A. pyramidalis* spreads less and is a little taller than *A. replans*. It has attractive foliage and prefers a damp location.

How to Grow. In warm southern climates, ajugas grow best in some shade. In cool climates, they prefer sun. They are happiest in a rich, moist soil, although most will tolerate dry shade. Crown rot, a fungal disease that causes the plants to wilt and die, is often a problem in areas with high humidity; look for a spot with well-drained soil and good air circulation. Ajugas are quite vigorous and can quickly creep into adjacent lawn areas; keep them separate with an edging strip, or be prepared to trim the edge 2 or 3 times a year. Propagate by division in spring.

Uses. Ajugas are ideal for covering large areas quickly. They are especially useful under trees and shrubs.

Asarum spp.
uh-SAR-um.
Wild ginger. Spring. Zones 3 to 9.

Characteristics. Height: 10 inches. Spread: 15 inches. Wild gingers produce carpets of heart-shaped foliage and interesting, brown-speckled, spring flowers that hide beneath the leaves. The root has a spicy, gingerlike aroma. Canada wild ginger (*Asarum canadense*) is a deciduous species with broad, medium to dark green leaves; it is quite hardy. European wild ginger (*A. europaeum*) has shiny, dark green, evergreen leaves; it is slightly less hardy (Zones 4 to 8). Mottled wild ginger (*A. shuttleworthii*) produces beautiful evergreen leaves that are spotted with silver. This species is more heat-tolerant and less hardy (Zones 7 to 9) than European wild ginger.

How to Grow. Wild gingers prefer shade and humus-rich, slightly acid soil that is moist but well-drained. To propagate, divide the plants in spring.

Uses. Wild gingers are ideal groundcovers for shady rock gardens and terrace gardens, as well as woodland and naturalized gardens.

BUGLEWEED. See *Ajuga* spp.

Convallaria majalis
kon-vuh-LAIR-ee-uh muh JAL-iss.
Lily-of-the-valley. Spring. Zones 2 to 8.

Characteristics. Height: 10 inches. Spread: 12 inches.

The sweet, fragrant, nodding white flowers of lily-of-the-valley are a symbol of spring. In addition to the flowers, the deciduous plants offer attractive, broad leaves and a vigorous, spreading habit that makes them great groundcovers. The variegated form 'Aureovariegata' has leaves with striking yel low stripes. 'Fortin's Giant' features larger flowers. 'Prolificans' is a double flowered form. 'Rosea' bears pink flowers.

How to Grow. Plant lily-of-the-valley in a partially to fully shaded site with moist to dry soil that has been amended with organic matter. Mulch with compost each autumn to keep the soil rich. In cool climates and moist soil, lily-of-the-valley can become a weed because it is such a strong grower. To keep it under control, or to expand your plantings, divide the plants in fall or spring after flowering.

Uses. Lily-of-the-valley is ideal for a shade garden. Choose a spot where its spreading won't be a problem.

CREEPING JENNY. See *Lysimachia nummularia*
CREEPING JUNIPER. *See Juniperus horizontalis*
ENGLISH IVY. See *Hedera helix*

Gaultheria procumbens

gall-THEER-ee-uh proh KUM-benz.
Wintergreen. Summer. Zones 3 to 8.

Characteristics. Height: 4 inches. Spread: 12 inches.

This attractive, creeping, evergreen groundcover is a native woodland wildflower. It has leathery, rounded leaves that turn reddish in autumn. The leaves and fruit smell like wintergreen when crushed. The small white to pink, pendulous summer flowers are followed by large red berries.

How to Grow. Wintergreen must have partial to full shade and moist, acid soil that is high in organic matter. It is slow-growing and doesn't transplant well; leave established plants to form hand some clumps.

Uses. Wintergreen is great for woodland and shade gardens.

Hedera helix

HED-er-uh HE-liks.
English ivy. Evergreen. Zones 5 to 10.

Characteristics. Height: 6 to 8 inches. Spread: 3 feet. English ivy creates a lovely evergreen groundcover under trees and in shady spots where few other plants will grow. Although it is a vigorous plant, it is not terribly invasive. 'Thorndale', also known as Baltic ivy, features large, attractive leaves. It is very hardy and is useful for stabilizing slopes and preventing other erosion problems. 'Gold Heart', one of the most beautiful ivies, is popular for its heart shaped, gold-striped leaves and its reliable growth habit.

How to Grow. English ivy tolerates a wide range of conditions, including full sun, deep shade, and poor soil. However, it prefers humus-rich, moist soil in partial shade. Cut the plants back as needed to keep them from spreading out of bounds. To propagate, dig up and transplant rooted stems or take cuttings in summer.

Uses. This groundcover is excellent for dry shade under trees or on slopes. Add extra interest by interplanting it with small bulbs, such as crocuses and dwarf daffodils.

HENS AND CHICKS. See *Sempervivum* spp.

Hypericum calycinum
hy-PEAR-ih-kum kal-ih-SIGH-num.
Aaron's-beard. Summer. Zones 5 to 8.

Characteristics. Height: 18 inches. Spread: 24 inches. This fast-growing, evergreen or semievergreen groundcover produces blue-green leaves and brilliant yellow blossoms with showy stamens on low, arching branches. It blooms on new wood and flowers over a long season.

How to Grow. Aaron's-beard grows well in full sun or partial shade and lean, well-drained soil. It performs best in the cooler parts of its range. If the plants lose their leaves over winter, shear them back by one-half to two-thirds to promote fresh, new growth. To propagate, divide the plants in fall or spring.

Uses. Use Aaron's-beard to cover hillsides, slopes, or berms.

Juniperus horizontalis

jew-NIP-er-us hore-ih-zon-TAL-iss.
Creeping juniper. Evergreen. Zones 3 to 9.

Characteristics. Height: 6 inches. Spread: 6 feet.

Creeping junipers are widely grown as groundcovers for hot, dry sites. Many cultivars with different foliage colors are available. One of the most popular is blue rug juniper (*Juniperus horizontalis* 'Wiltonii' or 'Blue Rug'). It offers intense steel blue foliage that hugs the ground on fast-growing, trailing branches. In winter, the foliage takes on a purplish cast.

How to Grow. The plants demand full sun and good drainage. They are very tolerant of heat and dry, sandy sites. Slightly acid soil (pH 5.0 to 6.0) is ideal. Creeping junipers aren't especially easy to propagate at home; buy new plants to expand your plantings, or try cuttings in fall.

Uses. Creeping junipers are ideally suited for covering hot, sunny slopes.

LILYTURF. See *Liriope* spp.

Liriope spp.

ler-EYE-oh-pee.
Lilyturf. Summer. Zones 5 to 10.

Characteristics. Height: 10 to 24 inches. Spread: 18 inches.

Creeping lilyturf (*Liriope spicata*) forms thick mats of arching, narrow leaves. As a groundcover, it has a wonderful grassy texture. Spikes of pale lavender flowers appear in summer. Blue lilyturf (*L. muscari*) has slightly wider leaves and grows taller (up to 2 feet); it is less vigorous and has a somewhat coarser look. Mondo grasses (*Ophiopogon* spp.) closely resemble lilyturf but are less hardy.

How to Grow. Lilyturfs are adaptable and easy to grow. They will grow in sun or shade; they appreciate some moisture but can take well drained to droughty soil. The plants tolerate heat well and adapt to seaside conditions. If the leaves turn brown after a harsh winter, shear them back in early spring. To propagate, divide the plants in spring or fall. The round, black seeds that follow the flowers will often self-sow, and you can lift and move seedlings when they appear.

Uses. Lilyturf is well suited to growing on slopes or banks, and under trees or shrubs. It also makes a nice edging.

Lysimachia nummularia
ly-sih-MAK-ee-uh num-yew-LAH-ree-uh.
Creeping Jenny. Early summer. Zones 3 to 8.

Characteristics. Height: 2 to 4 inches. Spread: 2 to 3 feet.

This ground-hugger has small, rounded, green leaves and 1-inch-wide, bright yellow, fragrant flowers, which appear in early summer. It is a good, dense groundcover, although it can become invasive. The golden form, 'Aurea', is especially beautiful and is less vigorous.

How to Grow. Creeping Jenny thrives in moist soil and partial to full shade. To propagate, divide the plants in spring.

Uses. Grow creeping Jenny along streams or pools, where it can spread freely.

Sempervivum spp.

sem-per-VY-vum.
Hens and chicks. Summer. Zones 3 to 8.

Characteristics. Height: 8 to 10 inches. Spread: 16 inches.

Hens and chicks are loved for their charming, evergreen rosettes, which consist of fleshy leaves with pointed tips. The thick, upright, flower stalks are topped with starry, purplish red flowers in summer. New plants are produced around the base of mature rosettes—hence the name "hens and chicks." The "hens" often die after flowering, but the "chicks" quickly fill in the space.

How to Grow. Hens and chicks tolerate a wide range of growing conditions, including hot, dry, and rocky places. They can take sun or light shade and grow best in well-drained, neutral soil.

Uses. Try a patch of hens and chicks along or in a wall or walkway. They also make superb additions to rock gardens.

Vinca spp.

VING-kuh.

Periwinkle. Spring. Zones 4 to 9.

Characteristics. Height: 4 to 6 inches. Spread: 24 inches.

Periwinkles are widely used groundcovers with glossy, evergreen leaves and rich blue flowers that appear in spring. The nonflowering trailing stems take root as they creep across the ground. Common periwinkle (*Vinca minor*) has small leaves. The cultivar 'Alba' has white flowers. Greater periwinkle (*V. major*) produces large leaves and is less hardy (generally Zones 7 to 10). 'Variegata' has cream-and-green leaves and is a popular addition to hanging baskets and window boxes.

How to Grow. These plants prefer loose, humus-rich soil with plenty of moisture. They can grow in full sun or shade but generally do best in partial shade. Weed carefully the first few years, until the plants get established. To propagate, divide the plants in spring or fall.

Uses. Periwinkles are ideal for controlling erosion on shady slopes and for covering the soil under trees and shrubs.

WOODRUFF, SWEET. See *Galium odoratum*
WILD GINGER. See A*sarum* spp.
WINTERGREEN. See *Gaultheria procumbens*

CHAPTER TEN

VINES

Vines have much to offer the adventurous gardener. Trained up trellises are allowed to spread gracefully over the ground, vines grow quickly to provide cover, shade, or privacy. They make a beautiful backdrop for borders and foundation plantings, and they can provide vertical accents for flower beds. Vines can also add seasonal interest—for example, when allowed to twine through trees and shrubs.

WHAT ARE VINES?

Vines are plants that need support to hold themselves upright. Some can grab onto a support by themselves; others will need some help from you to hang on. You'll know what kind of assistance your vines need by seeing how they grow. There are three basic ways vines can climb.

CLINGING VINES

The first group includes climbers that are self clinging. Some, such as English ivy (*Hedera helix*), have aerial roots; others, including Virginia creeper (*Parthenocissus quinquefolia*), have adhering tendril tips. These vines need little training and are able to climb walls, trellises, and tree trunks without additional support.

TWINING VINES

The second group consists of twining vines, which climb by wrapping themselves around a support. Some, including clematis, have twining petioles (leaf stems) or tendrils that need wire, string, or netting for support. Other twining vines, such as trumpet honeysuckle (*Lonicera sempervirens*) and wisterias (*Wisteria* spp.), wrap their whole stems around a support; they also need wires, poles, fences, or trellises to climb. If you want them to go up a trellis or thick post, you'll need to train the young vines in the right direction by securing the base of the plant to the support with strings or wire. When training a twining vine to cover a solid structure, such as a fence or wall, leave at least 1 inch of space between the wires or trellis and the structure. This will allow for good air circulation around the plant and greatly reduce possible disease problems. Also, attach the trellis to the wall or fence with hooks at the top and hinges at the base. That way, you can easily uncover the structure when you need to paint or do other maintenance.

CLIMBING ROSES

The third group includes long-caned roses that adapt well to vertical training. These plants don't actually climb, but they can hang onto rough supports (such as tree trunks) with their hooked thorns. Climbing roses need a sturdy support—along with pruning, training, and tying—to look their best. (To learn more about choosing and growing climbing roses, see Chapter 6, Roses.)

GARDENING WITH VINES

Versatile vines deserve a place in every part of the yard. Training them to grow up trellises, walls, arbors, and fences is both a traditional and an attractive way to display many vines. Leafy vines, such as crimson glory vine (*Vitis coignetiae*) and wisteria, are ideal for providing cool summer shade for porches, patios, and decks. These plants also make a perfect screen to add a sense of privacy or block an unpleasant view without the permanence or expense of a solid fence.

But don't forget that vines have much more to offer than just leaves. Flowering vines, such as morning glories (*Ipomoea* spp.) and clematis, are ideal for adding height and color to beds and borders. Train them to climb posts in the middle or back of the border, or create a tepee of bamboo poles for the vines to cover as a garden centerpiece.

TRAINING AND PRUNING VINES

Most vines will grow just fine without a lot of fuss. If they need some help holding onto their support, you can tie them with soft string. (Check the ties every few months to make sure they aren't cutting into the vine stems.) Woody vines benefit from some pruning and shaping to control their growth; regular pruning of very vigorous vines, such as wisteria, is especially important to keep them in bounds. For details on how and when to prune specific vines, see the individual plant portraits that follow.

PLANT PORTRAITS

The following plant portraits cover some of the best evergreen and deciduous vines for your garden. Most are relatively easy to find at nurseries and garden centers. Mail-order catalogs offer a wide selection of cultivars, along with species of unusual vines, so be sure to check them out.

GROWING TIPS AT A GLANCE

Each of the following plant portraits includes simple symbols to highlight special features you need to know about each vine. If you're not sure what any of the symbols mean, refer back to this key.

○ Full sun (more than 6 hours of sun a day; ideally all day)

◐ Partial sun (some direct sun, but less than 6 hours a day)

● Shade (no direct sun)

❧ Fragrant

ANEMONE CLEMATIS. See *Clematis montana*

Aristolochia durior
uh-riss-toe-LOW kee-uh DER-ee-or.
Dutchman's-pipe. Late spring. Zones 4 to 8.

Characteristics. Height: Up to 30 feet.

This twining, deciduous vine has heart-shaped leaves and unusual, 3-inch-long, brownish yellow flowers.

How to Grow. Dutchman's-pipe grows well in full sun to partial shade. Although it prefers moist, rich, well-drained soil, it will tolerate less ideal conditions. After flowering, trim the vines as needed for shape. To rejuvenate old or overgrown vines, cut the plants to the ground in late winter.

Uses. Train Dutchman's-pipe up a tree, fence, or stump. It is often used as a fast-growing screen on a porch or arbor.

Clematis X jackmanii

KLEM-uh-tiss jak-MAN-ee-eye.
Jackman clematis. Summer to fall. Zones 4 to 8.

○

Characteristics. Height: 6 to 14 feet.

The original large-flowered clematis, Jackman clematis is a thin-stemmed, deciduous vine. It climbs by wrapping its leafstalks around its support. It is known for its profusion of rich violet-purple flowers, which are 4 to 7 inches across. The flowers bloom on the current season's growth, over bright green leaves.

There are many fine cultivars to choose from. 'Comtesse de Bouchaud' bears large mauve-pink flowers in summer and is known to be very free-flowering. It is especially lovely growing up a tree trunk. 'Duchess of Edinburgh' has medium double, white flowers and is well suited for growing over shrubs or on walls. 'Ernest Markham' has large, magenta-red flowers with light brown anthers; it is one of the best red-flowered clematis. 'Superba' is the most popular clematis because of its large, dark purple flowers and free-flowering habit. 'Nelly Moser' bears distinctive mauve-lilac flowers with a deep pink bar and red anthers.

How to Grow. This vine prefers moderately moist soil with good drainage; dig in plenty of compost or aged manure before planting. Clematis grow best with their tops in the sun and their roots in the shade. To satisfy these seemingly incompatible conditions, choose a sunny spot where the base of the plant will be shaded by a shrub or a planting of perennials. Or, mulch the plants to keep the roots cool. Avoid planting Jackman clematis in extremely hot, exposed areas. If the individual stems or entire plants wilt suddenly, remove and destroy the affected parts; there is no cure for clematis wilt. Since plants bloom on the current season's growth, prune in February or March, leaving a strong pair or two of buds at the base of each stem.

Uses. Train Jackman clematis on fences or walls, or up through shrubs. It also makes an interesting groundcover when allowed to sprawl.

BOSTON IVY. See *Parthenocissus* spp.

Clematis montana

KLEM-uh-tiss mon-TAN-uh.
Anemone clematis. Late spring. Zones 5 to 9.

○

Characteristics. Height: 20 to 30 feet.

Anemone clematis is a fast-growing woody vine that climbs with twining leaf stems. The green leaves are roughly toothed and made up of three leaflets. New growth is tinged with purple. The white to pink, 2-inch-wide flowers are borne singly or in clusters; most have a vanilla scent. The feathery seed heads that follow are ornamental. The variety *Clematis montana* var. *rubens* is variable but usually has deep mauve-pink flowers with creamy stamens.

Other early-flowering clematis include *C. alpina*, which climbs to 6 feet and bears bell-shaped, violet-blue, nodding flowers; and Armand clematis (*C. armandii*), a fast-growing, evergreen species suitable for warm climates (Zones 8 and south). Armand clematis has large, glossy leaves with prominent veins and fragrant white flowers that appear in early spring. The feathery seed heads are decorative. *C. macropetala* grows to 10 feet tall and offers bright blue, 4-inch-wide flowers in early spring, followed by silvery seeds in fall.

How to Grow. Plant anemone clematis and other early-flowering species in full sun, but keep the roots covered with mulch or a groundcover. The soil should be fertile, well drained, and evenly moist. Provide wire or string supports to prevent the brittle stems from breaking. Prune the current season's shoots back to 2 or 3 buds after flowering. These plants are subject to clematis wilt; remove and destroy infected parts.

Uses. Both anemone and Armand clematis can climb high into trees and cover large trellises. Train smaller early-blooming species on fences or posts.

CLIMBING HYDRANGEA. See *Hydrangea anomala* subsp. *petiolaris*
CYPRESS VINE. See *Ipomoea* spp.
DUTCHMAN'S-PIPE. See *Aristolochia durior*
HONEYSUCKLE, TRUMPET. See *Lonicera sempervirens*

Hydrangea anomala subsp. petiolaris

hy-DRAN-jee-uh uh-NOM-uh-luh pet-ee-oh-LAIR-iss.
Climbing hydrangea. Summer. Zones 5 to 8.

Characteristics. Height: Up to 75 feet.

This self-clinging vine attaches to structures with aerial rootlets. It has large, circular leaves and showy flower clusters. Each cluster is made up of many small, fragrant, white flowers surrounded by larger petal-like bracts.

How to Grow. Plant climbing hydrangea in full sun or partial shade and fertile, moist, well-drained soil. It can be slow to establish itself, but it's worth the wait. Prune lightly in early spring to remove damaged growth or to shape the plants.

Uses. Climbing hydrangea is excellent for growing on a wall, arbor, porch, or tree.

Ipomoea spp.

ih-poh-MEE-uh.

Morning glory, cypress vine. Summer. Zone 10.

○

Characteristics. Height: Up to 20 feet.

These plants are fast-growing, soft-stemmed, twining vines. They are hardy in frost-free areas; elsewhere, they are grown as annuals. Common morning glory (*Ipomoca purpurea*) is popular for its broad, heart-shaped leaves and showy purple or reddish, white-throated, funnel-shaped flowers. 'Heavenly Blue' bears gorgeous true-blue flowers. Cypress vine (*I. quamoclit*) offers dainty, fernlike foliage and striking, brilliant red, star-shaped flowers that attract hummingbirds. Cardinal climber (*I. X multifida*) produces small scarlet trumpets.

How to Grow. Morning glories and cypress vines thrive in full sun and average, well-drained soil. Soak the seeds overnight, then sow them outdoors after the last spring frost, when the soil is warm.

Uses. Train morning glories, cypress vines, and cardinal climbers on strings or wires to cover walls, fences, trellises, or arbors.

JACKMAN CLEMATIS. See *Clematis X jackmanii*

Lonicera sempervirens
lon-ISS-er-uh sem-per-VY-renz.
Trumpet honeysuckle. Summer. Zones 3 to 8.

Characteristics. Height: 12 to 20 feet.

Trumpet honeysuckle is a twining vine that is evergreen in the South and semievergreen or deciduous in the North. It has 3-inch-long leaves and scentless, scarlet-and-yellow, tubular flowers that are 2 inches long and bloom in summer. The flowers are followed in autumn by bright red berries, which are popular with birds. 'Magnifica' blooms later and features red flowers. 'Sulphurea' has true yellow blooms that continue flowering well into fall.

How to Grow. Trumpet honeysuckle prefers rich, moist soil but will grow in any good garden soil. It thrives in full sun or partial shade and tolerates urban conditions. Prune as needed after flowering to keep the plants in bounds.

Uses. Allow trumpet honeysuckle to climb up a trellis or arbor, or let it scale a support on the side of a building. It also grows well with climbing roses.

MORNING GLORY. See *Ipomoea* spp.

Parthenocissus spp.

par-then-oh-SIS-us.
Boston ivy, Virginia creeper. Summer. Zones 4 to 8.

Characteristics. Height: 30 to 50 feet.

These vigorous, deciduous vines have adhesive-tipped tendrils that cement themselves to walls; they need no support to climb. Boston ivy (*Parthenocissus tricuspidata*) has shiny, 3-lobed leaves that are 8 inches wide. Clusters of small, greenish, summer flowers are followed by dark blue-black berries. 'Purpurea' produces leaves that remain purple throughout the growing season. 'Veitchii' has smaller leaves that are purplish when young. Virginia creeper (*P. quinquefolia*) is a similar species with 5-leaflet leaves. Also commonly called woodbine, or simply American ivy, it produces small flowers in summer, followed by clusters of blue-black berries. Both species turn brilliant scarlet or crimson in fall.

How to Grow. These vines grow in any good garden soil, in sun or shade. They tolerate city conditions. Trim as needed during the summer to remove damaged growth or to shape the plants.

Uses. Both Boston ivy and Virginia creeper are excellent for covering walls, fences, and tree trunks. The berries are attractive to birds.

TRUMPET HONEYSUCKLE. See *Lonicera sempervirens*

VIRGINIA CREEPER. See *Parthenocissus* spp.

Wisteria spp.
wis-TEER-ee-uh.
Wisteria. Spring. Zones 4 to 9.
○

Characteristics. Height: 30 feet or more.

Wisterias are large, vigorous, twining vines that require a strong (preferably metal) structure to support their weight. Japanese wisteria (*Wisteria floribunda*) is the most widely planted species. It produces a spectacular spring show of lightly fragrant, lavender-blue flowers in long, cascading clusters. 'Macro-botrys' bears very fragrant flowers in clusters up to 3 feet long. Chinese wisteria (*W. sinensis*) offers blue violet, less-fragrant flowers; the clusters are 6 to 12 inches long.

Wisterias thrive in full sun and fertile, moist, well-drained soil. When purchasing a wisteria, try to buy a named cultivar, because seedlings will vary in their flowering habits. Every year, prune the plants back severely after flowering. Pruning will encourage them to bloom more abun dantly and keep them in bounds; if left unchecked, the vines can take over structures and cause severe damage.

Uses. Train wisterias to climb large, strong structures such as freestanding arbors or pergolas. They can also be trained on sturdy wires affixed to concrete or brick walls. They are powerful twining vines, and with time will pull apart all but the sturdiest structures. They will also pull down down spouts and gutters if left to ramble at will.

PART III

THE PRACTICAL GARDENER

Once you have developed a design that appeals to you and have selected the plants ou would like to grow, it's time to get your hands dirty. Sure, planting and caring for a garden takes work, but it's work that's enjoyable and relaxing. It's very good exercise, too.

In the chapters that follow, you'll learn all the basic techniques you need to know to have a healthy garden. Chapter 11 covers everything from preparing the soil, making compost, multhing, and fertilizing, to growing plants from seed, plating, and propagating. You will also find chapters on handy tools and pest and disease control. As you read these pages and work in your garden, keep in mind that you'll learn much of what you need to know just going out and experimenting with different plants and techniques, to see which works best for you. That's because gardening conditions vary so much from one area to another. So use the basic guidelines that follow, but don't be afraid to experiment. Above all, have fun!

CHAPTER ELEVEN

PLANTING AND CARING FOR YOUR GARDEN

Once you've finalized your planting plan, it's time to get out and get started. Spend some time preparing the soil thoroughly so your carefully chosen plants will grow and thrive. Get the plants you need, either by growing them from seed or by purchasing healthy transplants. Plant them at the right depth and spacing, then stand back to watch them produce masses of beautiful blooms, tasty vegetables, or pungent leaves.

During the growing season, keep your plants vigorous and productive with good care, including mulching, fertilizing, watering, staking, pinching, and deadheading. If the urge to increase your perennial gardens strikes, propagate your existing plants with easy techniques such as division and cuttings. At the end of the season, prepare your garden for winter with a good fall cleanup. Pretty soon, the new seed and plant catalogs will start arriving, and it will be time to start the fun all over again!

PREPARING THE SOIL

The hardest work, and by far the most important for successful gardening, is preparing a site for planting. It's especially challenging when you're starting a site that's never been planted before. But if you do it right the first time, you'll see your plants growing strong and healthy, and you'll know it was worth the effort.

The goal in soil preparation is to develop a fertile, loose, crumbly soil. This kind of soil provides seeds and plants with what they need to grow: essential nutrients; aeration for strong and healthy root development; and good drainage so that roots get as much moisture as they need but aren't waterlogged. If you are starting with a clay or sandy soil, don't expect to have the fluffy kind of soil that's ideal for gardening the first season. It takes several years of steady work to transform poor or mediocre soil into great garden soil. But no matter what kind of soil you're starting with, you can improve it every time you dig.

DIG IN!

You can dig your garden beds virtually any time of year, as long as the soil is ready. Obviously, you can't dig when the ground is frozen. Soil that is either too wet or too dry isn't in prime condition for cultivation, either. Working the soil when it's too wet can destroy its good, crumbly structure and leave it tight and compacted— less-than-ideal conditions for good root growth. (This is especially a problem if your soil is on the clayey side.) If the soil is too dry, it will be harder for you to dig, and you may be left with a powdery soil that's prone to compaction and crusting.

So how do you know when the ground is ready to dig? Pick up a clump of soil in your hand, squeeze it, and roll it into a ball. Then tap the ball with your fingers: If it falls apart into smaller pieces, the soil is ready to be worked. If the ball does not come apart, your soil needs at least a few days to dry out. If the soil is dry and will not even form a ball, then water it well, wait a day, and perform the test again. If your soil is so clayey that the soil ball won't fall apart even after the ground has dried out some, try digging a few shovelfuls. If the soil feels very sticky and clings to your tools and boots, wait another few days (and remember to work in lots of organic matter to loosen the soil when you finally do dig!).

When both you and your soil are ready, begin by removing any weeds or other unwanted vegetation. Rake it away and place it in your compost pile. If you don't have a compost pile, this is a great time to start one!

You can loosen the soil by hand-digging or by using a rotary tiller. For most flowers, bulbs, and vegetables, it is sufficient to work the soil to a depth of at least 10 to 12 inches. However, the deeper the soil is loosened, the better, especially for large or deep-rooted plants. Once you've dug your beds deeply, you don't need to do it again every year. In vegetable gardens and annual flower beds, just scatter some organic matter over the surface and dig it into the top few inches with a garden fork.

Using a Rotary Tiller: A rotary tiller can make soil preparation much easier on your back and takes much less time than it does to do the job by hand. If you don't want to spend the money to purchase a tiller, keep in mind that many home rental centers have tillers for rent.

By tilling in several passes and setting the blades deeper at each pass, you can usually loosen the soil to a depth of 6 to 8 inches. While this is a help, it's not the last step in soil preparation. For best results, you should still hand-dig the area to break up the soil at least 2 to 4 inches below that.

Digging by Hand: If you choose to dig by hand, use a shovel to turn over the top 10 to 12 inches of soil. "Turning over the soil" means just that—taking each shovelful of soil and turning it over. Break up soil clods by hitting and separating them with a garden fork. Then dig over the area again with a garden fork to loosen the lower level where the shovel didn't reach. Remove any large to medium-sized rocks from the area; you can leave a few smaller rocks, since they help the soil drain.

There is another method of garden bed cultivation called double-digging. Double-digging involves loosening the soil to a depth of as much as 24 inches. To do this, you make a series of trenches and refill one trench with soil from another, along with generous amounts of organic matter.

Double-digging is hard work, and there is still some debate about whether all the extra effort is really worth it. It probably is worth the effort if you have heavy, poorly drained clay soil that needs intensive improvement. Double-digging also provides ideal conditions for root crops, such as carrots and potatoes. If you want to try this method, follow these steps:

1. After removing the existing vegetation, spread a 1- to 3-inch layer of organic matter over the planting area.
2. Take a sharp, flat-bladed spade and dig a trench about 2 feet wide, 1 foot deep, and as long as you want the new garden bed to be. Put the soil from this trench in a garden cart, or lay a sheet of plastic near the trench and place the soil on the sheet. Remove any large stones or other debris as you dig.
3. Add an inch or two of organic matter to the bottom of the trench. Also apply lime or any other soil amendments your soil may need (as indicated by the soil test you took back when you were investigating your garden site).
4. Using a garden fork, dig the organic matter and amendments into the soil at the bottom of the trench.
5. Dig another 2-foot-wide trench next to the first trench. Place the topsoil and organic matter into the first trench.

6. Repeat steps 2 through 5 until the entire bed has been worked. Fill the last trench with soil from the first trench.
7. Rake the bed, breaking up any surface clods to make a smooth, level surface.

While digging the trenches, never stand on the soil that you've already loosened. Your weight will compact the soil, which defeats the purpose of double-digging.

GETTING RID OF GRASS

Removing turf grass and weeds from new garden sites can be a big job. There are a few ways to approach this task, depending on how much time and energy you have.

If you can wait several months to plant, try smothering the grass with mulch: Mow the grass as short as possible, then cover it with a dense mulch, such as newspapers or old wool or cotton carpeting. Top that with a layer of more attractive mulch. After a few months, the grass should be dead, and you can dig or till the site to prepare it for planting.

If you want to plant soon, you need to take more direct action. For a relatively small area, you can remove the sod by hand. Slide a sharp spade between the grass and the soil to sever the grass roots. Pull up the sod pieces, shake off the loose soil, and toss the pieces upside-down onto your compost pile. As you expose the soil, carefully pick out any remaining weeds or weed roots. Don't be tempted to simply till live turf into the soil; tilling will only chop up the weed and grass roots and spread them all over the area, leaving you with serious weed problems in your new beds.

IMPROVE YOUR SOIL WITH ORGANIC MATTER

Soil improvement is an ongoing process; it doesn't stop after the first digging session. To achieve any kind of success in gardening, you must put as much time and care into growing rich, healthy soil as you do in designing your garden and selecting your plants.

All kinds of soil benefit from regular and generous additions of organic matter. What exactly is organic matter? Organic matter is just dead plant or animal tissue, material such as rotting vegetables, leaves, stems, and roots. As it breaks down, it releases nutrients and humus. Humus promotes good soil structure by helping soil particles stick together. Soil organisms are a critical part of this process, since they help to break down the organic matter.

Peat Moss: Peat moss is often recommended as a soil amendment, especially for loosening clay soil. It does not, however, have any significant nutrient value, so you still need to mix in manure or compost.

Animal Manures: Manures from cows, horses, chickens, and rabbits are excellent sources of organic matter for any garden. Manure adds nutrients, especially nitrogen, and it also improves soil structure.

Fresh manure can "burn" tender plant roots, so wait several months to plant after applying it, or use manure that has been aged until it's dry and odorless. Animal manures, even if aged, often carry weed seeds, so don't be surprised to see some new weeds cropping up in your garden not long after you have spread manure.

Compost: A compost pile, made from all your yard and fruit and vegetable scraps, is your best source of organic matter for your garden. There is nothing difficult or expensive about making compost—you simply mix together different kinds of organic matter and allow it to decompose. The organic matter is right at your fingertips, since it is constantly being produced in your yard and kitchen. Compostable items include leaves (shredded, if possible), vegetable and fruit scraps from the kitchen, shredded woody stems, spent annual and perennial plants, dead flowers, wood ashes, eggshells, coffee grounds, grass clippings, and manure from cows, horses, chickens, and rabbits.

If properly tended, a backyard compost pile will not be a source of unpleasant odor or a hangout for rodents. To prevent animal pest problems, avoid adding meat, fat, bones, or dairy products to your pile. Other materials to keep out of your pile include diseased plants, diseased fruits and vegetables, weeds that have gone to seed, corocobs (unless shredded first), citrus fruit, coal or charcoal ashes, and manure from dogs, cats, or humans.

GETTING YOUR PLANTS

Now that you've prepared an ideal site, you're ready to get your plants. You can start them yourself from seed, or buy them from a local or mail-order source. Your choice will depend on what kinds of plants you need, how much time you have, and what kind of budget you're working with.

PURCHASE GROWING PLANTS

Shopping at a local outlet or through a mail-order catalog is obviously the most direct and fastest way to get the plants you need. As long as you know what to look for in plants, you can buy them from any source.

Buying by Mail-Order: Buying plants through catalogs can be a little intimidating, since you can't see what you're buying until it arrives at your doorstep. But when you order from an established, reputable company, you can be fairly sure that you'll get good-quality plants at fair prices. Keep in mind that if a particular nursery has unbelievably low prices, the quality of the plants may be unbelievably poor. If you're nervous about buying by mail-order, try placing a small order the first year to see if you like what you get.

Most mail-order nurseries will ship your plants at the right planting time for your area. When the plants arrive, they will probably appear a little bedraggled; bareroot plants may even look like they are dead. Read the packing slip that comes with the plants to find out how to handle them. If you can't set out your plants right away, pot them up in a mix of potting soil and compost so they can keep growing.

Buying at a Nursery or Garden Center: Shopping for your plants at a retail outlet is fun and easy. The choice is usually more limited than what you can buy through mail-order, but you'll see exactly what you're getting for your money. It can be hard to resist impulse buying when confronted with rows of great-looking plants, but be strong and stick to the lists you made back in the planning stages. Otherwise, you may end up bringing home plants that you don't have the right location or any room for.

As you find the plants on your list, inspect them carefully. If possible, purchase younger plants that haven't yet flowered. A plant can be permanently stunted if grown for too long in a container that's too small. If it hasn't set flowers yet, you'll know it is still young and hasn't matured too quickly.

Gently lift each plant out of its container and inspect the roots. You should see some healthy-looking, white roots on the outside of the rootball. If you don't see any roots, the plant may be unhealthy; put it back. Also, avoid buying plants that are pot-bound. If the roots are thickly matted and circling around each other, the plant has outgrown its container. If the plant is too large to take out of the container, check to see if roots are starting to grow out of the bottom of the pot—another sign that the plant is pot-bound.

START YOUR OWN PLANTS FROM SEED

Growing your own garden plants from seed takes more time and planning than buying them, but it's a tremendously rewarding experience. There's a special feeling of satisfaction when you see the plants you've nurtured from tiny seeds finally burst forth with beautiful blooms or bountiful produce. Growing plants from seed also lets you grow new or unusual plants that haven't yet made it to your local nursery. Best of all, buying seed is much cheaper than buying plants, so you can fill your garden for a fraction of the cost of using store-bought plants.

Some plants—such as melons, pumpkins, squashes, and many wildflowers—are so tough that you can sow them directly in the garden where you want them to grow. And some grow so quickly and easily, there is no need to start them early or go through the process of transplanting; basil, beans, and nasturtiums are among this group of fast-growing plants.

Other plants appreciate a little pampering, however. Starting these plants indoors from seed will give them ideal growing conditions so they'll grow and bloom quickly when you set them out. Indoor sowing is practically a must for slow-growing annuals and vegetables; otherwise, they might not bloom or produce a usable harvest before frost. These include broccoli, peppers, eggplant, tomatoes, cabbage, brussels sprouts, melons, onions, ageratum, begonias, geraniums, impatiens, petunias, salvias, and snapdragons.

Many perennials can be grown from seed sown indoors or out. They generally take a year or two to become established and bloom from seed, so they require more patience than annual flowers and vegetables.

Providing the Right Conditions: The key to successful seed starting indoors or out is understanding the conditions your seeds need to grow. When given the necessary amounts of water, warmth, and light, most seeds will readily germinate and grow into healthy plants.

One of the most important requirements for seeds to grow is adequate moisture. Soil that is either too dry or too wet can be fatal to seeds and seedlings. Seeds sown indoors need a growing medium that is loose enough to hold a good supply of air and water for healthy root growth. Seeds sown outdoors need a prepared seedbed for best germination. Air circulation around the tops of the seedlings is important for minimizing the chance of disease problems developing. For most garden seeds, a soil temperature between 70° and 80°F is ideal for good germination. A heating mat (sold in many garden supply catalogs) is handy for keeping indoor-sown seeds at the optimal temperature.

Some seeds need light to sprout and should not be covered with soil. However, most seeds germinate best in darkness, under a light covering of soil. After germination, all seedlings need adequate light to grow well. A greenhouse or sunspace is ideal for indoor sowing. If you don't have either one, fluorescent lights are also fine for growing seedlings. Or you can grow your seedlings in an unshaded southern window, as long as the air temperature there is not too cold.

Selecting a Growing Medium: Do not use regular garden soil to start seed indoors; it is usually too heavy and could contain disease organisms that harm seedlings. The ideal growing medium for starting seeds holds some moisture but is well aerated, is free of disease and weeds, and is noncrusting. (The medium does not need to be nutrient-rich. In fact, it's better if it isn't. Seeds don't need nutrient-rich medium to germinate, and it tends to encourage problems with diseases.)

Horticultural vermiculite is great for starting seeds because it has all of these qualities and is inexpensive. You can also buy a commercial soilless mix from garden centers and garden supply catalogs. A soilless mix contains perlite, vermiculite, and/or peat, and sometimes a fertilizer, but not any actual soil.

Choosing a Container: Almost any kind of container that is at least 2 to 3 inches deep is fine for starting seed indoors. If the container is less than 2 inches deep, there is more of a chance that the soil mixture will dry out too quickly. Ideally, the container should have drainage holes; if there are no holes, be sure you don't overwater, or the seedling roots will be sitting in water and the seedling will die.

Traditional containers include wooden or plastic trays (often called flats), multipart plastic containers (called cell packs), peat pots and pellets, and soil blocks made from a soil-block mold. Garden supply catalogs often sell special seed-starting containers that are especially good for keeping the soil and seedlings from drying out. Some of the best containers are made from disposable materials readily found around the house—for example, milk cartons, plastic jugs, aluminum pans, and plastic trays.

Wash all containers—especially ones that have been used previously—in warm, soapy water. Then rinse them in a 10 percent bleach solution (1 part chlorine bleach to 9 parts water) to reduce the chance of disease problems. (Allow wooden containers to soak for at least 30 minutes in the bleach solution.) Finally, set the containers out to dry.

Deciding When to Sow: The sowing date depends on the last frost date for your area. (This is actually an average of when the last frost usually occurs.) If you don't know the date for your area, check with your local Cooperative Extension Service office or ask at your local garden center.

Depending on the plant, you'll start most indoor-sown seeds about six to eight weeks before the last frost date and most outdoor, direct-sown seeds around or after this date. There are some exceptions to this rule, so be sure to check the seed packets as soon as you get them to find the best sowing time for your particular seeds. Perennials, for example, are often sown outdoors in midsummer. If they're grown indoors, they generally need to be sown in midwinter.

Sowing Seed Outdoors: At the right sowing time for your seeds, make a seedbed in your prepared planting area by raking the surface smooth. Plant the seed at the appropriate depth, as indicated on the seed package. If you are making rows, follow the instructions on the package for the recommended spacing between rows. Always plant twice as many seeds as you need plants, since some seeds may not germinate, some may be eaten by animals, and some may get washed away by heavy rains. You can always thin plants out later if they get too crowded. Use a waterproof marker to write the plant name and the sowing date on a label, and place the label in the sown area.

Annual flowers and vegetables can be sown outdoors right where they are to grow, but for perennials, it's often best to prepare a separate nursery bed for seedlings. In a nursery bed, you can sow seed for many different perennials—or annuals, for that matter—in rows, and tend them all with one trip to the garden. This makes keeping them watered and weeded easier than if they were growing in beds spread around your yard. Select a convenient spot for your nursery bed to make it easy to tend your seedlings. A corner of your vegetable garden is often ideal. Once seedlings are large enough to manage on their own, you can transplant them into beds and borders.

Gently water the seedbed using a watering can or a hose with a fine-mist nozzle, so seeds don't scatter. Water every day (unless it rains) to keep the seedbed moist until the seedlings are well established. If the weather is very warm when you sow outdoors, you can mulch the seedbed with a light layer of straw or moistened burlap to keep in moisture. (Remove the burlap once seedlings appear.) When the seedlings are a few inches high, thin them to the spacing suggested on the seed packet, by cutting out unwanted plants with scissors. From this point on, direct-sown seeds just need regular garden care.

Sowing Seed Indoors: Sowing seed indoors is a bit more involved, but it usually provides great results.

To start, fill your chosen containers with growing medium. Tap the containers on a hard surface once or twice to settle the medium, then water them thoroughly and allow them to drain.

Use a ruler or other straightedge to make very shallow furrows in the surface of the moist medium. The furrows should be at least 2 inches apart and about twice as deep as the diameter of the seed you're going to sow there. (You can also check the seed packet for the recommended sowing depth.) Sow the seed thinly and evenly down the furrow. Press the seed very gently into the soil, and cover it lightly with more growing medium.

Another method is to sow the seed thinly and evenly over the entire soil surface. Lightly press the seed into the soil and cover it with about ⅛ inch of soil. If the seeds are very tiny, don't worry about covering them; pressing them lightly into the surface is enough.

After sowing, use a misting bottle to thoroughly moisten the surface. Label each container with the name of the seed it contains. To provide ideal conditions for sprouting, cover the containers with burlap, newspaper, or aluminum foil. For seeds that need light to germinate, use a clear plastic or glass covering.

Most seeds germinate best in warm soil temperatures, so place the containers in a warm area—for example, near a kitchen stove, radiator, or woodstove, or on top of the refrigerator. (Never place the pots or trays directly on or in front of a heat source, or the soil may dry out too quickly.) To be sure the growing medium stays at a consistently warm temperature, use an electric heating mat made specifically for starting seeds.

Once the seeds have sprouted, remove the covering for several hours each day. After a few days—or sooner, if you see any mold growing on the surface of the medium—take the cover off entirely.

When the seedlings appear, it's also time to reduce the soil temperature. Turn down the heating mat, or move the seedlings to a bright, but cooler spot. Most seedlings will grow well between 60° and 70°F. The exceptions are the cool-weather plants, including lettuce, spinach, onions, pansies, primroses, petunias, and snapdragons; they prefer growing temperatures between 50° and 60°F. Many gardeners believe that seedlings grow stronger and healthier if nighttime temperatures are 5° to 10°F lower than daytime temperatures.

For best growth, most seedlings need at least 12 to 16 hours of light each day. If there is not enough natural light available, seedlings will do fine under fluorescent light. Use the longest tubes possible to fit over the space you have provided for the growing seedlings. A double row of tubes is the best system and will emit enough light for a tray up to 16 inches wide. Hang the fixtures so the lights are 4 to 6 inches above the seedlings. Keep adjusting the height of the lights as the plants grow. Turn the lights off at night; plants also need darkness for proper development. If you like, you can set up a timer to turn the lights on and off automatically.

Thinning Out Seedlings: After the seedlings have developed at least two "true" leaves (those that appear after the first "seed" leaves), you can either thin them out to grow on in the germination container, or transplant them to a larger growing container. If the seedlings are not thinned or transplanted at this time, they will begin to crowd each other, resulting in weak, spindly plants. Overcrowded conditions can also cause poor air circulation around the plants, which may in turn lead to disease problems.

The best way to thin seedlings is to cut off the stems of unwanted plants at the soil level with scissors. That way, you won't disturb the root growth of the remaining seedlings. Always select the largest, strongest, and healthiest-looking seedlings to remain.

Remove enough seedlings so the remaining ones have at least 1 inch between them (more for larger plants). The remaining seedlings can then grow until they are ready to be transplanted into larger containers or directly into the garden.

Transplanting Seedlings: Seedlings are ready to be transplanted when they have developed two to four true leaves. Once they have reached this stage, they need more space to grow; without the additional space, they'll become leggy and weak. Depending on the plant, they can be transplanted to a larger container or directly into the garden.

Transplanting seedlings into deeper containers will help ensure stronger plants and good root systems. Seedlings that were started in large individual containers do not need transplanting before going directly into garden beds.

Before transplanting, thoroughly water the seedlings. Fill the transplanting container with premoistened growing medium. Prepare a planting hole in the middle of the medium that is large enough to hold the entire root system of the seedling. Next, take a fork or spoon and gently lift up the seedlings to be transplanted. Carefully separate the tiny plants, disturbing the roots as little as possible. Lift each seedling gently by the leaves—never by the stem—and set it in its planting hole. If the seedlings are leggy, plant them a bit deeper than they were in the germination container. Pat the soil medium back into the hole around the roots; it is important that the roots have proper contact with the soil. Label each new container with a waterproof marker.

Water the transplants as necessary to keep the soil evenly moist. Apply a liquid fertilizer about once a week at half the recommended strength. Keep the young plants in bright sunlight or under fluorescent lighting.

Hardening Off Seedlings: Transplants need to be hardened off before being planted directly outdoors. Hardening off plants is the process of gradually acclimating indoor-grown plants to tougher outdoor conditions. It takes anywhere from one to two weeks, depending on the plant and your climate.

Start the process around the last frost date. (Check the seed packet or the plant portraits in Part Two of this book for the best timing for specific plants.) The plants should have developed at least six true leaves by this time. Place them outdoors during the daytime, in a sheltered area that is out of the wind and direct sunlight. For the first two or three days, keep the plants outdoors for about 3 hours, then bring them back in. After this period, keep them outside for about 5 hours each day for the next several days. Make sure they are well watered and protected from any animal pests.

If the plants seem to be doing well at this point, leave them out all day and night. (Move them to a sunny spot if they are full-sun plants.) If frost threatens while you are hardening off your plants, bring them indoors overnight. After the last frost date, move the hardened-off plants to the garden.

Planting Your Garden

Now that you have a good collection of healthy plants, you're ready to get them in the ground. If you can, choose an overcast day for planting so the plants are less stressed while they're adjusting to their new growing conditions. If the soil is very dry, water the area a day or two before planting. Also, water container plants thoroughly before planting.

Set the plants out at the proper spacing, arranged according to how you had them on your garden plan. Avoid the temptation to overplant to get an instant, more mature, garden effect. If the plants have good growing conditions, they will quickly fill in their allotted space, and you will have a better-looking and healthier garden in the long run.

For easiest planting, start at the back of the garden and work toward the front. Set boards over the area to walk and kneel on so you don't compact the soil.

Setting Out Container-Grown Plants: To remove a plant from a container, set one hand over the top of the pot, with the plant's stems between your fingers. Turn the pot over so it is resting on your first hand, then use your other hand to pull off the container. If the plant's roots are circling around the outside of the container, use your fingers to gently untangle and loosen them.

If you are setting out plants in peat pots or peat pellets, you can plant the entire pot directly into the ground. With peat pots, however, it's best to peel off the upper rim and use a sharp knife to cut a few slits in the sides to help roots grow out.

Use a trowel or shovel to dig a hole about half again as wide as the root area and a little deeper. The hole should accommodate the root system of the plant without bending the roots. The plant should sit as deep in the ground as it did in the container before planting. (If the plant is a bit leggy, you can set it slightly deeper for better support.) Fill around the roots with the soil you removed from the hole. Firm the soil lightly, then water thoroughly.

If the soil needs a fertility boost, scatter some compost or a balanced fertilizer near the base of each plant after planting. Always follow the package directions for the exact amount needed. Never add fertilizer—especially chemical fertilizers—directly into the planting hole, since it can burn the roots. After you've planted the whole area, add a layer of mulch to the bed.

Planting Bareroot Perennials: Plant out bareroot perennials by digging a hole large enough to hold all the roots without bending them. Build a little cone or pyramid of soil inside the planting hole so that the top of the mound is just even with the soil surface. Set the crown of the plant (the point where the roots meet the stem) on top of this mound, and spread the roots evenly over the sides. Fill around the roots with soil, making sure you get good contact between the soil and the roots. After planting, water thoroughly and mulch.

MULCHING

Mulch is an essential part of successful gardening. It can be any material that you spread over a garden area to help retain soil moisture, moderate soil temperatures, prevent soil erosion, and keep weeds down. Mulch materials are usually divided into two groups: inorganic and organic. Inorganic mulches include black and clear plastic sheeting and polyester landscape fabrics. Organic mulches include materials such as compost, grass clippings, straw, and bark. The kind you choose will depend on what you want it to do and where you want to use it.

Inorganic mulches are very effective for keeping the soil moist and weeds smothered, but they are not very attractive. Plastic mulches can also be harmful around permanent plantings. Recent research indicates that the roots of many plants, such as trees and shrubs, do not grow as deep or as well under plastic mulches as they do under landscape fabric or an organic mulch. This can lead to shallow-rooted trees that are more likely to blow over in high winds. And shallow rooted plants in general are less drought-tolerant, since roots near the surface will dry out and die faster than roots extending deeper into the soil. Over time, plastic mulches can also encourage fungal disease problems and reduce soil oxygen levels.

Plastic and fabric mulches can be handy if you use them properly. For example, you can use black plastic for the vegetable garden to provide nice, warm growing beds for heat-loving crops such as sweet potatoes, peppers, eggplants, and squash. Use landscape fabric around trees and shrubs, and cover it with an attractive organic mulch, such as shredded bark or pine needles. But if you decide to use landscape fabric, keep in mind that it is difficult or impossible to remove around trees and shrubs because plant roots grow up into the fabric. Removing it damages roots.

In most parts of the garden, organic mulches are your best choice. Not only do they look very natural, they also add nutrients and organic matter to the soil as they break down. Pine needles will help to keep the soil acidic, so they are an ideal mulch for acid-loving plants such as rhododendrons, azaleas, and camellias. Straw is great for vegetable gardens, but it's too coarse for ornamental plantings. Shredded bark, wood chips, and compost mulches blend in well in many garden settings.

Applying Mulch: Before mulching, prepare the area by removing any existing weeds. Water thoroughly if the soil is dry.

Spread organic mulches about 2 to 3 inches deep around annuals, perennials, and vegetables, and 3 to 4 inches deep around trees and shrubs. Leave a few inches between plant stems and the mulch. Some settling will occur after you first apply the mulch; replenish the mulch as needed throughout the year to maintain the proper depth. For wintertime protection in northern zones, you can apply a deeper layer of mulch in late fall. Just be sure to remove the extra winter layer in early spring as the weather warms up.

If you are using black plastic in your vegetable garden, spread it over the prepared area several weeks before planting. (To make later watering easier, install a drip irrigation system before applying the plastic. For information on drip irrigation, see "Watering" on page 486.

When you are ready to plant, make slits—in the form of a cross—where you want to set transplants in the ground. Plant the transplants in the center of each cross, and water well.

When using a landscape fabric, lay it in strips around plantings of trees, shrubs, and roses. Leave a few inches of unmulched space around the base of each plant for good root growth. Mulch piled around plant stems can also cause disease problems. Top the fabric with a layer of organic mulch to help it last longer and to make it look more natural.

FERTILIZING

If you have been amending your soil regularly with compost and other organic matter, it is on its way to becoming naturally fertile. However, even with naturally fertile soil, there are times when plants need a boost of fertilizer for proper growth and development. For example, if you grow corn in the same place for several years, the area may be low in nitrogen, since corn is a heavy nitrogen user. To fertilize effectively, you need to know what kinds of nutrients to apply, the best time to apply them, and how much to use.

Deciding If You Need to Fertilize: Too much fertilizer can be as bad as too little, so don't be tempted to apply it just on general principles. It is difficult to determine exactly which nutrients your soil may be deficient in unless you have it professionally tested in a lab. Ideally, you should do a soil test when you are planning the garden and preparing the soil for planting. But if you didn't do it then, or if it's been a few years since you tested the soil and the plants look like they may need some help, take samples for testing now. Contact your county Cooperative Extension Service office for directions on how and where to send soil samples for testing. The results will indicate any nutrient imbalances and give recommendations on how to correct them.

Even if you have fertile soil, there may be times when your plants could use a nutrient boost, depending on the weather and on the particular kinds of plants. Container plants often need frequent fertilizing, since the space available for their roots is limited. If you notice any plants with yellowish or bronzy leaves, fewer-than-normal flowers, or particularly slow growth, try giving them a dose of liquid fertilizer to see if they perk up.

In general, trees and shrubs don't need extra fertilizer unless the soil is poor. Annual flowering plants and vegetables need more fertilizer than perennials. Lawn and ornamental grasses usually benefit from some additional nitrogen each year. Herbs, native plants, and wildflowers need very little, if any, fertilizer, especially if they are growing in fair to good soil.

Understanding Your Fertilizer Options: Fertilizers come in many different forms. They may be derived from organic materials or synthetic; they can be solid or liquid. Each kind has advantages and disadvantages. Organic gardeners only use fertilizers that are derived from organic materials.

Pound for pound, manures, compost, and other bulky organic materials supply less nitrogen, phosphorus, and potassium than chemical fertilizers. They also release their nutrients much more slowly. However, organic fertilizers provide a good balance of many different kinds of nutrients. They also add organic matter, which naturally promotes good soil structure and drainage. Yearly additions of these materials to already-fertile soils usually provide enough nutrients to grow most garden plants.

For a slightly more concentrated nutrient source, you can apply processed organic fertilizers. These materials include blood meal, bonemeal, fish meal, cotton-seed meal, and hoof-and-horn meal. While processed organic fertilizers break down fairly slowly in the soil, they release their nutrients faster than nonprocessed organic fertilizers.

Synthetic (chemical) fertilizers release their nutrients in a matter of hours or days, instead of weeks or months for some organic fertilizers. A scattering of balanced chemical fertilizer applied several times during the growing season will provide fast-growing vegetables, annual flowers, and container plants with nutrients immediately. You can also buy slow release chemical fertilizers, which break down gradually over the season to provide a steady supply of nutrients.

If your plants need a fast-acting nutrient boost, a dose of liquid fertilizer may be in order. Use a liquid-form organic fertilizer, such as fish emulsion or seaweed extract, or a chemical fertilizer that is made to dissolve quickly in water. Mix the materials according to package directions and spray them on the leaves of your plants. The plants will absorb the nutrients through their leaves and put them to use right away. In most cases, you'll notice improved growth within days. Liquid fertilizers are good for a quick fix or midsummer boost, but don't rely on them completely for fertilizing your plants. Concentrate on improving the natural fertility of the soil so your plants won't need this special treatment repeatedly.

Buying Fertilizers: Any fertilizer on the market must provide information about its N-P-K ratio, that is, the percentage of nitrogen (N), phosphorus (P), and potassium (K) it contains. When the three numbers are the same, such as 5-5-5 or 10-10-10, the fertilizer is said to be "balanced." If one number is higher than the others, as in 20-10-10, then you know that the fertilizer contains a higher concentration of that particular nutrient (in this case, nitrogen). This kind of fertilizer is useful if you know your soil is low in a certain nutrient. Organic fertilizers have a lower nutrient analysis than chemical fertilizers and will be marked as "certified organic" or "organic."

Besides indicating the balance of nutrients, the N-P K ratio also tells you how many pounds of nutrients the material contains. For example, if you have a 100-pound bag of fertilizer that is marked 20-10-10, this means there are 20 pounds of nitrogen, 10 pounds of phosphorus, and 10 pounds of potassium. The rest of the ingredients are "filler" materials.

Deciding When to Fertilize: Fertilize your garden beds naturally each fall by incorporating compost, shredded leaves, grass clippings, or manure (or a combination of these) into the soil. These materials will break down over the winter and release nutrients for spring planting.

Spring is a good time to apply more fertilizer if your soil needs extra nutrients. (Have a soil test done if you're not sure.) When preparing beds for planting, work in organic or chemical fertilizers as needed. Feed established perennials and roses with a balanced, slow-release fertilizer when they first begin to grow in early spring. At the same time, fertilize rhododendrons, azaleas, and other acid-loving plants with an acidic fertilizer, such as cottonseed meal.

After setting out annual, perennial, and vegetable transplants, give them a dose of a liquid fertilizer high in phosphorus to help them develop a good root system quickly. Vegetables and annual flowers benefit from an additional application of fertilizer during the growing season. Scatter a balanced granular fertilizer around the plants and scratch it into the top ½ inch of soil. Do not put fertilizer directly on the leaves or stems, as it can "burn" the plants.

During the growing season, give container plantings and other fast-growing plants a dose of liquid fertilizer if they need a nutrient boost. Stop fertilizing all plants by late summer. Otherwise you may encourage them to produce tender new growth that won't have time to harden off before cold weather arrives.

Applying Fertilizers: When applying packaged fertilizer, always follow the label directions for exact application amounts. It's better to apply fast-acting chemical fertilizers in several small doses than in one large dose. Use a measuring cup to scatter the right amount of chemical fertilizer around each plant. If you're fertilizing with compost or other bulky organic materials, the amounts don't have to be as exact; just apply a 1- to 3-inch layer over the area, and dig or till it into the soil.

When working with dry fertilizers, wear gloves to protect your hands and a mask to avoid breathing the dust. Apply liquid fertilizers with a hand mister or pump sprayer to thoroughly cover the leaves.

APPLYING ORGANIC FERTILIZERS

Chemical fertilizers are generally sold in tidy, labeled boxes or bags, so it is easy to find out how much to apply. But if you're dealing with organic fertilizers, it's not so easy to tell. Here are some guidelines to help you:

Alfalfa Meal: 40 to 50 pounds per 1,000 square feet

Animal Manure: 30 pounds per 1,000 square feet

Blood Meal: 10 to 30 pounds per 1,000 square feet

Compost: 1- to 3-inch layer

Cottonseed Meal: 20 to 30 pounds per 1,000 square feet

Earthworm Castings: 8 pounds per 1,000 square feet

Fish Emulsion: 2 ounces per gallon of water to cover 1,000 square feet (repeat 2 or 3 times during the season)

Fish Meal: 20 pounds per 1,000 square feet

Granite Dust: 10 pounds per 1,000 square feet

Seaweed Extract: 1 ounce per gallon of water to cover 1,000 square feet

WATERING

Improper watering is the number one cause of garden plant deaths. Plants use water for all of their vital functions. The roots need water so they can absorb dissolved nutrients. Plant stems and foliage need water to remain upright and transport food within the plant. Plants also use water to keep themselves cool in summer.

Water requirements can vary widely, depending largely on the soil, the plant, and the weather. Clay or loam soils retain more water than sandy soil, so they don't require as much watering. Mulched soil of any kind will stay moist much longer than bare soil.

Most plants thrive when the soil is evenly moist, but some can tolerate either extreme. For example, rose moss (*Portulaca grandiflora*) and coneflowers (*Echinacea* and *Rudbeckia* spp.) thrive under the hot, dry conditions that would cause a meltdown for plants like impatiens, ferns, and roses. You took these different needs into consideration when you were choosing plants for your garden. But during periods of high heat mixed with little rainfall, even drought-tolerant plants may need a little extra watering.

When to Water: Plants respond much better if given one good deep watering when the soil surface becomes dry, rather than frequent, light waterings. The only exception is seeds, whether started indoors or out—they do require frequent watering so that the soil surface doesn't dry out. Young transplants also need more frequent watering than established plants for the first several weeks after planting.

Most garden plants do fine with about 1 inch of water per week, either from rainfall or irrigation. If there is not enough natural rainfall, a sprinkler or irrigation system left on for about 1 hour should be enough each week. To check how long it takes for your sprinkler to emit 1 inch of water, set a coffee can in the garden. To check a drip irrigation system or soaker hose, set a can into the ground below part of the hose. Turn on the water at the tap and let it run until there is 1 inch of water in the can. If plants are spaced very close together, as in an intensively planted vegetable bed, allow the water to run an extra 20 minutes or so. If you notice puddles building up, stop watering in that area until the extra water drains off.

Throughout the growing season, you may need to water your garden plants about once a week if rain is lacking. During very hot weather, water whenever the top 1 inch of soil is dry. Drought-tolerant plants can get by with less water; experiment to find out exactly how much they need to survive.

The best time of day to water is either early morning or late evening. If you water in the late morning or afternoon, you will lose a lot of water to evaporation Watering in the middle of a hot, sunny day can also scald and discolor foliage. Plants susceptible to fungal problems, like roses and delphiniums, should be watered in the morning so the foliage doesn't remain damp throughout the night. However, if you notice any plants wilting due to lack of moisture, water them immediately! If you must water plants in the middle of the day, water at soil level to reduce leaf scald.

How to Water: The home gardener can choose from among many different kinds of irrigation equipment. For example, a sprinkling can or hose-attached mist nozzle is fine for watering seedbeds, container plantings, and hanging baskets, and for emergency spot watering.

Overhead sprinklers are best suited for lawns. They are not recommended for ornamental or vegetable gardens, because they lose a lot of water to evaporation. They also get the foliage wet, which can lead to plant disease problems.

A soaker hose or drip irrigation system, or a combination of the two, is the best choice for giving garden plants a regular deep watering at soil level. Drip irrigation involves using a main hose with emitters or special valves that connect to a network of attached tubes. These tubes emit water directly into the root area of plants. Soaker hoses are simply garden hoses that are porous throughout their entire length. Soakers are especially efficient for watering vegetable and flower gardens, and are usually spaced about 2 feet apart. Both drip systems and soaker hoses can be buried under mulch.

STAKING

Tall or floppy plants like tomatoes, peonies, dahlias, sunflowers, and hollyhocks need support as they grow. Staking will extend the life of these plants by preventing the stems from breaking due to wind or rain. Staking plants will also give your garden a more well-groomed and tidy appearance. There are two kinds of staking: peripheral and single.

Peripheral staking involves setting a circle of supports around a clump or group of plants. These are usually plants that grow fairly tall but have thin or sprawling stems, such as peonies, snapdragons, and tomatoes. Metal cages, which come in a range of sizes, are probably the easiest and most effective way to stake a wide variety of flowering plants and vegetables. The cages are hidden by leaves as the plants grow.

If you don't have cages, you can make your own out of stakes and twine. While the plants are still young, space four or five stakes evenly around the clump, and hammer them into the ground. Attach strong twine to one of the stakes, near the base, and string it around the other stakes to enclose the clump. As the plants grow, continue adding twine further up the stakes and around the plant clump. You can also place twine diagonally within the staked area for further support. As the plants mature, they will eventually cover the twine and stakes. Single staking is best for supporting very tall plants, as well as plants with very large flowers, such as sunflowers, delphiniums, dahlias, and hollyhocks. Set a tall, sturdy stake next to the plant just as it begins to grow. Hammer the stake about 6 inches into the ground and roughly 3 inches away from the center of the plant. As the plant grows, tie the stem to the stake every foot or so with twine or plant ties. Be careful not to crush the stem as you tie it.

Staking should be as inconspicuous as possible. Dark-colored metal, wooden, or bamboo stakes are excellent for any style of staking. Twiggy branches stuck in the ground around clumps of plants also work well for support and give a lovely, English-cottage look to the garden.

PINCHING AND DEADHEADING

Pinching controls the shape of your plants, especially those that have leafy stems and a somewhat bushy habit, such as coleus, petunias, phlox, basil, and mint. To make these plants look fuller, pinch off the shoot tips several times during the season. To prevent your chrysanthemums from flowering too early, keep pinching off the flower buds until midsummer.

Deadheading, which involves removing spent flowers and developing seedpods, is another important technique for keeping plants looking their best. Take a box or bucket and a pair of garden shears with you every time you walk through your garden, and pinch or cut off dead flowers and new seedpods. (When you've collected a few, toss them into the compost pile.) This will encourage your plants to produce more blooms and will keep the garden looking fresh. And by deadheading herbs, you can encourage them to produce more of their desirable leaves. Deadheading can also help cut down on disease problems in the garden. Do not deadhead if you want to save seed, or if you want flowers such as cleome, foxgloves, and hollyhocks to self sow for next year.

PROPAGATING PERENNIALS

Once you've been bitten by the gardening bug, you'll probably want to grow more and more plants. But while your desire for more plants may be unlimited, your budget probably isn't. The solution? Grow your own plants!

You may already be raising your own annual and vegetable transplants from seed. The same techniques will work for growing a wide range of wonderful perennials. (For a review, see "Start Your Own Plants from Seed" beginning on page 461.) You can also propagate perennials using other methods, including division, cuttings, and layering. The advantage of these three options is that they will give you plants that are identical to the original plants. Seedlings often look similar, but can vary somewhat in height and color.

Dividing: One of the easiest ways to propagate perennial plants is to simply dig them up and divide them. Besides giving you more plants, division will keep your garden from getting crowded and overgrown. Most ornamental perennials—including bulbs, ornamental grasses, and groundcovers—need to be (or at least benefit from being) divided every three to four years.

The best time of year to divide is in early spring, just after the plants have begun to grow again, or in the fall. To reduce plant stress, try to divide on overcast days. Water the area around the plants you want to divide. Take a shovel or spading fork and dig around each plant. As you dig, try not to disturb the root system of the plant too much.

Lift up the entire rootball area of the plant and shake off as much soil as possible. Usually, the rootball will naturally divide itself as you begin to gently pull it apart with your hands or cut it in half with a sharp knife. An easy way to separate larger rootballs is to stick two pitchforks into the middle of the rootball area so they are both pointing outward in opposite directions. Then gently pull the handles in opposite directions— the rootball should come right apart. Repeat as needed. For really tough rootballs, such as those of big ornamental grasses, you may need to use an ax to chop the pieces apart.

Depending on how large the rootball is, you should get two to four good-sized divisions—maybe more, if the plant hasn't been divided for many years. Make sure each section has some roots and some buds or top growth. Replant divisions as soon as possible, according to their recommended spacing. If the plant has top growth, cut it back by about a third. Mix a little phosphorus into the planting holes, set one clump in each hole, and water thoroughly. If you're dividing in the spring, top-dress with a balanced fertilizer.

If you don't have the time to replant your extra divisions, pot them up and keep them watered until you can plant them. If you don't need them, pot them up and give them away to your gardening friends and neighbors. Many church, school, or horticultural organizations would welcome your extra plants for their spring plant sales!

Hardy bulbs such as tulips, daffodils, hyacinths, snowdrops, and crocuses can be divided after flowering, when the foliage is turning yellow and the bulbs are going dormant. If you cut into or scrape the bulbs as you dig them up, throw them away; they'll probably rot anyway. Gently pull apart the bulbs and the roots. Replant them at the proper depth and spacing.

Tender bulbs, corms, and tubers should also be divided as they go dormant in the fall. But instead of replanting them right away, allow them to dry, then place them in containers or paper bags filled with peat moss or sand. Label all of the containers with the bulb name and color. Store them in a cool, dry, frost-free area until it's time to replant in spring.

Taking Cuttings: When you want to propagate a plant but don't want to dig it up or disturb its root system, you can take cuttings from the shoot tip or the stems. Tip cuttings include the top growing point of the plant. Stem cuttings take part of the stem without the top growing point.

Take cuttings of perennial plants starting in early to late spring. Tip and stem cuttings should be 4 to 6 inches long, depending on the size of the plant (short cuttings from shorter plants, and long ones from taller plants). Make the cuts at a 45-degree angle using a clean, sharp knife or razor blade. (Wipe the blade with rubbing alcohol to sterilize it before cutting.) Strip the leaves from the lower half of each cutting, leaving two to four sets of leaves. Also, remove flowers and seedpods from tip cuttings. Work quickly, before the cuttings wilt. To keep the cuttings from wilting, you can mist them frequently as you're preparing them.

Some propagators like to dip the base of cuttings into a rooting hormone powder before sticking them into the rooting medium. Plants will root without the hormone, but it can stimulate the development of a vigorous root system. Rooting hormone powders are readily available from most garden centers.

Stick prepared cuttings into a container filled with moistened vermiculite or perlite, or a 50/50 combination of the two. Use a pencil to make a hole in the medium for each cutting. Set the bottom third to half of the stem in the hole, and gently firm the medium around it. Space the cuttings far enough apart so they aren't touching. After you've set all the cuttings in the medium, water and mist them. Then cover the container with a tent of clear plastic to keep the humidity level high. If necessary, support the plastic with stakes or wire hoops so it doesn't rest on the cuttings. Place the covered container in a warm and partially shaded area; avoid exposing the cuttings to direct sunlight.

Depending on the plant, the cuttings should begin to form roots in two to three weeks. You can check on their progress by tugging on them lightly—the more resistance there is, the greater the root development. Once the cuttings have begun to develop a strong, vigorous root system with roots over 2 inches long, you can transplant them into the garden or into a container with a soilless potting mixture. To get them off to a good start, feed them with a dilute dose of liquid fertilizer.

Growing Root Cuttings: Some perennials—including Oriental poppy (*Papaver orientale*), hardy geraniums (*Geranium* spp.), and garden phlox (*Phlox paniculata*)—can even grow new plants from root pieces. For most plants that can be propagated this way, it's best to take cuttings in early spring, when the plants are eager to start growing again. (Propagate Oriental poppy in summer, while it is dormant.) Unpot or dig up the plant that you'll be propagating. You don't need to sacrifice the mother plant for root cuttings, as long as you leave about half of the roots and cut back about a third to half of its top growth (if it has any). Be sure to use a clean, sharp knife to do the cuttings.

For plants with very fine, hairlike roots, cut the root pieces into 2- to 4-inch sections and scatter them directly onto a wellprepared soil bed outdoors, or into a tray filled with a soilless potting mixture. Lightly cover the pieces with about ½ inch of the soil or potting medium, and gently water with a fine-mist nozzle. Keep the area well moistened until the roots begin to form plantlets.

For larger and fleshier roots, such as those from Oriental poppies and plume poppies, dig up the plants and cut the roots with a sharp, clean knife into sections about 3 inches long. Stick them into a rooting medium of equal parts perlite and soilless potting mixture. Stick the roots into the mixture vertically, with the root end that was closest to the center of the plant sticking about ¼ inch out of the medium. Keep the cuttings well moistened and misted. Once the roots have formed leafy growth, plant them where they are to grow, or hold them over in a coldframe during the winter and plant them out the following spring.

Layering: Whether you know it or not, you may already be propagating plants in your garden by layering. Many plants—including roses, sedums, azaleas, rhododendrons, and clematis—propagate themselves naturally through layering.

Layering occurs when one of a plant's branches touches the soil and eventually forms roots. You can mimic this natural process quite easily with plants that have sprawling or vining stems. Gently bend a stem until part of it behind the tip touches the ground.

(Don't bend the branch sharply, or you may break it or cut off nutrients and water to the growing area.)

Take a knife or razor blade and slightly nick the bottom section of the branch where it touches the soil. Cover the nicked section with 2 to 3 inches of soil. If necessary, place a rock over the soil to hold the branch down. It usually takes at least several months for enough roots to form so you can cut the branch away from the mother plant. At that point, you can dig up the new plant to transplant it, or just leave it where it is to add to the existing planting.

CONTROLLING WEEDS

Weeds are to gardeners what mosquitoes are to campers—pesky intruders that make an otherwise pleasant pursuit an unpleasant experience indeed. In the war against weeds, you need to be vigilant, or else they will quickly claim victory in your garden.

The best way to get the upper hand with weeds is to stop them early in the season. Take some time to weed thoroughly in early spring, when weeds begin to come up. Follow by adding or replenishing mulch to a depth of about 2 to 3 inches around established and new plants. If weeds are a particular problem in a garden bed or pathway, lay landscape fabric over the area and cover that with a few inches of organic mulch.

To keep ahead of weeds before they become large and numerous, make it a practice to weed all garden areas at least once a week. The easiest time to weed is when the ground has dried out slightly after a rain or after the area has been irrigated. Take a sharp, long-handled hoe and rake it firmly across the soil surface over weeds; smaller weeds should come right out of the ground. Hoe harder under larger weeds, or hand-pull them. If it is a sunny day, you can leave pulled weeds where they are—the sun and heat will dry out the roots. Or, if you want to be tidy, gather the weeds and add them to the compost pile.

Some weeds have deep roots that allow them to survive a simple hoeing; when you hoe off the top, the root will just send up another batch of leaves and flowers. For weeds with long taproots, such as dandelions and thistles, use a trowel or taproot weeder. A taproot weeder has a long, metal probe that is perfect for digging down under the base of the plant and pulling up the entire root.

Chemical weed killers, known as herbicides, can be used to eliminate large weedy areas or individual weeds. Herbicides do save considerable labor and time. However, they can also harm microorganisms in the soil, contaminate groundwater, and injure fish and other wildlife if they end up in rivers, streams, and ponds. Avoid using herbicides unless you have a very severe weed problem that you can't control any other way. Organic gardeners stay away from nearly all commercial herbicides with the exception of soap sprays.

There are two types of herbicides: selective and nonselective. Selective herbicides are used mostly by large-scale farmers and kill only certain types of weeds or grasses. Nonselectives, in various concentrations, will kill any plant. They are popular for controlling weeds in patios and pathways where you don't want weeds to grow.

You can apply herbicides directly onto plant foliage or onto the soil. Preemergent herbicides are applied to the soil to kill weed seeds before they sprout. They are usually applied in the spring or early summer, after the garden has been planted and mulched.

Always read the label to make sure the herbicide will control the kinds of weeds you want it to. When applying herbicides, follow the exact directions on the label and wear protective clothing, such as a long-sleeved shirt, long pants, rubber gloves, rubber boots, and goggles. Never apply herbicides on a windy day, as they can drift off and damage nearby plants. If you've treated an area with herbicides and have composted the weeds, do not use this compost for at least one to two months, to allow the herbicide time to break down. Most important, make sure herbicides are clearly labeled as poisonous, and keep them out of children's reach.

WINTERIZING THE GARDEN

The process of getting your garden ready for winter starts while you are still enjoying the late-summer sun. At this time, stop fertilizing and decrease watering so plants will grow more slowly and stop producing new growth. Also, in all areas but Zones 9 to 11, stop pinching back plants; otherwise, new growth may be damaged by an early frost.

In fall, weed the garden beds one last time. Dig up and compost frost-nipped annuals. (Be sure to discard any diseased plants.) Cut perennial leaves and stems to the ground, and rake all of the old plant parts out of the bed to help prevent disease and insect problems next year. Lift tender bulbs, such as dahlias and glads, for indoor storage. To build up the soil for spring planting next year, add compost or other organic matter to the vegetable garden and annual flower beds.

Right after the ground freezes, apply or replenish a

winter layer of mulch over perennials and bulbs to keep the cycles of freezing and thawing from pushing the plants out of the ground. Evergreen boughs are excellent for this purpose, and they are easy to clear away in the spring before plants begin to grow and flower.

Winterizing your garden doesn't have to mean an end to your garden enjoyment. You may decide to leave some plants in the garden all winter so you can enjoy their attractive seed heads or berries. If you leave tall ornamental grasses standing until early spring, you can admire their lovely straw color against the snow and listen to the sound of the wind swirling through them. While you're appreciating the garden from the warmth and comfort of indoors, grab your notebook and seed catalogs, and start thinking about your great new plans for next year!

CHAPTER TWELVE

TOOLS AND EQUIPMENT

There's no way around it: great gardens take hard work. Fortunately, you can make that work as painless as possible by using high-quality tools and equipment made for the job at hand.

BUYING THE RIGHT TOOLS

How can you tell the difference between a good-quality tool and an average or poor one? For starters, check the price. A very low-priced tool is probably low in quality, too. If you see three shovels at varying prices from the same place, you're usually better off buying one of the higher-priced models. Chances are, it will last longer and therefore be less expensive in the long run.

The second thing you should check is the weight of the tool. A heavier tool is often better than a lighter one, because higher grades of metal are heavier. If you aren't especially strong, however, you may prefer lightweight tools. To be sure you get a good tool, regardless of its weight, check the label: It should say that the tool is made from "tempered," "heat-treated," or "forged" metal. Buy stainless steel metal tools if you can afford them. Although they are the most expensive, they won't rust and are an excellent investment if you plan to use them for many years.

The third step is to see how the metal tool is attached to the handle. The best-quality tools have a "solid shank," "solid socket," or "solid strap" handle construction, which means that the whole metal part of the tool is one piece. Also, make sure the metal part of the tool is secured to the handle with rivets. If it isn't, the tool head may pop off the handle when you're doing heavy work.

Next, take a good look at the handle. The best tools usually have all-wooden handles. Ash and hickory are the preferred types of wood; avoid buying tools with handles made of Douglas fir, which is a poor-quality wood. Also, make sure there are no knots, cracks, or flaws in the wood.

Finally, "try on" the tool before you buy it. Try out the weight of the tool, as well as the feel of the handle. Look for handles that fit your hand well and are comfortable. If you're looking at trowels or other ground-level tools, check that the grip area of the handle is long enough so you won't scrape your hand against the ground when you use the tool. For longer-handled tools like hoes, shovels, and rakes, buy the handle size that matches your height best.

KEEPING TOOLS IN TOP SHAPE

Once you find the right tools, you'll want to make them last. Carefully collect and clean off all garden tools after you are finished for the day, then place them in a dry, well-organized garden storage shed or garage. Before storing the tools, be sure to wipe off all metal parts with an oiled cloth to keep them rust-free. Keep a sharpening stone or hand file in the storage area for regular tool and blade sharpenings, or have the tools professionally sharpened once or twice a year.

No matter how careful you are, it's almost inevitable that you'll misplace tools at one time or another. One way to prevent this from happening is to paint all the tool handles a bright color. They'll be easier to spot lying around your yard, and they'll also be easier to identify if you loan them out to neighbors or friends.

STARTING YOUR TOOL COLLECTION

What are the basic tools every gardener needs? And how do you know which tools are best for which jobs? In gardening, there are four primary kinds of tools: digging, weeding, raking, and pruning. It's also handy to have a wheelbarrow or garden cart, watering equipment, and a few other miscellaneous items. As you gain more experience, you may need or want to acquire more specialized garden tools. However, the following tools should suffice for most gardening tasks.

DIGGING TOOLS

The essential digging tools all gardeners should have include a trowel, spade, shovel, and short-handled spading fork.

Trowel: A good trowel is indispensable for planting, transplanting, and smaller plant-dividing jobs. The sturdiest trowels are of one-piece construction and have a stainless steel blade. Trowels come in regular and narrow sizes. Narrow trowels are useful for digging between closely spaced plants and for planting bulbs. Some trowels have inches marked along the blade to help you gauge how deep to plant various bulbs.

Spade: A spade has straight sides and a rectangular shape with a sharp, flat edge. For some jobs—such as digging, planting, and transplanting perennials, trees, and shrubs—spades and shovels can be used interchangeably. But a spade is the tool of choice for jobs where a sharp, clean cut is important, such as when you need to lift sod, edge beds, or work in closely planted areas to divide or transplant larger plants. A spade is also the best tool for digging into compacted soil or into beds with large roots from nearby trees or shrubs. If you can't afford to buy both a spade and a shovel, purchase the spade, which is more versatile.

Look for a spade with a "Y-D" handle. This type of handle, which divides at the top and is linked by a horizontal grip at the end, gives you a better grip than "T" handles. The spade should be solidly constructed, with a stainless steel or carbon-steel blade. Stainless steel can be expensive but is the best. The carbon-steel blade is just about as good and should also last a lifetime. Keep the blade sharp so it will be easier to use.

Shovel: Shovels are useful for larger digging and lifting jobs, such as digging up large beds, removing soil from an area, filling in soil around newly planted trees or shrubs, working compost into a bed, or moving sand, cement, or other material from one area to another.

Shovels come in long- and short-handled types. The long-handled ones are used for most garden tasks, since they give greater leverage and require less stooping than short-handled shovels. The highest-quality shovels are made from high-carbon, heat-treated steel with a forged construction.

The most useful type is probably the round-point shovel. Scoop shovels are larger, yet more lightweight and are used primarily for scooping up lighter-weight materials, such as sawdust, dry compost, manure, and leaves.

Short-Handled Spading Fork: This tool is indispensable for turning over already-loosened garden beds and for breaking up heavy soil and soil clods when you are preparing a site for planting. You can also use a spading fork for lifting and dividing bulbs and perennials, for lifting and moving dry materials such as hay and straw, and for digging up underground crops such as potatoes, peanuts, and beets.

A short-handled spading fork has four flat tines and is usually about 42 inches long. The best-quality ones are made from high-carbon tempered steel. Make sure the fork's tines have a bit of "spring" to them. This flexibility helps the tines absorb pressure so they won't get bent when you're digging into heavy or rocky soil.

A garden pitchfork is a slightly different type of fork that has slightly rounded and thinner tines. It is very useful for lifting lightweight, bulky materials such as hay, straw, and leaf mold.

WEEDING TOOLS

For many of us, weeding is the least enjoyable garden task. Fortunately, there are many tools you can use to make the job a little easier. Some of the most common "weed weapons" include a hoe, hand fork, and asparagus weeder.

Hoe: This ancient device is one of the most effective weeding tools and a good all-around garden tool. Use it to scrape weed seedlings from the soil and to hack out annual weeds and other fairly shallow-rooted weedy plants. You can also use a hoe to break up soil clods, cultivate already loosened soil, make furrows to plant seeds, or hill up soil around seedlings and plants. A scuffle hoe is a special type of weeding hoe with a double-edged blade that cuts on both the push and pull strokes.

Garden hoes come in long- and short-handled types. For most people, the long-handled kind is easier to use, because it requires less bending over.

Hand Fork: This tool is handy for both eliminating weeds and cultivating the soil when you are sitting or kneeling in the garden. It is also useful for pulling rocks, leaves, and other debris away from the base of plants.

Asparagus Weeder: This tool has a long, narrow metal shaft with a V-shaped blade at the bottom. It is very handy for getting rid of dandelions, dock, and other taprooted weeds in lawns and borders without disturbing the grass or other ornamental plantings. Insert the blade into the soil an inch or so from the weed, and push it down into the soil to pop out the weed. Be sure to get the entire root; otherwise, the remaining piece may sprout a new plant.

RAKING TOOLS

A variety of gardening tasks involve raking, including preparing beds for planting, cleaning debris out of garden beds, and, of course, cleaning up dropped leaves in fall. These tasks require two different kinds of rakes: a bow rake and a lawn rake.

Bow Rake: Once the soil in a planting area has been cultivated and broken up with other tools, a metal-toothed bow rake is the best tool for smoothing over the site and removing small sticks and stones from the surface. It is also useful for evenly scratching fertilizer, lime, or other soil amendments into the soil. Never use a bow rake on a lawn, as it can easily tear up the grass.

Before purchasing a rake, test it out to be sure the handle length and weight are comfortable for you.

Lawn Rake: A lawn rake ranks up there with a trowel and hoe as an essential garden tool. This fan- or broom-shaped rake is lighter than a bow rake and is useful for collecting leaves, grass clippings, twigs, and other light-weight lawn and garden debris.

Rubber-tipped lawn rakes are handy for removing debris in flower beds without harming the plants. Avoid purchasing plastic rakes, because they tend to break in cold weather. Bamboo lawn rakes are a better choice, since they are sturdy, inexpensive, and lightweight. They also have a natural "springy" feel to them.

PRUNING TOOLS

Pruning tools range from small handheld shears for cutting fresh flowers to large loppers and saws for pruning off tree and shrub limbs. High quality tools will help make your cutting chores much easier and safer than cheap tools. Essential pruning tools for most home gardens include hand pruners, long-handled loppers, hedge shears, and short-handled grass shears. If you prune trees and shrubs regularly, you should also have a pruning saw.

Hand Pruners: It's a good idea to carry pruning shears with you whenever you're out in the garden. You'll use them for innumerable tasks, from snipping off spent blooms and harvesting fresh flowers and herbs to trimming small twigs, cutting back perennials and roses, and snipping pieces of twine.

There are two types of hand pruners: bypass and anvil. The bypass type has two curved blades that cut like a pair of scissors. Anvil-type pruners have only one cutting blade, which cuts against a straight, flattened edge. Bypass types tend to make cleaner cuts, while anvil types give you better stability for cutting woody plant parts. Choose the kind that feels best to you.

Long-Handled Loppers: This tool gives you additional leverage and cutting strength for pruning small-to medium-size shrub and tree branches that are too large for hand pruners. The long handles extend your reach so that you don't have to step into a wide garden bed or use a ladder. Like hand pruners, long-handled loppers come in anvil and bypass types.

Hedge Shears: These are mostly used to prune and shape shrubs and to cut back or deadhead perennials. While hand pruners can be useful for cutting back one or two plants at a time, hedge shears are easier and faster to use for cutting back larger perennial plantings. This tool is also suitable for cutting back taller grasses or weeds where a lawn mower can't reach.

Short Handled Grass Shears: These shears are a smaller, one-hand version of hedge shears. They are used for cutting back grass along edgings, walkways, and borders, and around places where a lawn mower can't reach. If you have to do a lot of this kind of trimming in your garden, you may want to invest in electric- or battery-powered shears or string trimmers. (String trimmers are especially effective and easy to use; just use caution when working around the base of trees or shrubs, as the fast-spining plastic line can nick and damage the bark of woody plants.)

Pruning Saws: When loppers aren't big enough for a pruning job, you need a pruning saw or bow saw. These handheld tools will quickly cut through woody branches if you keep them sharp. They are both equally effective, although the pruning saw can sometimes be easier to maneuver when you're working around crowded stems.

WHEELBARROWS AND GARDEN CARTS

Wheelbarrows and carts are invaluable for moving heavy loads of soil mix, mulch, peat moss, compost, garden debris, gravel, and cement.

The single front wheel of a wheelbarrow makes it easier to maneuver than a garden cart, which has two wheels. There are generally two kinds of wheelbarrows available: those for professional construction jobs, and those for garden use. The construction types are heavier and sturdier and can support more weight than the lighter garden models. Unless you are unable to lift a heavier wheelbarrow, the professional kind is better, since it is more durable. No matter which kind of wheelbarrow you choose, make sure it has good bracing on the legs. Keep the wheel well oiled, and don't allow water to sit in metal wheelbarrows, or they may rust. Store wheelbarrows and carts in a dry location.

When using a wheelbarrow, be careful to keep the load

balanced; otherwise, it may tip over. If the load shifts and the wheelbarrow becomes difficult to control, just let it tip over; if you try to keep it upright, you may end up straining your back or other muscles. Also, to avoid back injury, never lift more than you can easily manage.

A garden cart allows you to carry heavy loads with more relative ease than a wheelbarrow, since the weight is distributed over two wheels instead of just one. Carts can usually hold more material than wheelbarrows, although they are more difficult to unload. Be careful when using them on inclines; a heavily loaded cart can easily push or pull you downhill!

WATERING TOOLS

The right kind of watering equipment will help ensure that your plants get the right amount of moisture and will help you conserve water. Equipment can range from a basic watering can to fancy, electrically timed drip irrigation systems. For the average home garden, you can get by with a watering can, a regular hose, and a soaker hose, plus a hose reel and hose guides, several hose nozzles, and possibly a sprinkler.

Watering Can: A galvanized steel watering can is both attractive and functional. Make sure the nozzle is fairly large so it doesn't clog up too much and so it can be cleaned out easily.

For many gardeners, a 2-gallon type is the easiest to lift when full. A smaller can with a misting nozzle is handy for watering freshly planted seeds and seedlings.

Watering cans are especially useful for watering container plantings in areas you can't reach easily with a hose.

Hoses: Garden hoses are made of many different materials, including rubber, nylon, vinyl, canvas, and polyester fabric. When buying hoses, keep in mind that the rubber types with good-quality fittings are the most durable. Avoid plastic hoses, which can crack or break in cold weather.

Soaker hoses look like regular garden hoses, except that they have small holes along their entire length. They are used to slowly deliver a steady flow of water at ground level or just under the soil surface. These hoses are easier to use than drip emitter systems, since they don't clog up as much as emitters do. Soaker hoses come in lengths of 25 to 500 feet. Place them in the garden permanently, or move them as necessary to water the entire garden. It is important to adjust the water pressure, since the hose may burst open if the pressure is too high. Start with a low water flow, then raise the pressure gradually until water is oozing out slowly over the whole length of the hose.

Hose Reels and Guides: While hoses are necessary for getting water to different parts of the garden, they can cause problems when they kink, knock over plants, or twist into knots. You can make your hoses much easier to manage with a hose reel and hose guides.

A hose reel keeps your hose neatly coiled in a roll, preventing it from getting knotted up and making it a much simpler task to wind up the hose when you're finished with it. Hose guides are metal or wooden stakes that are placed in strategic spots in the yard to guide hoses around plants and borders. As you drag the hoses around, the guides keep them from damaging your plants.

Nozzles: There are many kinds of hose nozzles to choose from. The best are those that allow you to adjust the flow of water at the free end of the hose. With fan-type nozzles, you can use a gentle spray for seedbeds and seedlings, and a stronger flow for irrigating more established plants. A watering wand can also make watering much easier. This long wand has a nozzle at one end and attaches to the hose at the other end. It is great for watering outdoor hanging baskets and for spot-watering hard-to-reach plants in wide borders. The wand also allows you to deliver water at soil level without getting the plants' foliage wet.

Sprinklers: Sprinklers are most useful for watering large lawns and gardens that need frequent irrigation. They are not as efficient as soaker hoses or drip irrigation systems for ornamental and vegetable gardens.

Oscillating sprinklers are handy for distributing water evenly over a wide swath of garden or lawn. Most of these sprinklers can cover about a 55-by-65-foot area. Avoid buying cheap models, since they tend to pause at the extremes of their arc and cause puddling at those spots.

Revolving sprinklers whirl water around a circular area. At high water-pressure levels, most revolving types can cover a 50-foot circular area. They can water a smaller area if you reduce the water pressure.

Impulse sprinklers shoot water straight up through a nozzle. As it shoots up, it is deflected by a little metal arm that goes back and forth, scattering the stream of water into smaller droplets over a given area. These sprinklers are most often used to water large lawns. At higher water pressures, they can cover a diameter of lawn up to 100 feet. When used to water ornamental beds, they are usually placed atop 4- to 6-foot stands.

In general, the highest-quality sprinklers are made of

stainless steel or brass. Choose one that is easy to clean (debris can clog the emitter holes) and that is appropriate for the size of your lawn.

When you use the sprinkler, adjust the water pressure as necessary so the water can be absorbed by the soil. If water is coming out faster than it can soak into the soil, it will run off and be wasted. If you notice runoff, turn the sprinkler off for an hour or two to let the water soak in.

MISCELLANEOUS EQUIPMENT

Open up any gardening supply catalog, and you'll see dozens of products designed to make gardening easier and more successful. Having these items readily available, in a well-organized storage space, will save you from having to hunt them down each time you are ready to go out and work in the garden.

Sprayers: Fertilizers, pesticides, and herbicides are often applied in a spray form. If you need to spray small seedlings, houseplants, or just a small area of your garden, you can buy a simple plant mister or simply recycle a used window cleaner-type plastic bottle. For most jobs, though, a simple compressed-air sprayer is the best choice.

A home garden compression sprayer varies in capacity size but usually holds 1 to 5 gallons. Of course, if you have a large garden, you may want to go with a large sprayer. However, remember that 1 gallon of water weighs about 8 pounds, so don't get a larger sprayer if you can't comfortably tote around the extra weight.

The compression sprayer is very simple to operate: Simply pump the handle up and down several times to compress the air inside the pump. Push in the attached trigger to release the spray solution through the wand and spray nozzle. (For safety's sake, don't let a compressed sprayer sit in the hot sun too long before using it; the heat could cause the sprayer to explode.) Plastic compression sprayers are fine for most home gardens, although metal sprayers are, of course, more durable. Try to find a sprayer with a good mist nozzle; a fine mist is the best way to deliver most fertilizers and other chemicals to plants.

Instead of a compression sprayer, you can purchase a hose-end sprayer that is attached to the end of a hose nozzle. The sprayer either comes prepackaged with a concentrated solution or gives directions on how to prepare your own concentrated fertilizer or pesticide solution. The sprayer attachment releases the solution it contains into the stream of water coming from the hose. This kind of attachment is very efficient for frequent fertilizing jobs. It is also a handy device if you have trouble carrying around the heavier compressed air sprayer.

If possible, buy one sprayer for fertilizing and another for pesticides and herbicides. Never use fertilizers in sprayers with any amount of residue from pesticides or herbicides. In fact, the safest practice is to have a sprayer marked for each specific pesticide or herbicide you use. If you can't afford to buy more than one sprayer, thoroughly clean and rinse the sprayer and all nozzle parts after each application. No matter what chemical spray you are using, mix only the amount you will need for the immediate job. Do not store and try to reuse any of the unused chemical solution.

Mechanical Spreader: A mechanical spreader is a very useful device for evenly distributing dry fertilizer or lime over a large lawn or vegetable garden. Most home-garden types of spreaders are pushed by hand. An oscillating shuttle device at the bottom of the spreader disperses the particles evenly, which is virtually impossible to do if you scatter material by hand.

Tool Sharpeners: Nothing is as frustrating for a gardener and damaging to a plant as dull garden tools. Buy a hand file or other sharpening tool, and use it according to the package directions. Or have your tools professionally sharpened once or twice a year.

Gloves: For general garden work, lightweight cotton gloves are the most comfortable on hot days and for easier tasks like pulling annual weeds. Keep a good pair of leather gloves for tough garden jobs, such as pruning roses or other prickly shrubs. If you are working around poison ivy, wear rubber gloves, a long-sleeved shirt, long pants, and rubber boots. Thoroughly wash all of these items in warm water and detergent before putting them back on again.

Boots: If you are using a shovel, spade, pitchfork, or other sharp digging implement, wear sturdy footwear, such as leather work boots. Wear rubber boots when spraying pesticides and herbicides in the garden.

Knee Pads: Sometimes gardening seems like a rough contact sport! Knee pads can go a long way toward making many weeding and planting tasks much more comfortable. They will also extend the life of your favorite gardening pants and keep all your jeans from getting grass stains at the knees!

Kneeling Bench: This item is excellent for lending support as you get up and down while weeding or planting an area. It is a padded device that also acts as a little bench when turned upside down.

CHAPTER THIRTEEN

PEST AND DISEASE PORTRAITS

Part of the joy of caring for a garden is watching it change through the seasons and the years. Perennials grow into large, showy clumps; groundcovers fill in to form attractive carpets; vegetables mature into plum roots, succulent leaves, or juicy fruits. But there are some changes that are not for the better: those caused by pests and diseases attacking your plants. Fortunately, there are simple techniques you can use to keep these unwelcome visitors to a minimum.

With these detailed portraits of pests and diseases, you'll learn how to identify pests and disease, and how to deal with them before they damage your garden.

PEST PORTRAITS

APHIDS

Characteristics: Aphids are tiny, soft-bodied, pear-shaped insects that suck the juices from leaves, stems, flowers, and fruit. They come in a variety of colors, including green, yellow, red, brown, black, gray, and white. (They are often the color of the plant on which they are feeding.) Most species have wings, but they do not generally fly away when they are discovered. Aphids are parthenogenetic, which means that the females can reproduce even if no males are present. They can also give birth to female aphids that are already pregnant. It's no wonder aphids are so prolific!

Aphids prefer succulent new growth. You'll usually find them on leaf and flower buds, or on the undersides of new leaves. They are most damaging on young plants, since they can severely disfigure young foliage; they are not as troublesome on mature plants. However, some species transmit viral diseases, which can be much more serious than the damage caused by the aphids.

Aphids secrete a sticky substance called honeydew,

which attracts ants. The honeydew can be troublesome when it falls from trees onto cars, plants, or garden furniture. Also, a black sooty mold can grow on the honeydew. While this fungus does not harm leaves directly, it is unsightly and can keep light from reaching the foliage, thereby preventing photosynthesis.

Symptoms: Look for yellowish leaves, leaves with curled edges, sticky leaves and stems, black mold, or ants. The aphids themselves are easy to spot when you look closely; they cluster on succulent new growth and on the undersides of leaves.

Host Plants: Aphids are practically everywhere and can attack any kind of plant.

Controls: If you are not squeamish, you can try squashing the aphids right on the plant with your fingers. You can also wash them off with a strong spray of water. Aphids have many natural predators, including ladybugs, green lacewings, praying mantids, and parasitic wasps. You can also trap aphids on yellow sticky boards. If your plants are seriously infested, you can spray or dust with insecticidal soap, pyrethrin, or rotenone. When applying pesticides, don't forget to spray the undersides of the leaves; just treating the tops may not help at all.

APPLE MAGGOTS

Characteristics: Apple maggots are the larvae of dark brown flies that are about ¼ inch long.

The flies lay their eggs on the skins of apples, and the maggots hatch and eat into the fruit. The maggots are small white or yellowish worms that measure about ¼ inch long. They are one of the most serious orchard pests in the Northeast and Canada.

Symptoms: Apples have slight depressions where the maggots enter the fruit. Unfortunately, it's often difficult to detect damage until you cut or bite into the apple.

Host Plants: Apple maggots attack apples, apricots, cherries, peaches, pears, and plums. Blueberries are attacked by a similar pest, the blueberry maggot.

Controls: The trick is to control the female flies before they lay eggs on the fruit. To do this, hang round, red sticky traps around susceptible plants before the flowers open.

BEETLES

Characteristics: Approximately 40 percent of all insects are beetles. They have hard shells and two pairs of wings, and come in many sizes, shapes, and colors. Their larvae, sometimes called grubs, can be damaging to plant roots. Beetles feed on organic matter, other insects, and plants. Some, including ladybugs and ground beetles, are beneficial to the garden. Most garden pest beetles either devour plants completely or chew holes in foliage, flowers, stems, and buds. Some beetles are damaging in the garden not because they eat plants, but because they carry diseases. For example, bark beetles are vectors of chestnut blight and Dutch elm disease fungi, which have nearly eliminated the American chestnut and American elm trees from the landscape.

There are many garden beetle pests. Asparagus beetles are either blue-black with 4 white spots and reddish edges, or red or brown with 12 black spots. Mexican bean beetles are yellow with black spots; they feed on beans, peas, and squash. Colorado potato beetles are yellow with black stripes and orange heads. They lay bright yellow eggs on the undersides of leaves. Their feeding can completely devastate potatoes and related crops, including tomatoes and eggplants. Cucumber beetles are yellow with black stripes or spots. They feed on many plants, including asparagus, beans, corn, tomatoes, potatoes, eggplants, and vine crops such as squash and cucumbers.

Flea beetles are small and black with yellow or white markings. They get their name from their tendency to jump like fleas when disturbed. They chew holes in foliage and transmit serious viral and bacterial diseases. Japanese beetles are the scourge of rose gardens in the East. The adults are metallic green with copper-colored wings and black heads. They feed on roses, zinnias, and beans, as well as a wide range of other plants. Their comma-shaped, dark-headed, white grubs feed on turf-grass roots.

Symptoms: You may see holes in leaves, buds, or flowers, or whole plants may be defoliated. Japanese beetles tend to leave lacy-looking foliage. Beetles are easy to detect, since they feed on the plants both day and night.

Host Plants: Some species, such as asparagus beetles, only bother specific plants. Others will eat whatever they can find. All beetles have their favorites. Most plants can be bothered by some kind of beetle.

Controls: Cover vegetable crops with floating row covers to keep beetles from reaching the plants. Handpick beetles from other plants in the moming, before the pests are warm enough to fly away, and drop them in a bucket of soapy water. Biological Controls, such as milky disease spores and BTSD, are valuable for controlling some beetles, including Japanese beetles, Colorado potato beetles, cucumber beetles, and flea beetles; check garden supply catalogs or garden centers to see what is available. To control serious infestations, you can spray or dust with neem, pyrethrin, sabadilla, ryania, or rotenone. Check the label to make sure the product you buy will be effective against the pest you need to control. Some pesticides and biological controls are targeted for grubs and must be applied at the proper time, or they will be ineffective.

BORERS

Characteristics: Borers are the wormlike larvae of beetles and moths. They bore holes into the stems or roots of trees, shrubs, or perennials, and feed on the plant tissue. There are many species, some of which are named after the plants they feed on. The species commonly found in gardens are rose borers, raspberry root borers, raspberry caneborers, iris borers, peachtree borers, European corn borers, dogwood borers, lilac borers, bronze birch borers, and squash vine borers. They can be very serious pests, because they are almost impossible to control once they are inside the plant. They cause vine crop plants like melons to wilt and can kill trees by girdling the trunk under the bark. They often enter woody stems through a cut or bruise. Trees with thin, easily damaged bark, such as dogwood and birch, are particularly susceptible to borers.

Symptoms: Borers leave a hole with frass, or sawdust, where they enter the plant. They cause vine crops such as squash and melons to wilt suddenly. If you cut the stem of affected vine crops or cane plants lengthwise, you can find the borers in their tunnels.

Host Plants: Specific borers attack certain plants. All vine crops—including cucumbers, melons, pumpkins, and squash—are susceptible to squash vine borers. Bearded irises are susceptible to iris borers. Other plants that can be damaged by borers include apricots, blackberries, cherries, corn, peaches, plums, raspberries, birches, dogwoods, and roses.

Controls: There are no good controls for borers once they are in the plants. Sometimes you can insert a wire into the tunnel and kill the borer in the plant. Injecting BT into the hole may also control borers. To prevent damage, clean up garden debris in the fall, and avoid wounding trees with lawn mowers, string trimmers, and other equipment.

CABBAGE LOOPERS

Characteristics: Cabbage loopers are the larvae of night flying brown moths with a silver spot on each forewing. These green caterpillars have yellow stripes on their backs; as they move, their back curves into a loop. They chew large holes in the foliage and heads of many vegetable crops, especially members of the cabbage family. They can eat whole seedlings to the ground.

Symptoms: Large, jagged holes appear in the foliage of infested plants, or seedlings are eaten. Green, looping worms are evident on the foliage.

Host Plants: Many plants are prone to damage, including beans, broccoli, brussels sprouts, cabbage, cauliflower, collards, kale, kohlrabi, lettuce, parsley, radishes, rutabagas, and turnips.

Controls: Rotate crops and don't grow them in the same bed for 5 years. Use floating row covers to keep pests off the plants. Or dust uncovered plants with diatomaceous earth, and handpick pests that appear. Beneficial insects—including lacewings, Trichogramma wasps, and ladybugs—attack cabbage loopers. Organic pesticides, including rotenone and pyrethrin, are effective as a last resort.

CABBAGE MAGGOTS

Characteristics: Cabbage maggots are the larvae of insects that resemble houseflies. The flies lay their eggs at the base of the stem of the plant. The small, white, blunt-headed maggots hatch and tunnel into the roots, interrupting the plant's ability to take up food and water from the soil. Cabbage maggots can kill young plants or severely disfigure radish and turnip roots. They are most active in cool weather.

Symptoms: The lower leaves turn yellow, and young plants stop growing, wilt, and die for no apparent reason.

Brown, slimy tunnels are evident in plant roots, especially in radishes and turnips.

Host Plants: Susceptible crops include beets, broccoli, brussels sprouts, cabbage, cauliflower, celery, collards, kale, kohlrabi, peas, radishes, rutabagas, and turnips.

Controls: Grow radishes to lure adult flies away from other cabbage-family plants. Crops planted in midsummer for fall harvest are less prone to damage. Parasitic nematodes can attack cabbage maggots.

CABBAGEWORM, IMPORTED

Characteristics: The imported cabbageworm, also called imported cabbage butterfly, causes the same kind of damage as the cabbage looper. The adult is a butterfly with white or yellow wings marked with black spots. The damage is caused by the larvae, which are green caterpillars with a narrow orange stripe down their backs. They feed on the foliage and heads of members of the cabbage family.

Symptoms: You'll see large, ragged holes in foliage and heads, along with green caterpillars.

Host Plants: Imported cabbageworms attack broccoli, cabbage, kale, lettuce, mustard, and nasturtiums.

Controls: Cover vegetable crops with floating row covers to prevent damage. Handpick pests from uncovered plants, or spray them with BTK. Imported cabbageworms also have various natural predators, including Trichogramma wasps and praying mantids.

CORN EARWORM

Characteristics: The corn earworm is the larval stage of a brown moth. The worm is a 1½-inch, white, green, or red caterpillar with short spines. Early in the season, corn earworms feed on leaves and buds. Later generations enter the corn ears through the silks and feed on the kernels at the tips of the ears. This pest also feeds on many other crops. On tomatoes, it is called tomato fruitworm; on cotton, it is called bollworm.

Symptoms: Corn plants may be stunted and have damaged ears. Tomato fruits are damaged at the stem end.

Host Plants: Corn earworms feed on beans, corn, lettuce, okra, peanuts, peppers, squash, and tomatoes.

Controls: Corn cultivars with tight husks are considered generally resistant to this pest. Green lacewings, parasitic wasps, and beneficial nematodes are effective controls. Do not weed out smartweed if you have it, since it works as a trap crop. Spraying with BTK before the worms crawl too far into the ears may help.

CUTWORMS

Characteristics: Cutworms are among the most frustrating of all garden pests, because they come out at night and literally cut seedlings down to the ground. These 1- to 2-inch-long, soft bodied, gray or brown caterpillars curl up when they are touched. They live in the soil during the day and come out at night to feed. They also eat the roots of seedlings, causing the young plants to wilt and die. Cutworms mature into brown, night-flying moths.

Symptoms: Seedlings are cut to the ground, or they wilt and die.

Host Plants: Virtually all kinds of vegetable and flower seedlings are susceptible, including beans, cabbage-family crops, eggplants, lettuce, peppers, potatoes, and tomatoes.

Controls: Once cutworms strike, there is nothing you can do but replant. To prevent damage, place stiff paper collars around the base of the plants. (Push the collar into the soil a bit to keep the pests from crawling underneath.) A ring of diatomaceous earth sprinkled around the plants creates an abrasive barrier. Handpick the worms at night. Beneficial nematodes and Trichogramma wasps attack cutworms. Check garden supply catalogs and garden centers for a BTK bait that controls cutworms.

GYPSY MOTH

Characteristics: Gypsy moth caterpillars grow up to 2½ inches long and are covered with tufts of hair. They are dark, with red-and-blue markings and a yellow head. They mature into moths with a 1½-inch wingspan. The male moth is brown and the female is white. They are prevalent in the eastern United States and have also been found in British Columbia and the Pacific Northwest.

Gypsy moths were introduced from Europe to New England in 1869 as a potential replacement for the silkworm. They have no natural enemies in North America and have devastated forest trees and residential landscapes. They can defoliate whole stands of trees in a couple of weeks. The foliage of many hardwoods can grow back, but repeated attacks can kill the trees. Evergreens may die if they are defoliated in one season. Fortunately, gypsy moths produce only one generation in a year.

Symptoms: The caterpillars eat foliage and are evident on trees and shrubs.

Host Plants: Gypsy moths feed on hardwood forest trees, hemlocks, spruces, white pines, fruit trees, and many shrubs.

Controls: Sticky tape around the base of trees prevents the larvae from climbing the trunks. Handpicking works when the infestation is not severe and the pests are within reach. Trichogramma wasps and beneficial nematodes can be effective. Spraying with BTK can help, too.

HARLEQUIN BUG

Characteristics: Harlequin bugs are small, shiny, black, beetlelike insects that are triangular in shape and have red markings on their backs. When they are squashed, they give off a bad odor. They suck the juices from foliage, sometimes causing plants to wilt and die. Harlequin bugs lay rows of distinctive, keg-shaped, black-and-white-striped eggs on the undersides of leaves.

Symptoms: Leaves have yellowish, blackish, or whitish spots; young plants wilt. You'll see the adult bugs, as well as their eggs, on the undersides of the leaves.

Host Plants: Susceptible crops include broccoli, brussels sprouts, cabbage, collards, eggplants, kale, kohlrabi, radishes, and turnips.

Controls: Plant turnips, mustard, or radishes as trap crops to lure pests away from other crops. Protect susceptible vegetable crops with floating row covers. On uncovered plants, you can control infestations with insecticidal soap, pyrethrin, sabadilla, or rotenone.

LEAFHOPPERS

Characteristics: Leafhoppers are small, wedge-shaped insects that jump like fleas when they are disturbed. They are green, brown, or yellow and sometimes have red or yellow markings. These pests suck the juices from plants and spread diseases as they feed. They leave behind a sticky honeydew, similar to that left by aphids.

Symptoms: Leafhoppers generally feed on the undersides of leaves and hop when disturbed. Damaged foliage has a mottled appearance and is glazed by the honeydew, which attracts a black sooty mold. The plants may show signs of yellows or a viral disease.

Host Plants: These pests feed on many plants, including beans, beets, carrots, potatoes, spinach, squash, tomatoes, fruit trees, raspberries, asters, and marigolds.

Controls: Clean up garden debris. Use floating row covers to keep leafhoppers off vegetables. Green lacewings and Trichogramma wasps attack leafhoppers. If infestations occur, try using organic controls, such as insecticidal soap, pyrethrin, sabadilla, or rotenone.

LEAFMINERS

Characteristics: Leafminers are the larvae of small black flies. These larvae tunnel under the surface of leaves and form blotches or squiggly lines on the leaves. Besides disfiguring foliage, leafminers carry fungal diseases, such as black leg and soft rot. Like borers, they are difficult to control once they have entered the plant tissues, because contact pesticides cannot reach them.

Symptoms: Blotches or lines appear on the foliage of susceptible plants.

Host Plants: Many plants are susceptible to leafminers, including beans, cabbage, lettuce, peppers, radishes, spinach, turnips, arborvitae, birches, columbines, and hollies.

Controls: Clean up garden debris each fall. In vegetable gardens, till the soil thoroughly to expose overwintering larvae, and protect the crops with floating row covers. On uncovered plants, leafminers are difficult to control except when they are in the adult fly stage, which occurs in early spring. Handpick the eggs on the undersides of the foliage; they are white, the size of a pinhead, and laid in lines of 3 to 5 eggs. Pick off and destroy foliage that shows signs of damage.

MEALYBUGS

Characteristics: Mealybugs are sucking insects that feed on the stems and leaves of plants. They are small and oval-shaped, and look as if they are covered with a powdery white wax. They release honeydew, which attracts ants and supports the growth of black sooty mold. Some species carry viral diseases.

Symptoms: Plants are weakened and have yellowish leaves. The insects are plainly visible on stems and leaves (especially in the crotches of branches).

Host Plants: Many houseplants and greenhouse plants are attacked by mealybugs. Outside, fruit trees, grapes, persimmons, azaleas, and wisterias are particularly susceptible.

Controls: After mealybugs begin to feed, they cover themselves with a waxy coating that is difficult to penetrate with insecticides. These pests are easiest to control in the crawler stage, after the eggs hatch but before they begin feeding. Green lacewings are useful predators.

Insecticidal soaps, neem, and light horticultural oils can be effective against serious infestations.

MITES

Characteristics: Mites are tiny spider relatives that suck the juices from plant foliage. They are most active in hot, dry weather and multiply quickly when conditions are favorable. The strength of mites is in their numbers, and they are unbelievably prolific: They can produce a new generation in 2 weeks, and up to 8 generations in a single season. If allowed to go unchecked for several weeks, they can quickly infest and kill a plant.

Symptoms: Mites cause distorted growth, especially on stem tips, and stippling on foliage; damaged leaves eventually turn yellow and drop. Mites may also make tiny webs that are visible between the leaves. If you suspect that a plant has mites, hold a piece of white paper under a leaf and shake the plant; the red, black, or brown mites should fall on the paper and move around. If you see more than 5 of these insects, you should take action immediately.

Host Plants: Many house-, greenhouse, and garden plants are susceptible to mites. Some that are particularly prone to infestation include dwarf Alberta spruce, roses (especially miniature types), strawberries, and many fruit trees.

Controls: Green lacewings, ladybugs, and predatory mites are natural predators. A strong blast of water on the undersides of leaves can knock mites off a plant. Insecticidal soap sprays are also effective.

SCALE

Characteristics: Scales are sucking insects similar to mealybugs. They find a feeding site on a stem or leaf base, attach themselves to the site with their mouthparts, and begin feeding. They secrete a hard, shell-like covering, or a waxy, cottony coating. The shell-like species are called armored scales. This group includes oystershell scale and euonymus scale. The cottony types include cottony-cushion scale and tortoise-shell scale. Serious scale infestations can kill branches and even entire trees. Scales excrete sticky honeydew, which favors the growth of black sooty mold.

Symptoms: The leaves of infested plants turn yellow; the branches weaken and die. Scale insects are visible on plant stems and foliage. Their honeydew is sticky and often has black sooty mold growing on it.

Host Plants: Scales can attack a wide range of both indoor and outdoor plants. In the landscape, particularly susceptible plants include fruit trees, ashes, beeches, birches, bittersweets, camellias, dogwoods, euonymus, hollies, lilacs, maples, and pachysandra.

Controls: Scale is difficult to control once it has attached itself to its feeding place. Green lacewings are natural predators. In the crawling stage, scales can be controlled with insecticidal soap. Oil sprays can also help control scales.

SLUGS AND SNAILS

Characteristics: These ground-dwelling mollusks can be devastating to many kinds of plants. They commonly grow 2 to 4 inches long, although they can reach up to 8 inches long on the West Coast. Slugs can be brown, orange, tan, black, purplish, or yellow, with stripes or spots. Snails are very similar to slugs but have hard shells. Both slugs and snails prefer moist, cool locations. They are hermaphrodites, which means that each slug or snail has both male and female parts. They can live for several years and produce one generation each year. They feed mostly at night, starting about 2 hours after sunset.

Symptoms: Slugs and snails chew ragged holes in plant foliage and can devour young seedlings. They leave a characteristic trail of slime. Sometimes you can find them during the day under boards or stones.

Host Plants: Slugs and snails feed on most garden plants, especially those in cool, shady areas and those with foliage close to the ground. They love cabbage, coleus, geraniums, hollyhocks, hostas, marigolds, primroses, and snapdragons, just to name a few.

Controls: Sprinkling a ring of diatomaceous earth, crushed eggshells, or wood ashes around plants can be an effective way to keep these pests off your plants. Traps can also work. Buy special traps, or make your own by sinking shallow dishes into the soil, so the rim is flush with the soil surface; fill the traps with beer. Some gardeners leave wooden boards in the general area where slugs and snails feed; the pests will collect under the boards during the day, so you can easily remove and destroy them. You can also go out at night with a flash-light and handpick the pests from plants. Sprinkling salt on slugs is not a good idea, because the salt can also harm your plants.

TARNISHED PLANT BUG

Characteristics: Tarnished plant bugs are brown, flat, ¼-inch, oval-shaped bugs with irregular markings in white, yellow, red, and black. They have a characteristic yellow triangle with a black dot on the lower third of each side. These pests suck the juices from plant parts and inject a toxin that deforms foliage and flower buds. They also carry fire blight disease, which can be devastating to fruit trees and shrubs.

Symptoms: Roots, shoots, and flowers may be deformed, and the pests themselves are usually present. Black spots and pitting may be evident on stem tips, flower buds, and fruit. These pests can stop fruit production altogether, especially on dwarf fruit trees and strawberries.

Host Plants: Tarnished plant bugs attack a wide range of plants, including strawberries, fruit trees, and vegetables. They also feed on China asters, chrysanthemums, dahlias, marigolds, poppies, salvias, sunflowers, zinnias, and other flowers.

Controls: Clean up the garden in autumn, since the insects overwinter in plant debris. Protect vegetable crops and strawberries with floating row covers. Hang sticky traps near fruit trees to catch these pests. For serious infestations, you can spray or dust with pyrethrin, sabadilla, or rotenone.

THRIPS

Characteristics: Thrips are very small, barely visible, slender insects with feathery wings. They feed by sucking the juices from leaves, stems, flower buds, and fruit. They can also spread disease pathogens as they feed.

Symptoms: Thrip feeding causes streaking on foliage and scarring on fruits; the leaves may eventually wither and die. White- and light-colored flowers may be discolored; severely infested flowers are deformed or destroyed.

Host Plants: Many plants are affected, including beans, corn, onions, squash, blueberries, fruit trees, chrysanthemums, and gladioli.

Controls: Green lacewings, ladybugs, and predatory mites are natural enemies of thrips. Use diatomaceous earth or garlic sprays to keep the pests off your plants. Insecticidal soaps, pyrethrin, or rotenone can be effective against infestations.

TOMATO HORNWORM

Characteristics: These big green, white-striped caterpillars are the larvae of a large gray or brown moth with 5 orange spots on each side of its body and a wingspan of up to 4 or 5 inches. The moths can hover like hummingbirds as they sip the nectar of funnel-shaped flowers, such as those of petunias and flowering tobacco. Plants are damaged by the caterpillars, which are 3 to 5 inches long and have a black horn at the end of their bodies. They feed voraciously on tomatoes, tobacco, and other members of the tomato family.

Symptoms: Tomato hornworms chew large holes in leaves and fruit. Brown droppings are visible on foliage and stems. You may also see the pests near the damage.

Host Plants: These pests feed on dill, eggplants, peppers, potatoes, tomatillos, and tomatoes.

Controls: Tomato hornworms can be controlled by handpicking; keep an eye out for them so you catch them before they cause too much damage. (If you see a tomato hornworm with white cocoons along its back, it has already been parasitized by Trichogramma wasps and its days are numbered; leave it on the plant so the parasites can hatch and attack other hornworms.) Plant dill as a trap crop to lure the pests away from your crops. Pyrethrin and rotenone are effective against serious infestations.

WEEVILS

Characteristics: Weevils are beetles with hard shells and characteristic long snouts. There are many species, and they feed on a wide range of plants. They generally feed at night and live in the soil during the day, so you may never see them unless you look for them at night with a flashlight. The adults chew on foliage and fruits; their larvae feed on leaves, roots, stems, and fruits. Bean weevils feed on seeds. Weevils are parthenogenetic and do not need males to reproduce.

Symptoms: Look for foliage with notched edges or

large holes (with only the midvein remaining). Other symptoms include chewed fruit or zigzag patterns where larvae entered the roots, stems, or fruits. The weevils are evident at night.

Host Plants: Many plants are host to weevils, including beans, carrots, peas, rhubarb, blueberries, fruit trees, strawberries, cyclamen, dogwoods, magnolias, rhododendrons, roses, spruce trees, tulip poplars, and yews.

Controls: Clean up garden debris in the fall to remove overwintering sites for the pests. Rotate vegetable crops to prevent overwintering weevils from attacking susceptible plants. Sprinkle diatomaceous earth around plants to form a barrier. Beneficial nematodes can help to control the pests. Weevils are difficult to control with contact sprays unless you catch them at night; pyrethrin or rotenone may be effective.

WHITEFLIES

Characteristics: Whiteflies are small, white flying insects that feed on the undersides of plant foliage. They suck the juices from leaves, stems, and flower buds, and leave behind a honeydew on which black sooty mold grows. They also carry diseases. Whiteflies are one of the worst insect pests in greenhouses.

Symptoms: Whiteflies tend to fly away in a cloud when you shake an infested plant. They cause stippling on foliage, which eventually turns yellow and dies. The leaves may be covered with sticky honeydew and black sooty mold. Whiteflies also distort flower buds and weaken plants.

Host Plants: Many plants are susceptible, especially tomatoes, flowering tobacco, geraniums, heliotrope, petunias, and verbenas. Certain species feed on citrus plants, grapes, mulberries, strawberries, azaleas, ferns, and irises.

Controls: Use a forceful spray of water to chase whiteflies off foliage temporarily. Green lacewings, ladybugs, and Trichogramma wasps are natural predators; Encarsia formosa is recommended as a predator for greenhouse whiteflies. Indoors or out, you can trap these pests with yellow sticky boards. Insecticidal soap works when it hits the flies. (Try not to disturb them before spraying, or they will simply fly away and return later.) Neem, pyrethrin, and ryania sprays can also be effective.

WIREWORMS

Characteristics: Wireworms, the larvae of click beetles, are stiff, hard-shelled, dark brown or yellow worms. They resemble millipedes that have lost all but 3 pairs of legs. They feed on underground plant parts, including roots, stems, tubers, and seeds. These pests are particularly destructive to root crops but are also damaging to other vegetables and flowers. Wireworms are often found in areas that have recently been turned from grass into garden beds.

Symptoms: Plants wilt and may die. When you dig up an infested plant, you may see the worms in the roots or tubers.

Host Plants: Wireworms feed on many crops, including beans, beets, carrots, com, onions, peas, potatoes, radishes, asters, dahlias, gladioli, and phlox.

Controls: Clean up garden debris in the fall, and rotate root crops. Before planting new beds made from lawn areas, skewer pieces of raw potato on the end of sticks and bury them in the soil; after a week or two, lift out and destroy the infested pieces. Beneficial nematodes can be effective against wireworms.

DISEASE PORTRAITS

ALTERNARIA LEAF SPOT

Characteristics: Alternaria leaf spots are caused by fungi that attack many flowers, as well as fruit and vegetable crops. The fungi, which grow on both living and dead tissue, disfigure foliage and fruits. (They can also damage fruit in storage.) The spores are spread by wind and water, and overwinter on plant debris. The disease can spread in a wide range of temperatures—from 40° to 90°F—and prefers moist conditions. Infection is usually worse toward the end of the season as the disease builds up.

Symptoms: Dark brown, circular lesions form on main stems, leaf stems, leaves, and fruits. Leaves may drop prematurely. The spots may have concentric rings or may be long and narrow. Older leaves are normally affected more severely.

Host Plants: Many plants are susceptible to Alternaria, including beans, carrots, cabbage-family crops, cucumbers, potatoes, pumpkins, radishes, sweet potatoes, carnations, and zinnias.

Controls: Plant resistant cultivars, and rotate susceptible crops. Space plants properly to allow for good air circulation. Avoid wetting the foliage. If you see damage, remove infected plants and plant parts to prevent the disease from spreading. (Burn, bury, or dispose of infected plants in your trash; do not compost them.)

ANTHRACNOSE

Characteristics: Anthracnose is a fungus that causes sunken lesions to form on stems, leaves, and fruit. It needs warm weather to germinate and is most active when temperatures range from 78° to 86°F. The pathogen overwinters in the soil and on plant debris. It is spread by wind, water, and gardening tools.

Symptoms: Spots with sunken centers appear on leaves, stems, and fruit. Pink spores may be visible in the spots. The foliage may die.

Host Plants: Anthracnose infects many plants, including beans, cucumbers and other vine crops, rhubarb, tomatoes, blackberries, raspberries, hollyhocks, lupines, pansies, snapdragons, and sycamore trees.

Controls: Look for resistant cultivars. Rotate the planting sites of susceptible crops. Provide adequate air circulation, and avoid watering the foliage. If anthracnose has been a problem in past years, apply a preventive spray of sulfur- or copper-based fungicide on susceptible plants to keep the spores from germinating. Remove infected plants and plant parts to prevent the disease from spreading. (Burn, bury, or dispose of infected plants in your trash; do not compost them.)

APPLE SCAB

Characteristics: Apple scab is a serious disease that can cause entire apple and pear crops to fail in bad years. This fungal disease attacks leaves, fruit, and stems, causing small, poor-quality fruit and early leaf drop. It is worst in wet, cool weather, when the fungus can spread the fastest.

Symptoms: Yellow or light green spots form on young leaves and flower buds, and eventually turn darker. The leaves may be disfigured or destroyed; they become velvety looking as the spores develop. The spots can spread to form large areas of dead tissue. Fruit and foliage drop prematurely.

Host Plants: Apple scab affects both apples and pears.

Controls: Prevent problems by planting resistant cultivars. Remove infected foliage and fruit immediately to help keep the disease from spreading. (Burn, bury, or dispose of infected plants in your trash; do not compost them.) If you choose to spray, check with your local Cooperative Extension Service office for recommendations on suitable materials and when to apply them.

BACTERIAL SPOTS AND BLIGHTS

Characteristics: Spots and blights are caused by a number of different bacteria. They are most prevalent in high humidity and either warm or cool temperatures, depending on the disease. Bacterial spots and blights infect plants through wounded tissue or small holes in plant leaves. The pathogens overwinter in plant debris.

Symptoms: Irregular spots with a water-soaked

appearance (and sometimes a foul smell) form on leaves, stems, flowers, and fruit. Foliage, stems, and flowers may be killed quickly.

Host Plants: Many plants are susceptible, including beans, peas, peppers, tomatoes, fruits, zonal geraniums, nasturtiums, and tuberous begonias.

Controls: Clean up the garden in autumn. Rotate the planting sites of susceptible crops. Provide adequate air circulation, and avoid watering the foliage or wounding the plants. Keep garden tools clean, and disinfect them after using them on a plant you think might be infected. Bacterial diseases cannot be cured, so remove infected plants and plant parts as soon as possible to prevent the infection from spreading. (Burn, bury, or dispose of infected plants in your trash; do not compost them.)

BACTERIAL WILT

Characteristics: Bacterial wilt diseases clog the water-conducting tissues of infected plants, causing them to wilt and die. The bacteria enter plant tissue through wounds or natural openings in stems. They are spread by flea beetles, cucumber beetles, infected seeds, wind, or water. The bacteria are most active in warm, wet weather, when temperatures are above 75°F. The pathogen overwinters in plant debris and in the soil around infected plants.

Symptoms: Plants wilt even when they are not dry. Streaks may appear on the foliage. Sticky material may ooze from cut stems.

Host Plants: Bacterial wilt diseases infect many plants, including beans, corn, cucumbers and other vine crops, tomatoes, astilbes, bleeding hearts, cosmos, dahlias, dianthus, nasturtiums, and sweet alyssum.

Controls: Clean up plant debris in the fall. Rotate the planting sites of susceptible crops, and plant resistant cultivars. Avoid wetting the leaves. Control flea beetles and cucumber beetles, which can carry the disease. Remove infected plants and plant parts to prevent the disease from spreading. (Burn, bury, or dispose of infected plants in your trash; do not compost them.)

BLACK LEG

Characteristics: Black leg is a fungal disease that produces a dry rot. It causes sunken lesions to form on plant stems near the base; the spots may run together and girdle the stem. This disease is spread by infected seeds, rain, and garden tools, and is particularly damaging in warm, wet, or humid weather. The spores overwinter in plant debris in the soil.

Symptoms: Sunken lesions form around the base of the stem. Gray or black spots can appear on stems and leaves, and leaf margins may turn blue or red. Plants can wilt, fall over, and die.

Host Plants: Black leg most commonly affects potatoes and cabbage-family plants, including cabbage, broccoli, cauliflower, and kale.

Controls: Purchase seeds from a reputable seed company. Rotate the planting sites of susceptible crops, and grow resistant cultivars. Avoid wetting the leaves. If the disease was serious in past years, try a preventive copper spray. Remove infected plants and plant parts to prevent the disease from spreading. (Burn, bury, or dispose of infected plants in your trash; do not compost them.)

BLACK SPOT

Characteristics: Black spot is familiar to those who grow roses in the humid environments of midwestern, northeastern, and southeastern states. This fungal disease causes black spots to form on leaves; the spots spread and eventually cause the foliage to drop. The infections are worst in wet, humid weather in spring and fall, but can be a problem all summer in areas with high humidity. Black spot is spread by water and affects the leaves closest to the ground first.

Symptoms: Black spots form on the foliage, which turns yellow and drops. Whole plants can be defoliated by July in severely affected areas.

Host Plants: Black spot infects roses.

Controls: Select resistant cultivars. Choose a site with good air circulation, and allow ample space between plants. Avoid wetting the foliage. Remove infected plant parts to keep the disease from spreading. To prevent black spot, some rose growers use a regular spray schedule of fungicidal soaps, sulfur-based fungicides, or chemical fungicides.

BOTRYTIS

Characteristics: Botrytis is a fungal disease that affects fruits, flowers, leaves, and stems. It is also called gray mold, because one of the later symptoms of the disease is a fluffy, gray mold. The fluffy part releases the spores, which are spread by water. Botrytis is most prevalent in wet weather, especially in the cooler temperatures of spring.

Symptoms: Flower petals develop blighted tissue and become soft and watery; eventually, a gray mold develops. The leaves have spots that turn dry and white or brown. Fruits that form from infected flowers develop spots from the blossom end; these spots enlarge and eventually develop a gray mold. Botrytis on peonies causes the plant tissue to rot and emerging foliage to fall over or blacken at the tips. It can also prevent flower buds from opening.

Host Plants: A wide range of plants are susceptible, including beets, lettuce, onions, peppers, tomatoes, blackberries, raspberries, strawberries, African violets, azaleas, begonias, dahlias, geraniums, peonies, petunias, snapdragons, and many bulbs.

Controls: Look for resistant cultivars. Rotate the planting sites of susceptible crops. Provide a site with good air circulation, and avoid wetting the foliage. Remove infected plant parts to prevent the disease from spreading.

CLUB ROOT

Characteristics: Club root is a fungal disease that affects plant roots and causes wilting and stunted plant growth. It gets its name from the abnormal swellings it causes on roots. Club root is spread by water and wind, and can survive in the soil for 7 years without a host.

Symptoms: The only above-ground symptom is stunted growth. When you dig up affected plants, you'll see club-shaped swellings on the roots.

Host Plants: Club root attacks cabbage, broccoli, kale, and other members of the cabbage family.

Controls: The pathogen that causes club root prefers acid conditions, so try adding lime to the soil to raise the pH. Look for resistant cultivars, and rotate the planting sites of susceptible crops. Remove infected plants and plant parts to prevent the disease from spreading. Avoid planting susceptible crops in that area for at least 7 years.

DAMPING-OFF

Characteristics: Damping-off diseases can attack many types of plants of all ages, but they are most commonly a problem on seedlings. Several fungi can cause this condition. Some damping-off pathogens attack seeds before they sprout, preventing them from germinating; others attack seedlings after they emerge. The pathogen is present in the soil and can be spread by garden tools. It is most troublesome in moist conditions with poor air circulation.

Symptoms: Seeds do not germinate, or seedlings suddenly fall over and die. A brown, crimped area may be visible on the stem at the soil line.

Host Plants: Seedlings of all types are susceptible.

Controls: Use sterilized mixes when starting seedlings indoors. Take care not to overwater flats and pots of seedlings. Once the seeds have germinated, remove any covers and allow the soil to dry out a little between waterings. Thin the seedlings as soon as possible to prevent overcrowding, which encourages damping-off.

FIRE BLIGHT

Characteristics: Fire blight is a bacterial disease that attacks the stems of pear and apple trees, causing the limbs to look burned. It is spread by bees, tarnished plant bugs, aphids, and other insects, as well as by rain, dew, tools, and the wind. Infected tissue oozes a sticky substance that drips onto lower limbs, further encouraging the infection to spread. Fire blight can be devastating to some trees, especially fruiting and ornamental pears. The disease is worst in wet spring weather; it sometimes seems to stop magically in June.

Symptoms: Reddish, watersoaked lesions develop on branches, and branch tips wilt and curl. Limbs turn black, as if they have been burned. A sticky substance oozes from the infected branches. Flowers wither and die.

Host Plants: Fire blight attacks apples, pears, and ornamental members of the rose family.

Controls: Plant resistant cultivars. The disease prefers succulent growth, so be careful not to overfertilize. Many gardeners prune affected limbs at least 12 inches from the last affected tissue, although some pathologists recommend breaking, not pruning, the limb closer to the infected part. If you do prune, disinfect your pruners before using them on something else. Cut or break limbs during the winter, when the pathogen is dormant. An antibiotic streptomycin spray is now available to home gardeners for controlling the spread of the disease.

FUSARIUM WILT

Characteristics: Fusarium wilt disease is caused by a fungus that clogs the water-conducting tissues of plants, causing them to wilt and die. It thrives in warm, reasonably dry weather and is only active when soil temperatures are between 60° and 90°F. Fusarium is spread by water and cucumber beetles. It can live in the soil for 20 years without a host plant.

Symptoms: Plants may be one-sided, stunted, or wilted. Leaves turn yellow and drop off. The roots rot, and the plants eventually fall over and die. When the stem is sliced lengthwise, a red substance is visible in the tissue.

Host Plants: Fusarium attacks many different plants, including asparagus, cabbage, celery, corn, melons, peas, potatoes, radishes, spinach, and tomatoes.

Controls: Clean up garden debris in the fall. Plant resistant vegetable cultivars. (The "F" after the name of a tomato cultivar indicates a resistance to Fusarium.) Rotate planting sites, or grow susceptible crops in containers. Remove and destroy infected plants.

MILDEWS

Characteristics: Mildews are caused by fungi. Powdery mildew creates a powdery look on the top of plant leaves that does not wipe or wash off. Downy mildew causes similar symptoms but appears on the undersides of foliage. Powdery and downy mildews are very host-specific, which means that the powdery mildew you see on your lilacs will not spread to your phlox. This fact can be a relief to gardeners who plant a variety of plants, although similar conditions encourage powdery mildew in all susceptible plants. The diseases are most troublesome in late summer, in high humidity with poor air circulation. They prevent photosynthesis, thus weakening plants; the damage is more serious on some plants than on others. The later in the season the disease occurs, the less damage it tends to cause.

Symptoms: The foliage of infected plants develops a whitish tinge that looks like powder; it appears on the top or bottom of the leaves, depending on the disease. On some plants, such as roses, flower buds can be severely deformed.

Host Plants: Mildews can attack many different plants. Those most susceptible to pow dery mildew include cucumbers, melons, squash, blueberries, fruit trees, raspberries, strawberries, sage, tarragon, ageratums, asters, bee balm, begonias, black-eyed Susans, China asters, coralbells, cosmos, dahlias, delphiniums, lilacs, phlox, roses, salvias, sunflowers, yarrows, and zinnias. Plants particularly prone to downy mildew include beans, broccoli, lettuce, onions, radishes, spinach, turnips, vine crops such as cucumbers and squash, tarragon, asters, China asters, cornflowers (bachelor's buttons), forget-me-nots, poppies, salvias, and sweet alyssum.

Controls: Clean up garden debris in autumn. Rotate the planting sites of closely related crops. Choose a site with good air circulation, and avoid overcrowding. Plant resistant cultivars. Train vining crops to grow up trellises to keep them off the ground. Remove infected plants and plant parts to prevent the disease from spreading.

MOSAIC VIRUSES

Characteristics: Mosaic viruses do not generally kill plants but may cause stunted or abnormal growth. "Mosaic" refers to the various color pigments that are exhibited in the leaves when the disease causes the plant to stop making chlorophyll. (Chlorophyll is what makes a plant green and enables it to make food for itself.) Tobacco mosaic, which attacks members of the tomato family, is one of the most common forms.

Symptoms: Mottling and unusual colors on plant foliage are common symptoms of mosaic viruses. You may also see stunted or abnormal growth, low vegetable yields, and discolored flowers and fruit.

Host Plants: Mosaic viruses can infect many plants,

including cucumbers, lettuce, melons, peppers, potatoes, summer squash, tobacco, tomatoes, raspberries, orchids, and petunias.

Controls: Control insect vectors, including leafhoppers and aphids. Do not smoke in the garden or greenhouse. If you are a smoker, do not handle virus-susceptible plants until you have washed your hands. Plant resistant cultivars. (The "T" after the name of tomato cultivars indicates a resistance to tobacco mosaic virus.) Remove and destroy infected plants.

NEMATODES

Characteristics: Nematodes are microscopic worm-like organismsthat live in the soil. Some feed on decomposing plant matter, some feed on plants, and some feed on other nematodes and garden pests. The ones that feed on plants may damage roots, shoots, flowers, or leaves. They cause wilting and stunted growth as they interrupt the ability of plants to take up moisture and nutrients from the soil. These nematodes can severely deform the roots of root crops, such as carrots and potatoes. They tend to be scattered in the soil and may not damage crops that are within several feet of affected plants. If you suspect that nematodes are a problem in your garden, you can send a soil sample to your local Cooperative Extension Service office to have it checked.

Symptoms: Above ground, nematode symptoms include stunted growth and deformed leaves, flowers, and fruit. Root knot nematodes cause knotlike galls to form on roots; aboveground growth may be yellowed or stunted.

Host Plants: Many plants are susceptible, including beans, carrots, okra, potatoes, sweet potatoes, tomatoes, and strawberries.

Controls: Rotate planting sites of susceptible crops, and grow resistant cultivars. (The "N" after the name of tomato cultivars indicates a resistance to nematodes.) Apply beneficial nematodes to the soil to prey on the pest species. If you know nematodes are a problem, another option is to plant susceptible crops in containers.

RUSTS

Characteristics: Rust diseases are caused by various fungi. They produce rust-colored spores, usually on the undersides of foliage. (Don't confuse the brown or rust-colored spots scattered on the back of fern foliage with rust; the spots on the fronds are the fruiting bodies of the fern.) Rusts tend to have fairly specific hosts. Some, such as cedar-apple rust, need two hosts to complete their life cycle. Rust spores are commonly spread by the wind.

Symptoms: Rust-colored spores are evident on foliage, flowers, and fruit. Leaves may turn yellow and drop.

Host Plants: Many plants are susceptible to rust diseases, including asparagus, beans, apples, blackberries, pears, raspberries, ageratums, asters, black-eyed Susans, cannas, cedar trees, chrysanthemums, coreopsis, cornflowers (bachelor's buttons), cosmos, dianthus, four o'clocks, hollyhocks, irises, lilies, salvias, snapdragons, sweet alyssum, and yarrows.

Controls: Grow resistant cultivars, and rotate the planting sites of susceptible crops. Choose sites with good air circulation. Avoid wetting the leaves. Remove infected plants and plant parts to prevent spreading the disease from spreading.

SMUTS

Characteristics: Smuts are fungal diseases that are spread by wind. Different smuts have specific hosts; corn smut, for instance, will not infect turfgrass. Smuts can cause spots to appear on any plant part. These spots swell and form masses covered with gray membranes, which burst to release millions of black spores. The spores can live in the soil for many years until a susceptible crop is planted in the same spot. Corn smut, the kind you're most likely to encounter, actually looks much worse than it is. You can remove the infected part with little effect on the rest of the plant.

Symptoms: Swollen, gray masses form on leaves, stems, flowers, fruit, or seeds. The masses open to release sooty black spores. Corn smut is sure to attract attention and is easy to diagnose. On turfgrasses, smuts form gray lines that open to release black spores.

Host Plants: Smuts mainly attack grasses, including turigrass and corn. Dahlias and pansies may also be affected by smuts.

Controls: Rotate the planting sites of susceptible crops.

Provide adequate air circulation, and avoid wetting the foliage. Remove infected plants and plant parts as soon as you see them (try to catch them before the spores are released) to prevent the disease from spreading.

VERTICILLIUM WILT

Characteristics: Like Fusarium, Verticillium is a fungus that clogs the water-conducting tissues of plants, causing them to wilt and die. It thrives in cool, humid conditions. Verticillium can be spread by water and by gardeners when they cultivate the soil.

Symptoms: Look for stunted, one-sided, or wilted plants. Leaves turn yellow and drop off. The roots can be rotted, and plants may simply fall over and die. When the stem is sliced lengthwise, a tan substance is visible in the tissue.

Host Plants: Verticillium wilt can damage many plants, including eggplants, peppers, potatoes, rhubarb, tomatoes, mint, sage, blackberries, fruit trees, raspberries, and strawberries.

Controls: Plant resistant vegetable cultivars. (The "V" after the name of tomato cultivars indicates a resistance to Verticillium.) Rotate crops to different parts of the garden, or try growing them in containers.

Clean up garden debris in the fall. Remove and destroy infected plants.

YELLOWS

Characteristics: Yellows is caused by mycoplasmas, single-celled organisms spread by insect vectors, including leafhoppers. Like viruses, yellows diseases do not tend to kill plants, but they do stunt plant's growth.

Symptoms: Plants are stunted and may appear stiffer, more branched, and more upright than is characteristic of the plants. The plants and flowers have a yellowish look. Flowers may be deformed or may not develop at all.

Host Plants: Many plants are susceptible to yellows, including China asters, chrysanthemums, coreopsis, cornflowers, delphiniums, marigolds, nasturtiums, pansies, petunias, salvias, and sweet alyssum.

Controls: Clean up garden debris. Control leafhoppers, which spread the disease. Remove infected plants and plant parts to prevent the disease from spreading.

Antirrhinum majus
49

Calendula officinalis
55

Chrysanthemum ptarmiciflorum
'Silver Lace'
59

Cleome hasslerana
61

ANNUALS AND BIENNIALS

ANNUALS AND BIENNIALS

Consolida ambigua
63

Cosmos bipinnatus
65

Dianthus barbatus
67

Digitalis purpurea
70

Eschscholzia californica
73

Eustoma grandiflorum
74

Helianthus annuus
'Sunrise' and 'Sunset'
78

New Guinea impatiens
81

ANNUALS AND BIENNIALS

Lathyrus odoratus
85

Myosotis sylvatica
93

Pelargonium X *hortorum*
97

Petunia X hybrida
'Summer Madness'
100

Portulaca grandiflora
103

Tagetes tenuifolia
'Lemon Gem' and 'Tangerine Gem'
106

Tropaeolum majus
111

Zinnia
'Pinwheel Series'
119

ANNUALS AND BIENNIALS

PERENNIALS

Anemone X hybrida
134

Artemesia ludoviciana
'Silver King'
138

Aster novae-angliae
'Alma Potschke'
142

Baptisia australis
146

Begonia grandis
148

Campanula glomerata
150

Coreopsis grandiflora
'Early Sunrise'
156

Delpinium elatum hybrids
159

USDA Hardiness Zone Map

AVERAGE ANNUAL MINIMUM TEMPERATURE

Temperature (°C)	Zone	Temperature (°F)
-45.6 & Below	1	Below -50
-42.8 to 15.5	2a	-45 to -50
-40.0 to -42.7	2b	-40 to -45
-37.3 to -40.0	3a	-35 to -40
-34.5 to -37.2	3b	-30 to -35
-31.7 to -34.4	4a	-25 to -30
-28.9 to -31.6	4b	-20 to -25
-26.2 to -28.8	5a	-15 to -20
-23.4 to -26.1	5b	-10 to -15
-20.6 to -23.3	6a	-5 to -10
-17.8 to -20.5	6b	0 to -5
-15.0 to -17.7	7a	0 to 5
-12.3 to -15.0	7b	5 to 10
-9.5 to -12.2	8a	10 to 15
-6.7 to -9.4	8b	15 to 20
-3.9 to -6.6	9a	20 to 25
-1.2 to -3.8	9b	25 to 30
1.6 to -1.1	10a	30 to 35
4.4 to 1.7	10b	35 to 40
4.5 & Above	11	40 & Above

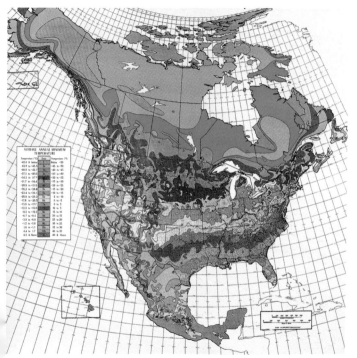

To get a full-color, 4-foot-square copy of this map, send a check for $6.50 to: Superintendent of Documents, Government Printing Office, Washington, D.C. 20402. Ask for Item #1417.

PERENNIALS

Dicentra spectabilis
163

Echinops ritro
165

Gaillardia X grandiflora
168

Geranium sanguineum
170

Hemerocallis hybrid
174

Hosta undulata
'Albo-marginata'
177

Iris siberica
"Dewful"
181

Paeonia lactiflora
'Mrs. Wilder Bancroft'
189

PERENNIALS

Papaver orientale
192

Perovskia atriplicifolia
194

Phlox paniculata
196

Primula X *polyantha*
199

Acidanthera bicolor var. *murielae*
214

Anemone blanda
216

Arisaema triphyllum
218

Convallaria majalis
223

BULBS

BULBS

Crocus sp.
225

Dahlia
'Claire de Lune'
228

Gladiolus hybrids
231

Hyacinthus orientalis
234

Iris danfordiae and *I. reticulata*
238

Lilium candidum
240

Narcissus
'King Alfred'
245

Tulipa
'Fringed Beauty'
249

BULBS

ROSES

Rosa
'American Pillar'
272

Rosa
'Gourmet Popcorn'
278

Rosa
'The Fairy'
282

Rosa chinensis
'Mutabilis'
284

Rosa damascena
'Semperflorens'
285

Rosa X *harisonii*
288

Rosa
'Apricot Nectar'
289

Rosa
'Love'
290

VEGETABLES

Asparagus
299

Carrot
'Short 'n Sweet'
316

Eggplant '
Purple Blush'
330

Honeydew melon
'Venus Hybrid'
337

Snap Peas
345

Hot peppers, mixed types
348

Potatoes
'Kennebec' and 'Red Pontiac'
351

Pumpkin
'Prize Winner'
355

VEGETABLES

HERBS

Caraway
382

Roman chamomile
385

Chives
386

Dill
388

Lavender
'Hidcote'
391

Sweet Marjoram
394

Rosemary
401

Sweet bay
405

HERBS

Convallaria majalis
417

Gaultheria procumbens
419

Hedera helix
420

Juniperus horizontalis
'Wiltonii'
422

Liriope spicata
423

Lysimachia nummularia
424

Sempervivum spp.
425

Vinca minor
426

Aristolochia durior
434

Clematis X *jackmanii*
435

Parthenocissus tricuspidata
442

Wisteria floribunda
443

PLANTS FOR EVERY PURPOSE

The lists that follow will help you get the most out of your garden. Use them to help you find the perfect plant for a problem site, fill your yard with flowers for cutting, or welcome butterflies and bees.

PLANTS FOR HOT, DRY AND SUNNY SITES

Have a hot, dry site where nothing seems to thrive? Tired of mowing that sunny slope all summer? Try creating a garden with any of the tough, drought-tolerant plants listed below for an attractive solution to these problem areas.

ANNUALS
Amaranthus tricolor (summer poinsettia)
Catharanthus roseus (vinca)
Centaurea cyanus (bachelor's button)
Chrysanthemum ptarmiciflorum (dusty miller)
Cosmos spp. (cosmos)
Eschscholzia californica (California poppy)
Helianthus annuus (sunflower)
Mirabilis julapa (four o'clock)
Portulaca grandiflora (rose moss)
Tagetes spp. (marigolds)
Zinnia elegans (common zinnia)

PERENNIALS

Achillea spp. (yarrows)
Artemisia spp. (artemisias)
Asclepias tuberosa (butterfly weed)
Centaurea montana (mountain bluet)
Coreopsis spp. (coreopsis)
Liatrus spp. (gayfeathers)
Echinops ritro (globe thistle)
Gaillardia X grandiflora (blanket flower)
Helianthus spp. (perennial sunflowers)
Hemerocallis hybrids (daylilies)
Perovskia atriplicifolia (Russian sage)
Phlox subulata (moss pinks)
Solidago spp. (goldenrods)
Stachys byzantina (lamb's ears)

BULBS

Sparaxis tricolor (harlequin flower)

HERBS

Lavender (*Lavandula* spp.)
Oregano (*Origanum* spp.)
Sage (*Salvia* spp.)
Thyme, common (*Thymus vulgaris*)

GROUNDCOVERS
Juniperus horizontalis (creeping juniper)
Sempervivum spp. (hens and chicks)

PLANTS FOR SHADY SITES

While few plants tolerate deep, dark shade, many can grow well in a spot with just a few hours of sun. A site that gets bright light but no direct sun can also provide good growing conditions for a wide variety of attractive annuals, perennials, bulbs, and herbs.

ANNUALS AND BIENNIALS
Ageratum houstonianum (ageratum)
Begonia semperflorens (wax begonia)
Catharanthus roseus (vinca)
Cleome hasslerana (spider flower)
Digitalis purpurea (foxglove)
Impatiens spp. (impatiens)
Lobularia maritima (sweet alyssum)

Lunaria annua (honesty)
Myosotis sylvatica (forget-me-not)
Viola X *wittrockiana* (pansy)

PERENNIALS
Alchemilla mollis (lady's-mantle)
Anemone X *hybrida* (Japanese anemone)
Aquilegia spp. (columbines)
Astilbe spp. (astilbes)
Baptisia australis (false indigo)
Begonia grandis (hardy begonia)
Campanula spp. (bellflowers)
Dicentra spp. (bleeding hearts)
Filipendula spp. (meadowsweets)
Hemerocallis hybrids (daylilies)
Hosta hybrids (hostas)
Liriope muscari (lilyturf)
Phlox divaricata (wild sweet William)
Phlox stolonifera (creeping phlox)
Primula X *polyantha* (primrose)

BULBS
Anemone spp. (anemones)
Chionodoxa spp. (glory-of-the-snow)
Convallaria majalis (lily-of-the-valley)

Crocus spp. and hybrids (crocus)
Ipheion uniflorum (spring starflower)
Lilium spp. (lilies)
Lycoris spp. (resurrection lilies)
Narcissus hybrids (daffodils)
Zantedeschia spp. (calla lilies)

HERBS
Lemon balm (*Melissa officinalis*)
Parsley (P*etroselinum crispum*)
Peppermint (*Mentha X piperita*)
Spearmint (*Mentha spicata*)

GROUNDCOVERS
Ajuga spp. (ajugas)
Alchemilla mollis (lady's-mantle)
Convallaria majalis (lily-of-the-valley)
Galax urceolata (wand flower)
Galium odoratum (sweet woodruff)
Gaultheria procumbens (wintergreen)
Hedera helix (English ivy)
Hosta spp. (hostas)
Liriope spp. (lilyturfs)
Lysimachia nummularia (creeping Jenny)
Vinca spp. (periwinkles)

PLANTS FOR CUT FLOWERS

Few things seem more indulgent than surrounding yourself with beautiful bouquets of cut flowers. Whether you set aside a separate cutting garden or just snip blooms from your beds and borders, you can always have a supply of great cut flowers—just try any or all of the flowers suggested below.

ANNUALS
Ageratum houstonianum (ageratum)
Antirrhinum majus (snapdragon)
Calendula officinalis (pot marigold)
Centaurea cyanus (bachelor's button)
Cleome hasslerana (spider flower)
Consolida ambigua (rocket larkspur)
Cosmos sulphureus (cosmos)
Dianthus spp. (pinks)
Digitalis purpurea (foxglove)
Eustoma grandiflorum (lisianthus)

Gypsophila elegans (annual baby's breath)
Helianthus annuus (sunflower)
Lathyrus odoratus (sweet pea)
Myosotis sylvatica (forget-me-not)
Papaver spp. (poppies)
Phlox drummondii (annual phlox)
Tagetes spp. (marigolds)
Trachymene caerulea (blue lace flower)
Tropaeolum majus (nasturtium)
Xeranthemum annuum (immortelle)
Zinnia elegans (zinnia)

PERENNIALS
Achillea spp. (yarrows)
Alchemilla mollis (lady's-mantle)
Amsonia tabernaemontana (blue starflower)
Anemone X *hybrida* (Japanese anemone)
Aquilegia spp. (columbines)
Artemisia spp. (artemisias)
Asclepias tuberosa (butterfly weed)
Aster spp. (asters)
Astilbe spp. (astilbes)
Baptisia australis (false indigo)

Campanula spp. (bellflowers)
Centaurea montana (mountin bluet)
Coreopsis spp. (coreopsis)
Chrysanthemum spp. (chrysanthemums)
Delphinium elatum hybrids (delphiniums)
Dianthus spp. (pinks)
Dicentra spp. (bleeding hearts)
Echinops ritro (globe thistle)
Filipendula spp. (meadowsweets)
Gaillardia X *grandiflora* (perennial blanket flower)
Helianthus spp. (perennial sunflowers)
Hemerocallis hybrids (daylilies)
Hosta hybrids (hostas)
Iris spp. (irises)
Liatris spp. (gayfeathers)
Liriope muscari (lilyturf)
Paeonia lactiflora (peony)
Papaver orientale (oriental poppy)
Perovskia atriplicifolia (Russian sage)
Phlox spp. (phlox)
Salvia spp. (salvias)
Solidago spp. (goldenrods)
Veronica spp. (veronicas)

BULBS

Acidanthera bicolor (Abyssinian gladiolus)
Anemone coronaria (Mediterranean windflower)
Convallaria majolis (lily-of-the-valley)
Dahlia hybrids (dahlias)
Gladiolus hybrids (glads)
Iris spp. (irises)
Lilium spp. (lilies)
Lycoris spp. (resurrection lilies)
Narcissus hybrids (daffodils)
Sparaxis tricolor (harlequin flower)
Tulipa spp. and hybrids (tulips)
Zantedeschia spp. (calla lilies)

HERBS

Anise hyssop (*Agastache foeniculum*)
Dill (*Anethum graveolens*)
Fennel (*Foeniculum vulgare*)
Lavender (*Lavandula* spp.)

PLANTS FOR DRIED FLOWERS

The first fall frost doesn't have to signal the end of your flowers! During the summer, collect and dry a variety of flowers and seedpods to enjoy indoors in fall, for arrangements, wreaths, potpourris, and other crafts. Here's a list of some of the best plants for drying.

ANNUALS
Ageratum houstonianum (ageratum)
Centaurea cyanus (bachelor's button)
Consolida ambigua (rocket larkspur)
Gypsophila elegans (annual baby's breath)
Lunaria annua (honesty)
Xeranthemum annuum (immortelle)

PERENNIALS
Achillea spp. (yarrow)
Artemisia ludoviciana 'Silver King'
    ('Silver King' artemisia)

Asclepias tuberosa (butterfly weed)
Astilbe spp. (astilbes)
Baptisia australis (false indigo)
Echinops ritro (globe thistle)
Filipendula spp. (meadowsweets)
Papaver orientale (oriental poppy)
Salvia spp. (salvias)
Solidago spp. (goldenrods)

HERBS
Anise hyssop (*Agastache foeniculum*)
Chives, garlic (*Allium tuberosum*)
Lavender (*Lavandula* spp.)

PLANTS FOR FRAGRANCE

Fragrance is a fairly personal thing. What smells heavenly to one person may be unpleasant to another. The plants listed below, however, are proven favorites for pleasing scents. Not all cultivars of these plants are fragrant, so try to sniff before you buy. On some plants, it's the flower that's scented; on others, it's the leaves. The list tells you what to check on each plant.

ANNUALS

Antirrhinum majus (snapdragon): flowers
Brachycome iberidifolia (Swan River daisy): flowers
Dianthus spp. (pinks): flowers
Heliotropium arborescens (heliotrope): flowers
Lathyrus odoratus (sweet pea): flowers
Lobularia maritima (sweet alyssum): flowers
Matthiola incana (stock): flowers
Mirabilis julapa (four o'clock): flowers
Nicotiana alata (flowering tobacco): flowers
Petunia X hybrida (petunias): flowers
Phlox drummondii (annual phlox): flowers
Tagetes spp. (marigolds): flowers and foliage
Trachymene caerulea (blue lace flower): flowers
Tropaeolum majus (nasturtium): flowers

PERENNIALS

Achillea spp. (yarrow): foliage
Artemisia spp. (artemisia): foliage
Chrysanthemum X morifolium (garden mums): flowers and foliage

Dianthus spp. (pinks): flowers
Hemerocallis hybrids (daylilies): flowers
Paeonia lactiflora (peony): flowers
Perovskia atriplicifolia (Russian sage): foliage
Phlox spp. (phlox): flowers
Primula X *polyantha* (primrose): flowers
Solidago spp. (goldenrods)

BULBS

Acidanthera bicolor (Abyssinian gladiolus): flowers
Convallaria majalis (lily-of-the-valley): flowers
Hyacinthus orientalis (hyacinth): flowers
Lilium spp. (lilies): flowers

HERBS

Anise hyssop (*Agastache foeniculum*): flowers
   and foliage
Basil (O*cimum basilicum*): foliage
Caraway (*Carum carvi*): foliage
Catnips (*Nepeta* spp.): foliage
Chamomile (*Chamaemelum nobile*): flowers
   and foliage
Dill (*Anethum graveolens*): foliage
Fennel (Foeniculum vulgare): foliage
Feverfew (*Chrysanthemum parthenium*): foliage

Lavender (*Lavandula* spp.): foliage and flowers
Lemon grass (*Cymbopogon citratus*): foliage
Marjoram, sweet (*Origanum majorana*): foliage
Oregano (*Origanum* spp.): foliage
Peppermint (*Mentha* X *piperita*): foliage
Sages (*Salvia* spp.): foliage
Spearmint (*Mentha spicata*): foliage
Sweet bay (*Laurus nobilis*): foliage

PLANTS THAT ATTRACT BEES AND BUTTERFLIES

Make your yard a haven for butterflies, bees, and other beautiful and beneficial insects. Below are some plants that are favorite food or shelter sources for these fascinating creatures.

ANNUALS

Ageratum houstonianum (ageratum)
Calendula officinalis (pot marigold)
Centaurea cyanus (bachelor's button)

Cosmos spp. (cosmos)
Gaillardia pulchella (annual blanket flower)
Helianthus annuus (sunflower)
Heliotropium arborescens (heliotrope)
Lobularia maritima (sweet alyssum)
Tropaeolum majus (nasturtium)
Zinnia spp. (zinnias)

PERENNIALS

Achillea spp. (yarrows)
Akea rosea (hollyhock)
Asclepias tuberosa (butterfly weed)
Aster spp. (asters)
Chrysanthemum spp. (chrysanthemums)
Coreopsis spp. (coreopsis)
Echinops ritro (globe thistle)
Helenium autumnale (sneezeweed)
Helianthus spp. (perennial sunflowers)
Hemerocallis hybrids (daylilies)
Liatris spp. (gayfeathers)
Nepeta X faassenii (catmint)
Phlox paniculata (garden phlox)
Salvia spp. (salvias)
Solidago spp. (goldenrods)

HERBS

Catnips (*Nepeta* spp.)
Chives (*Allium schoenoprasum*)
Dill (*Anethum graveolens*)
Fennel (*Foeniculum vulgare*)
Lavender (*Lavandula* spp.)
Mint (*Mentha* spp.)
Parsley (*Petroselinum crispum*)
Rosemary (*Rosmarinus officinalis*)
Sage (*Salvia officinalis*)

FLOWERS FOR CONTAINERS

Many plants can survive in pots, but some adapt better than others to life in a container. Here are some of the best choices for container gardens.

ANNUALS

Ageratum houstonianum (ageratum)
Antirrhinum majus (snapdragon)

Begonia X *semperflorens* (wax begonia)
Brachycome iberidifolia (Swan River daisy)
Calendula officinalis (pot marigold)
Callistephus chinensis (China aster)
Catharanthus roseus (vinca)
Centaurea cyanus (bachelor's button)
Chrysanthemum ptarmiciflorum (dusty miller)
Cosmos spp. (cosmos)
Cynoglossum amabile (Chinese forget-me-not)
Dianthus spp. (pinks)
Dyssodia tenuiloba (Dahlberg daisy)
Eschscholzia californica (California poppy)
Eustoma grandiflorum (lisianthus)
Gaillardia pukhella (annual blanket flower)
Helichrysum bracteatum (strawflower)
Heliotropium arborescens (heliotrope)
Impatiens spp. (impatiens)
Lobularia maritima (sweet alyssum)
Matthiola incana (stock)
Mirabilis jalapa (four o'clock)
Myosotis sylvatica (forget-me-not)
Pelargonium spp. (geraniums)
Petunia X *hybrida* (petunia)
Phlox drummondii (annual phlox)
Portulaca grandiflora (rose moss)

Tagetes spp. (marigolds)
Tropaeolum majus (nasturtium)
Viola X wittrockiana (pansy)
Xeranthemum annuum (immortelle)
Zinnia spp. (zinnias)

PERENNIALS

Achillea spp. (yarrows)
Aquilegia spp. (columbines)
Aster spp. (asters)
Chrysanthemum spp. (chrysanthemums)
Coreopsis spp. (coreopsis)
Dianthus spp. (pinks)
Hemerocallis hybrids (daylilies)
Nepeta X faassenii (catnips)
Primula X polyantha (primrose)

BULBS

Anemone spp. (anemones)
Arum italicum (arum lily)
Convallaria majolis (lily-of-the-valley)
Crocus spp. and hybrids (crocus)
Eranthis hyemalis (winter aconite)
Hyacinthus orientalis (hyacinth)
Iphieon uniflorum (spring starflower)

Iris spp. (irises)
Leucojum spp. (snowflakes)
Lilium spp. (lilies)
Lycoris spp. (resurrection lilies)
Narcissus hybrids (daffodils)
Ornithogalum spp. (star-of-Bethlehem)
Sparaxis tricolor (harlequin flower)
Tulipa spp. and hybrids (tulips)
Zantedeschia spp. (calla lilies)

HERBS
Basil (*Ocimum basilicum*)
Catnips *(Nepeta spp.)*
Chives (*Allium schoenoprasum*)
Coriander (*Coriandrum sativum*)
Dill (*Anethum graveolens*)
Lavender (*Lavandula* spp.)
Lemon grass (*Cymbopogon citratum*)
Oregano (*Origanum* spp.)
Peppermint (*Mentha* X *piperita*)
Pot marigold (*Calendula officinalis*)
Spearmint (*Mentha spicata*)
Sweet bay (*Laurus nobilis*)

BULBS
FOR ALL SEASONS

With a little planning, you can enjoy beautiful bulbs nearly year-round. Use the lists below to help plan your plantings for extended blooms. Some genera are listed under more than one season because they contain species that flower at different times.

WINTER OR EARLY SPRING

Crocus, some species and hybrids (crocus)
Eranthis hyemalis (winter aconite)
Ipheion uniflorum (spring starflower)
Iris spp. (irises)
Narcissus, early species (daffodils)
Tulipa, early species (tulips)

SPRING

Anemone blanda (Grecian windflower)
Anemone coronaria (Mediterranean windflower)
Arisaema, most species (Jack-in-the-pulpits)

Chionodoxa spp. (glory-of-the-snow)
Crocus, many species and hybrids (crocus)
Hyacinthus orientalis (hyacinth)
Narcissus hybrids (daffodils)
Tulipa, mid-season types (tulips)
Zantedeschia spp. (calla lilies)

SUMMER

Acidanthera bicolor (Abyssinian gladiolus)
Arisaema, some species (Jack-in-the-pulpits)
Begonia Tuberybrida hybrids
Dahlia hybrids (dahlias)
Gladiolus hybrids (glads)
Lilium spp. and hybrids (lilies)
Sparaxis tricolor (harlequin flower)
Zantedeschia spp. (calla lilies)

FALL

Crocus, some species (crocus)
Lycoris spp. (resurrection lilies)

Season-by-Season Guide to Garden Maintenance

Garden planting and maintenance times vary from zone to zone and within zones from year to year. There is too much variation in climates in this country for one calendar to suit all growing regions of the country. However, the following month-by-month guide is a good general guide for you to begin planning your own maintenance calendar.

EARLY SPRING

- Shop for the garden tools and equipment you will need for the coming season

- Remove winter mulch from perennials as the weather begins to warm up
- Weed early, and weed often!
- Turn or loosen the soil in annual flower beds and vegetable gardens
- Use a spading fork to carefully cultivate soil around plants in perennial beds
- Work manure, compost, and other organic matter into garden beds before planting
- Apply acidic fertilizers to azaleas and rhododendrons
- Rake and aerate your lawn; sow new grass seed as necessary
- Cut ornamental grasses to just above the ground if you didn't cut them down in fall
- Cut back all dead perennial parts that you left standing for the winter
- Start flower and vegetable seed for planting outdoors after the last frost
- Sow seed of lettuce, peas, and other fast-growing, cool-weather crops directly in the garden

MID-SPRING

- Plant perennials, roses, groundcovers, trees, and shrubs; mulch and water them thoroughly
- Weed garden beds and borders

- Divide and replant summer- and fall-blooming perennials
- Snip off spent flowers and developing seedpods from tulips, daffodils, and other bulbs
- Replenish mulch around established roses, and begin fertilizing them
- Prune any shrubs that have finished early-spring flowering
- Mow and fertilize lawns as needed
- Plant out seedlings of broccoli, cabbage, cauliflower, and other cool-season crops

LATE SPRING

- Start mowing your lawn regularly
- Begin harvesting your first crop of lettuce, spinach, and other early greens
- Continue planting perennials
- Set out hardened-off transplants of annual flowers, vegetables, and herbs; mulch beds as you finish setting out your plants
- Direct-sow annual flower seed
- Lay out irrigation lines in garden beds
- Water during dry spells to make sure your garden gets approximately 1 inch of water per week
- Remove spent flowers from rhododendrons and azaleas and other spring-flowering plants

- Set out stakes or hoops to support lilies, delphiniums, peonies, hollyhocks, foxgloves, and other tall plants
- Continue getting rid of annual and perennial weeds

EARLY SUMMER

- Keep watering and weeding as needed
- Continue planting out annual bedding plants and vegetables
- Scout for insect problems; take control measures as necessary
- Deadhead or cut back spent annual and perennial flowers
- Prune shrubs that have finished flowering
- Continue to fertilize your roses as necessary, and keep an eye out for pests and diseases
- Prune early-blooming clematis after flowering
- Harvest lettuce, peas, and other early vegetables
- If you plan to be away during the summer, make arrangements to have someone water your garden

MIDSUMMER

- Continue watering, weeding, and mulching
- Treat plants that aren't growing vigorously to a dose of fish emulsion or other liquid fertilizer
- Scout for pest and disease problems; control as necessary

- Continue fertilizing and spraying roses
- Remove faded flowers from annuals and perennials to prolong bloom time
- Stake tall-growing plants as needed
- Divide bearded irises after flowering if they are getting too crowded
- Prune wisteria after flowering
- Pinch off the shoot tips of chrysanthemums and asters to promote more branching and more blooms in fall
- Sow seeds of foxgloves, sweet William, and other biennial flowers in pots or an unused garden bed

LATE SUMMER

- Continue weeding, watering, and deadheading
- Dig up and discard dead or diseased plants
- Stop fertilizing all plants
- Continue treating pest and disease problems
- Prune hydrangeas after they finish flowering
- Trim summer-blooming clematis after flowering
- Sow seeds of spinach, lettuce, and other fall vegetable crops
- Transplant seedlings of biennial flowers to where you want them to bloom next year
- Freeze or can your garden's surplus vegetables

EARLY FALL

- Weed and water as necessary
- Start a compost pile if you don't have one already! Toss in unused produce, weeds (if they haven't gone to seed), spent flowers and plants, leaves, grass clippings, and other trimmings as you remove them from the garden
- Test your soil for pH and nutrient levels; add amendments as indicated in your results to balance the soil for next year
- Seed new lawn areas or lay new turf, making sure you keep the area well watered during spells of warm, dry weather
- Aerate established lawns
- In colder regions, begin planting crocuses, daffodils, tulips, and other spring bulbs; in warm climates, set out pansies, sweet alyssum, and other hardy annuals for winter bloom
- Plant perennials, roses, groundcovers, trees, and shrubs
- In cold-winter areas, pot up rosemary, chives, and other culinary herbs to enjoy inside for the winter
- Divide spring- and early-summer-blooming perennials
- Harvest late-season vegetables

MID-FALL

- Rake leaves. Add them to the compost pile, or shred them for use as a winter mulch

- Do one final weeding of the garden
- Apply slow-release fertilizer and lime to lawns as needed
- Remove spent annual flowers and vegetable plants from the garden, and toss them into the compost pile
- Unless you live in a frost-free area, dig up dahlias, cannas, glads, tuberous begonias, and other tender bulbs; let them dry for a few days, then store in slightly moist sand or peat moss in a cool, dry place
- Cut back frost-nipped perennials to within several inches of the ground
- Plant new hardy perennials
- Divide any perennials you didn't get to in early fall
- Incorporate compost and other organic matter into empty garden beds
- Plant hardy perennials, spring-flowering bulbs, bareroot roses, trees, and shrubs
- Direct-sow winter rye or other cover crops to protect the soil in empty garden beds for the winter

LATE FALL TO EARLY WINTER

- Add protective mulch to carrots, turnips, parsnips, beets, and other root vegetables you haven't finished harvesting
- Cut chrysanthemums and asters to the ground after flowering

- Continue incorporating compost and organic matter in garden beds
- Continue planting spring bulbs
- Continue raking and composting leaves
- In cold-winter areas, wait until the ground freezes to apply a thick layer of mulch to perennials, trees, and shrubs
- Place wire mesh around the base of woody plants to protect them from animal damage over winter
- Empty hoses of water and store them
- Order new seed and plant catalogs

MID- TO LATE WINTER

- Replenish winter mulch as needed
- Trim trees and shrubs (except spring-flowering kinds) as needed
- Make new plans for garden beds
- Send in seed and plant orders
- Begin sowing seeds indoors (usually late February)
- Look for any perennials that have been heaved out of the ground by freezing and thawing; push them back into the soil
- Gather all tools for cleaning, repair, sharpening, and oiling; store them in a dry, protected area